Welcome to
GET STARTED
WITH ARDUINO

Arduino and Arduino-compatible microcontrollers are essentially simple computers that we can easily embed in our projects. They enable us to sense input and create output in a huge number of ways. Buttons, touch-sensitive areas, environmental sensors, and more can feed into these computers. Lights, sound movements, and more can feed out. Controlling these with a little bit of programmable logic allows us to create devices with a huge range of interactions.

This all sounds very computer-y, but Arduinos are designed to be embedded, so are often hidden away in things that don't look like computers. We look at some fantastic projects that showcase the range of things you can make with these microcontrollers.

It's become a cliché to say that the only limit is your imagination, but these boards are sufficiently powerful and flexible to mean that it's very nearly true. You can add interactions, simple or complex, to almost any project. What's even better is that they're designed to be easy to use. Now you've picked up this book, it's time to get started and create your own amazing Arduino project.

Got a comment, question or thought about HackSpace magazine?

get in touch at
hsmag.cc/hello

GET IN TOUCH

hackspace@
raspberrypi.org

hackspacemag

hackspacemag

ONLINE

hsmag.cc

BEN EVERARD
Editor ben.everard@raspberrypi.org

EDITORIAL
Editor
Ben Everard
ben.everard@raspberrypi.org

Features Editor
Andrew Gregory
andrew.gregory@raspberrypi.org

Book Production Editor
Phil King

Sub Editors
David Higgs, Nicola King

DESIGN
Critical Media
criticalmedia.co.uk

Head of Design
Lee Allen

Designers
Harriet Knight, Sam Ribbits

CONTRIBUTORS
Matt Bradshaw, Jo Hinchliffe, Dr Andrew Lewis, Jenny List, Brian Lough, Graham Morrison, John Wargo

PUBLISHING
Publishing Director
Russell Barnes
russell@raspberrypi.org

Advertising
Charlie Milligan
charlotte.milligan@raspberrypi.org
+44 7725 368 887

DISTRIBUTION
Seymour Distribution Ltd
2 East Poultry Ave,
London EC1A 9PT
+44 (0)207 429 4000

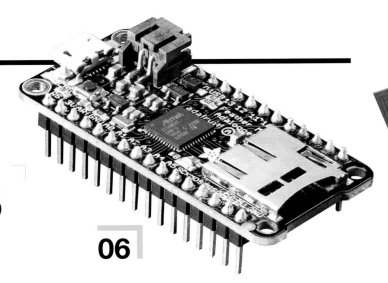

46

Contents

06

7-segment displays

138

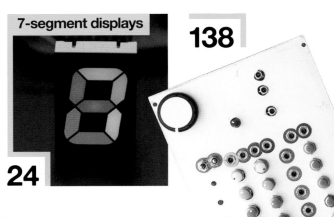

24

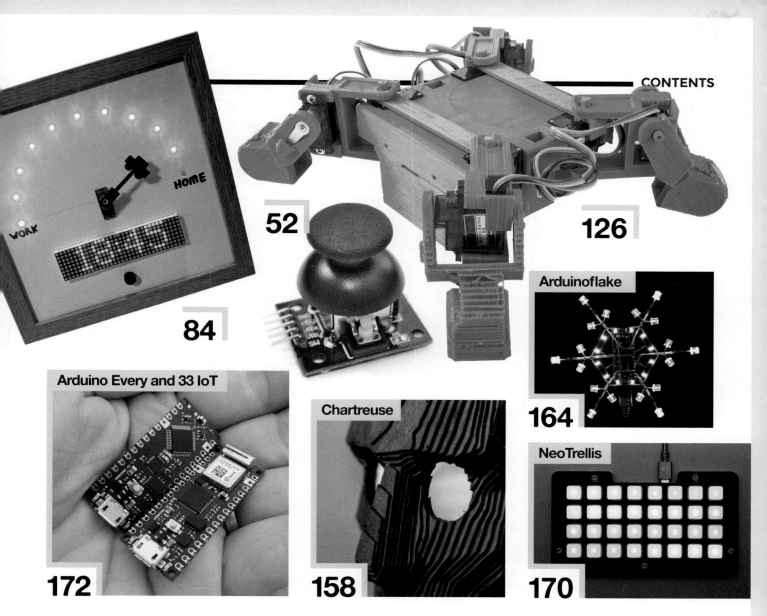

52

84

126

Arduinoflake
164

NeoTrellis
170

Arduino Every and 33 IoT
172

Chartreuse
158

THE ULTIMATE GUIDE TO
ARDUINO

Discover the boards, add-ons, and programming environment that make it easy to create interactive electronics projects

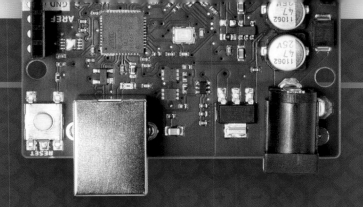

Arduinos are stripped-down computers. They've got a little storage, some RAM, and a processor all packed into a chip. You write code for them on a normal desktop or laptop, then upload this over USB to run on the board. They're cheap (ranging from a few pounds to a few tens of pounds), widely available, and easy to use.

While the word 'Arduino' can mean specifically boards that are designed and manufactured by the Arduino organisation, many other Arduino-compatible boards are available. These range from boards that are almost identical to official boards, to boards that are wildly different but that can still be programmed using the official software. We'll be looking at all boards – both official

and compatible – here, as few makers restrict themselves to just one type.

We use these boards to add tiny programmable brains to our project. They can be combined with LEDs to add visual effects, speakers to add sounds, motors to add movement, and a vast range of sensors to bring in information to be processed. It's a cliché to say that the possibilities are endless, but they really are.

What's more, the boards have been designed to be as easy to use as possible. The programming environment has many of the complexities of many programming tools, and they're designed so you can get started without having to know anything about electronics – add-ons known as shields can just be pushed on top.

Now, let's dive in and take a closer look at the hardware. →

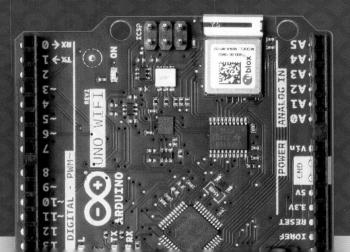

OUR FAVOURITE

ARDUINO-COMPATIBLE

BOARDS

Pick the best board for your next project

Arduinos are boards made by the Arduino LLC company. However, as the designs and software are open-source, there's a large number of 'Arduino-compatible' boards.** Exactly how compatible depends on the boards. All of them can be programmed from the Arduino IDE. Some of them are also pin-compatible with official Arduino boards, and can use the same hardware.

There are literally hundreds of Arduino-compatible boards, and we can't cover them all here, so let's instead take a look at a few of our favourites. Each one is specialised for a particular use.

ARDUINO UNO WIFI REV2

ARDUINO | €38.90 | store.arduino.cc

The Uno has been the board of choice for beginners for nine years. While it's been through a few revisions in that time, the first major change came out in 2018 with the Uno WiFi Rev2. Including WiFi makes this an ideal starter board for anyone looking to make internet-connected projects.

Perhaps the most attractive thing about this board is the number of add-on 'shields' that have been created for it over the years. There are hundreds – possibly thousands – of these that make it easy to add more features to your projects. Unlike many other boards in this form factor, the Arduino Uno WiFi is 5V, so is guaranteed to work with all shields built for the original Uno. □

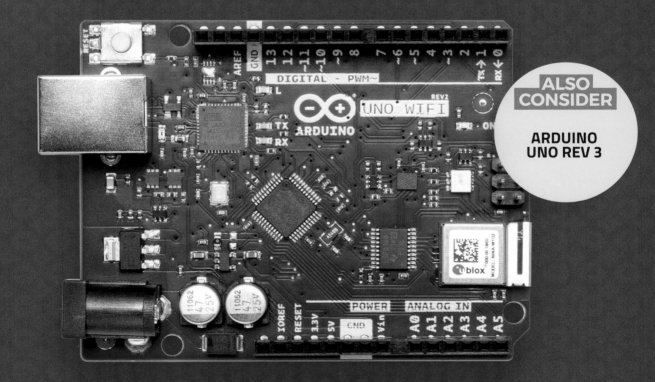

ALSO CONSIDER

ARDUINO UNO REV 3

ARDUINO MKR WIFI 1010

ARDUINO | €27.90 | store.arduino.cc

The MKR range makes it easy to build high-quality, reliable Internet of Things projects. Each board includes a battery charger and secure crypto element on a robust PCB. There's a range of official add-on boards designed for the needs of small and medium businesses, which includes the capability to connect to CAN buses and communicate via RS-485.

As well as this, there's extra software support in the form of Arduino IoT Cloud that makes it really quick to hook your projects up. There are a few MKR boards that connect to the wider world in different ways – including LoRa and Sigfox – but for most projects, good old-fashioned WiFi is the best option. □

ALSO CONSIDER

FEATHER HUZZAH

SPARKFUN ESP32 THING

BEST FOR
INTERNET OF THINGS

FEATHER M0 ADALOGGER

ADAFRUIT | $19.95 | adafruit.com

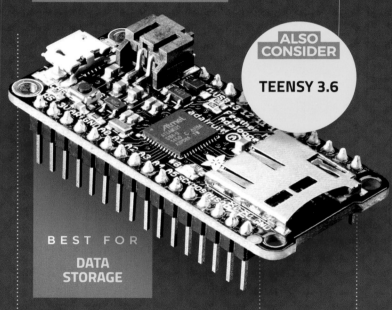

ALSO CONSIDER

TEENSY 3.6

BEST FOR
DATA STORAGE

Adafruit's Feather range is made up of lots of boards the same shape, with the same pinouts, but with different microcontrollers at their heart. This means that one set of accessories works with all of them.

One common set of builds that we do involves sensing and storing information. This could be environmental data – such as the amount of pollution in the air, or how much moisture there is in soil, or information about how a device is used. For this, SD cards are a great solution, as they're small, cheap, and easy to use with both microcontrollers and computers. The Feather M0 Adalogger has a microSD card reader on the board itself, so you don't need any extra hardware. □

METRO M4 FT. ATSAMD51

ADAFRUIT | $27.50 | adafruit.com

The original Arduinos all used AVR microcontrollers. These are easy to work with, but lack a bit of oomph compared with the more modern ARM Cortex-M series microcontrollers used in many newer boards.

Metro M4 Express keeps the traditional Arduino Uno form factor, but pops in a more powerful processor. When it comes to raw processing power, the Metro M4 Express flies past the Arduino Uno and even the faster official board, the Arduino Zero. As well as having a faster processor, it's got a floating point unit, so if you're doing maths, the advantages are twofold.

If you need to crunch through a lot of data, this is a great choice. ▢

ALSO CONSIDER

TEENSY 3.6 SPARKFUN REDBOARD TURBO OR **ARDUINO ZERO**

BEST FOR

PROCESSING POWER

GRAND CENTRAL M4 EXPRESS

ADAFRUIT | $37.50 | adafruit.com

ALSO CONSIDER

TEENSY 3.6

BEST FOR

LOTS OF INPUT AND OUTPUT

This feature-packed board has a whopping 54 IO pins, and sports the same blistering-fast processor as the Metro M4 Express. It's in the same form factor as the Arduino Mega and Arduino Due, so there's a range of add-ons already available, even though this board is brand new.

While this is quite a big board, there's a good chance that if you need this many IOs, then you're working on a big project. Whether it's to control lots of lights, lots of motors, or get lots of inputs from sensors, when we need lots of IOs, the Grand Central is now our board of choice. ▢

RASPBERRY PI 4

RASPBERRY PI | $35–$55 | raspberrypi.org

Many people have been using Raspberry Pi boards to run the Arduino IDE but, since March 2018, you've also been able to program Raspberry Pi devices directly from the Arduino software. This is particularly useful because it links into the cloud IDE so that you can control your Linux machines from anywhere on the web.

Unlike traditional microcontrollers, you can run multiple sketches simultaneously, and even install and remove software. This ability to manipulate machines with a few clicks makes it easy to update embedded systems without having to physically access them or learn to use remote administration tools aimed at sysadmins.

Head to **create.arduino.cc/devices** to get started. ⬚

BEST FOR
LINUX COMPATIBILITY

ALSO CONSIDER
BEAGLEBOARD

ESP8266

VARIOUS | $2–3 | various sites

ALSO CONSIDER
BLUE PILL
ESP32

BEST FOR
LOW PRICE

There's a wide range of boards that are built around the ESP8266 modules that provide USB connectivity and break out the IO pins. They're available on many direct-from-China websites for around £2 each. The stand-out feature at this price range is the WiFi connectivity. Usually, they come with a Lua firmware, but also support Arduino. There is essentially no manufacturer's support for these boards; however, there's an active community that provides libraries and tutorials for many common uses.

The pictured board has nine 3.3 V GPIOs and one analogue in; however, this can only take between 0 and 1 V (a simple voltage divider can be used if you've got a larger range than this). They're small, cheap, and well-connected – perfect when you just want to add the ability to remotely control an object. ⬚

TOP 10 ADD-ONS

Traditionally, Arduino add-ons have been called 'shields', and were designed to slot directly into the pins on boards in the Arduino form factor. However, as Arduino-compatible boards now come in many shapes and sizes, we can't be so restrictive. Here, we've included any hardware that can easily work with Arduino-compatible boards, regardless of form factor.

There are so many Arduino add-ons that it's impossible to pick one as 'best'. It depends on the form factor of your underlying board, your power requirements, and the features you need for your project. Here are ten of our favourites, but there are hundreds of others that can make great projects.

1. NeoPixels

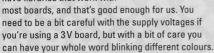

We're stretching the definition of Arduino add-on almost to its limit to include these, but they're easy to work with on Arduino and have libraries that work with most boards, and that's good enough for us. You need to be a bit careful with the supply voltages if you're using a 3V board, but with a bit of care you can have your whole word blinking different colours.

2. Core Memory Shield

Back in the early days of computing, RAM was made of loops of magnetic material. Wires crossed through these loops, and electrical pulses through these wires could induce and read magnetism. This way, small amounts of data could be stored. While we now have much faster, smaller, and cheaper forms of memory, you can still geek-out with old-fashioned ferrite core memory using this Arduino shield from **hsmag.cc/pzKiKq**.

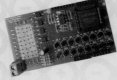

3. Grove Base Shield

This is a metashield. It doesn't have any hardware in itself, but it gives you the ability to add hardware easily to an Arduino Uno (or compatible) board. There are 16 ports that break out analogue inputs, UART connections, digital IO, and I²C into 'Grove connectors'. There's a range of Grove-compatible hardware that can then be plugged into this. It's easier to build up designs than using an evergrowing stack of shields, and more robust than using a breadboard.

4. CRICKIT

This add-on is available for several Arduino-compatible boards, including the Feather range from Adafruit, the Circuit Playground Express, the micro:bit, and the Raspberry Pi. It adds a bunch of input and output options, including a NeoPixel driver, touch sensors, motor drivers, servo controllers, and high-current IO. It's a great board to have on hand as it can be useful in so many projects.

5. OpenLog

If you've used Arduino, one of the first things you learned (after blinking an LED) was probably sending data to the serial monitor. This is a great way to get data from your Arduino to the computer it's plugged into. However, what if your Arduino isn't plugged into a computer? The OpenLog stores serial messages on an SD card, so you can log your data as usual and come back to get it later.

6. Adafruit Ultimate GPS FeatherWing

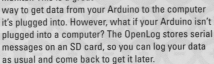

The GPS is truly one of the wonders of the modern world. We take it for granted now, but the ability to know your position to within a few metres anywhere in the world, or get an accurate idea of your speed, is miraculous. This FeatherWing includes a GPS receiver, a real-time clock, and a battery backup, which all makes it easy to use with any of the Feather range. You can get similar add-ons for other form factors.

7. MKR Motor Carrier

Controlling motion with electronics is an art form. At the simplest level, it's just a case of a small DC motor, but as you look for more power or more precision, you need to consider more factors. The MKR Motor Carrier from Arduino adds the ability to control four motors (two with encoders) and four servos to any of the MKR boards. There's also a charger for 2S and 3S LiPo batteries, which should keep your motors running when not near a power source.

8. Protoboard shield

If you design your own hardware, you may well have started out with a breadboard. This makes it really easy to prototype things, but it's not very permanent. One option is to design a PCB, but if it's a one-off project with simple hardware, then it can be much quicker to solder it together on some protoboard. You can find this in the right shape to slot straight into most popular form factors for Arduino-compatible boards. There are a few different formats. Shown is the official Arduino protoboard for the Mega form factor.

9. Nixie tube drivers

Nixie tubes are gorgeous numerical displays from the days before LEDs. Put enough volts into the right pins and you're rewarded with a digit glowing orange-red. They can be a little tricky to drive from Arduinos, as they require a few hundred volts to run. The exixe board packages up everything you need, and lets you control them via SPI. There's even an Arduino library to take the hassle out of using these retro displays. Get yours from **hsmag.cc/xtdbjd**.

10. 3D printer

Many 3D printers are built on Arduino-compatible systems. The popular Marlin firmware is designed to work on the Arduino Mega 2560 and the RAMPS 1.4 add-on board. Many 3D printers use other hardware, but it's all built on this Arduino-compatible platform, including the Anet A8 (pictured). In a sense, then, all these 3D printers are really just Arduino add-ons.

ARDUINO IDE

Let's get ready to program

Figure 1 →
Main interface

1. The main code area

2. Button to compile the code, but don't upload it to the board

3. Button to upload the code to the board (and compile if changes have been made)

4. Output from the compiler and uploader

5. Details of the currently connected board

The Arduino IDE is, for many people, the place where hardware programming happens. It is, by development environment standards, a fairly straightforward piece of software, but it does the basics well: There's code highlighting, tabs for multiple files, and the ability to manage the compilation and hardware options. Let's take a look at the main features.

Figure 1 shows the main interface with a program (known as a 'sketch' in Arduino-speak) that turns the built-in LED on and off every second. There are two functions: one called **setup** that runs when the board is turned on (or reset), and one called **loop** that runs repeatedly. This is the basic organisation of every Arduino sketch.

Perhaps the best feature of the Arduino IDE is its ability to support a vast range of different hardware. All this hardware requires different options to the software responsible for compiling and packaging the code, so you need to make sure that the software knows which hardware you're using. You can select the correct option in Tools > Boards (see **Figure 2**). If your hardware isn't listed there, you can add more boards via URLs (find the correct

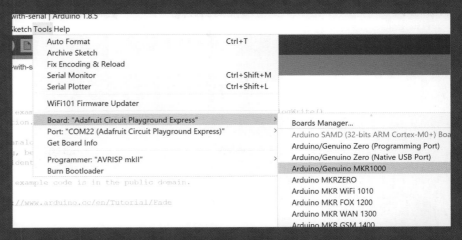

URL from your hardware supplier) in File > Preferences > Additional Board Manager URLs.

Libraries are packaged bits of code that are easy to reuse. There are hundreds of them for Arduino, most of which give you the ability to control hardware without getting bogged down in the nitty-gritty of how they work. The Library manager (in Sketch > Include a Library > Manage Libraries) gives you the ability to easily install and use these libraries (**Figure 3**). Many will also install example sketches (in File > Examples) that give you a chance to see how to use them.

One of the problems with embedded coding is that it can be hard to see what's going on. The serial monitor gives us a solution to this. It's a way of shovelling data through the USB connection between the computer and the board. Using the command `Serial.println()` (you'll also need `Serial.begin(9600)` or similar in your `setup()` function), you can send data from your board to the computer and display it using the serial monitor for text (in Tools > Serial Monitor) or the Serial plotter for numbers (in Tools > Serial Plotter). You can also send data in the other direction if you need to control your hardware from a computer. →

Figure 2 ⬆
As well as selecting the correct board, you'll also have to select the right port. You'll see the different options in Tools > Port

Figure 3 ⬇
Before diving into some complex coding, it's always worth asking yourself if there's a library that will make your life easier

PROGRAMMING LANGUAGE

The Arduino IDE uses a language based on C++. If you've programmed in any similar language before, take a look at the example sketches included with the Arduino IDE. They're well commented, and take you from the basics upwards. Alternatively, there are loads of great resources to help you get started from any level of programming experience (including none). Graham Morrison's excellent ten-part tutorial series can be found in this very book, starting on page 24.

SCHOOL OF MAKING ━━━━━━━━━━━━━━━

Add Arduino power to your projects

Get started with coding for the Arduino platform

John Wargo

🐦 @johnwargo

John is a professional software developer, writer, presenter, father, husband, and geek. He is currently a Program Manager at Microsoft, working on Visual Studio Mobile Center. You can find him at **johnwargo.com**

So you want to start programming microcontrollers and doing some cool projects with the hardware. You've selected Arduino as your starting platform, purchased a popular Arduino board, and you're ready to get started. What's next? In this short article, we'll show you how to get started coding for Arduino.

Arduino (**arduino.cc**) is a very popular hardware platform for computer-controlled hardware projects. Arduino is a small, inexpensive, programmable microcontroller that exposes a multitude of input and output (I/O) connections you can use to create computer-controlled circuits, wiring in switches, lights, sensors, and more. It's an open hardware platform, which means that the hardware specification is open source, so anyone with the means can design and distribute their own Arduino-compatible hardware. Therefore, there's a series of devices made by arduino.cc and a bevy of 'compatible' devices from other vendors as well.

To program an Arduino device, you'll code applications in a language similar to very old programming language called C; these applications are called sketches. Because the Arduino is basically a small computer system, although with limited processing speed and memory, the platform supports a subset of the capabilities of C. You'll code your Arduino applications in an integrated development environment (IDE); Arduino offers both a locally installed IDE or a cloud IDE to use for your projects. There are alternative IDEs available as well; you can find a list of options at **hsmag.cc/aQJqkJ**.

When creating sketches, you'll code your sketch in an IDE, then connect your Arduino-compatible device to your PC using an USB cable. With that in place, the IDE compiles your sketches into executable code, then downloads them to the Arduino device over the cable. As your sketch runs, you can pass data between the IDE and your Arduino device over a serial communication channel enabled in the IDE (shown in **Figure 1**). Once compiled code is deployed to the device, the device resets and, once the device completes initialisation, it executes the sketch.

An Arduino sketch consists, at a minimum, of two parts: code that runs once, and code that runs repeatedly. Let us show you.

In the Arduino IDE (described later), an empty Arduino sketch looks like this:

SERIAL COMMUNICATION

The serial communications capabilities of the Arduino platform expose additional capabilities for your sketches. At a minimum, you can use serial communication to send data back to the IDE while you're troubleshooting your sketches. To do this, open the IDE's Tools menu and select Serial Monitor. A new window opens, and any data written using the Serial commands (described at **arduino.cc/en/Reference/Serial**) will appear in the monitor window.

You can also use serial communications to transfer collected data (from sensors connected to the Arduino board) to another computer system like a Windows PC or a Raspberry Pi. Makers often do this since the Arduino supports analogue inputs and the Raspberry Pi does not. In this scenario, the Arduino becomes merely a data collection device, and the Raspberry Pi does whatever number crunching is appropriate for the project, potentially even displaying data on a connected screen or uploading the data to a remote server for processing.

Figure 1 ◈
Arduino
development
architecture

USB CABLE

- - - - Sketch Download - - - - - - ▶

◀ - - - Serial Communication - - - - -

Development
Workstation

```
/*
*/
void setup() {
}
void loop() {
}
```

The first part of the sketch is a comment block. Anything, absolutely anything you enter between the /* and */ characters is ignored by the Arduino compiler.

```
/*********************************
My First Arduino Sketch

by John M. Wargo
   December, 2017

Meatloaf meatball pork ground round fatback
kielbasa cow porchetta pork loin ball tip. Spare
ribs picanha drumstick pork jerky cupim alcatra
meatball beef ribs. Ball tip ground round
pastrami pancetta shank kevin.

*********************************/
```

In your sketches, you'll use this commenting approach when you have multiple lines of content you want displayed within the sketch. At a minimum, use a comment block at the beginning of the sketch to describe the sketch, as we've done in the example, using dummy content from the Bacon Ipsum generator (at **baconipsum.com**). You should also use block comments like this to describe important parts of your sketches.

You can also add single-line comments to your sketches. To do this, start any line in your sketch with double forward slash characters (//) or after any of your code. All content following the double forward slashes is ignored by the Arduino compiler. In the following example, a single-line comment precedes the definition of the **numCols** variable. The comment and the executable code are on separate lines, so we started the comment line with the double forward slashes.

```
//Number of columns in the table
int numCols;
```

Or something like this where the comment follows the definition of the **relayStatus** variable:

```
bool relayStatus;  //The current status of
the relay (on/off)
```

The sketch's **setup** function is defined with the following code:

```
void setup() {
}
```

Any code you add to this function (you'll add your code between the curly braces **{}**) is executed by the Arduino device as soon as you power it up and the hardware finishes initialising. This function is executed only once; you'll use this function to set up your sketch and execute the things that only need to be done when the sketch starts.

You'll normally use this to define the configuration of your hardware; as many input/output (I/O) connectors on the Arduino can be used for either input or output, you'll have to tell your sketch how you intend to use them. We'll show you an example of this in a little while.

The final component of a minimalist sketch is the **loop** function:

```
void loop() {
}
```

In this function, put any code that you want to run repeatedly on the Arduino. The Arduino executes the **setup** function once, then executes the **loop** function over, and over, and over again until either the Arduino explodes (it won't, we're just kidding) or you disconnect power from the device. You can put all your code in the loop, or break your code into smaller functions and call those functions from the **loop** function.

To see all of this in action, look at the following example. By default, the Arduino developer tools include a simple sample sketch called Blink. →

> **Arduino is a small, inexpensive, programmable microcontroller** that exposes a multitude of input and output (I/O) connections

YOU'LL NEED

◆ **An Arduino-compatible board**
An actual Arduino device is preferred as there's extra setup required for many Arduino compatible boards. The recommended starter board is the Arduino Uno (hsmag.cc/QKaKXM) or the newer, and more capable, Arduino Zero (hsmag.cc/KGJbVd)

◆ **Microsoft Windows, Apple macOS, or Linux**

◆ **Universal serial bus (USB) cable**
To connect the Arduino device to your computer system. Arduino on-device connectors vary; most use a micro-USB connector, but the Uno uses a USB A/B cable

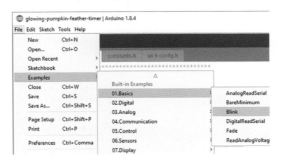

Figure 2 ◆
Opening the Arduino Blink sketch

SCHOOL OF MAKING

```
Blink | Arduino 1.8.4                                          —  □
File Edit Sketch Tools Help

Blink
 1 /*
 2   Blink
 3
 4   Turns an LED on for one second, then off for one second, repeatedly.
 5
 6   Most Arduinos have an on-board LED you can control. On the UNO, MEGA and ZERO
 7   it is attached to digital pin 13, on MKR1000 on pin 6. LED_BUILTIN is set to
 8   the correct LED pin independent of which board is used.
 9   If you want to know what pin the on-board LED is connected to on your Arduino
10   model, check the Technical Specs of your board at:
11   https://www.arduino.cc/en/Main/Products
12
13   modified 8 May 2014
14   by Scott Fitzgerald
15   modified 2 Sep 2016
16   by Arturo Guadalupi
17   modified 8 Sep 2016
18   by Colby Newman
19
20   This example code is in the public domain.
21
22   http://www.arduino.cc/en/Tutorial/Blink
23 */
24
25 // the setup function runs once when you press reset or power the board
```

Above
The Arduino Blink sketch

Most Arduino devices include an LED on board, hard-wired into one of the Arduino's I/O ports. The included Blink sketch enables you to quickly accomplish something with the Arduino – turning that on-board LED on and off repeatedly.

Note: The Blink sketch starts with a long and thorough introductory comment block that we're omitting here for brevity's sake. We'll show you how to open the sketch soon, so you'll be able to study the whole sketch in detail.

```
// the setup function runs once when you press
reset or
// power the board
void setup() {
  // initialize digital pin LED_BUILTIN as an
output.
  pinMode(LED_BUILTIN, OUTPUT);
}
```

Below
Configuring the IDE for the connected Arduino board

```
// the loop function runs over and over again
forever
void loop() {
  // turn the LED on (HIGH is the voltage level)
  digitalWrite(LED_BUILTIN, HIGH);
  // wait for a second
  delay(1000);
  // turn the LED off by making the voltage LOW
  digitalWrite(LED_BUILTIN, LOW);
  // wait for a second
  delay(1000);
}
```

In the **setup** function, there's only one executable line:

```
pinMode(LED_BUILTIN, OUTPUT);
```

Calling **pinMode** sets the configuration for one of the Arduino's I/O pins. In this case, its configuring the I/O pin defined in **LED_BUILTIN** for output mode. Remember, most Arduino boards have an on-board LED; the Arduino team has preconfigured the Arduino development environment to store the I/O pin associated with each Arduino board in a variable called **LED_BUILTIN**. Any time the sketch references **LED_BUILTIN**, the compiler replaces the reference with the actual pin number to which the LED is connected. The Arduino Zero has its LED wired to I/O pin 13, so for the Zero, the code is essentially:

```
pinMode(13, OUTPUT);
```

With this in place, the sketch knows that when working with pin 13, it will be outputting (sending a voltage) to the pin, not receiving input.

In the `loop` function, the code completes the following steps:

◈ Uses the **digitalWrite** method to set the output voltage on the **LED_BUILTIN** pin to **HIGH**. This means that the pin gets a voltage equivalent to the current operating voltage of the Arduino. Some Arduino devices operate at 3 V and others at 5 V; all that's important to know here is that with execution of this code, the Arduino is now powering the LED connected to the I/O pin at its brightest.

◈ Waits for 1000 milliseconds (1 second) using the **delay()** method.

◈ Uses the **digitalWrite** method to set the output voltage on the **LED_BUILTIN** pin to LOW. This translates to no voltage (0), essentially turning the LED off.

◈ Waits for 1000 milliseconds (1 second) using the **delay()** method.

Below ◈
Setting the IDE's communication port

Below ◈
Compile and Deploy buttons

When the code runs, it will turn the LED on for 1 second, then off for 1 second, repeating the process until you remove power from the device or deploy a different sketch.

Now it's time to see the sketch in operation. To do this, you'll start by installing the Arduino IDE on your computer system. Open your browser of choice and navigate to **arduino.cc**. On the site's top menu, click the Software link, then, on the page that opens, download the latest version of the Arduino IDE for your system's operating system. Once the download completes, launch the downloaded file to begin the software installation.

Once the installation completes, start the Arduino IDE. In the Arduino IDE, open the File menu, select Examples, then 01.basics, then Blink, as shown in **Figure 2** (page 17).

```
Archiving built core (caching) in: C:\
Users\JOHNWARGO\AppData\Local\Temp\arduino_
cache_950966\core\core_arduino_avr_uno_
c3bfe3f79ffbeab93536a1a484b588d9.a
Sketch uses 928 bytes (2%) of program storage
space. Maximum is 32256 bytes.
Global variables use 9 bytes (0%) of dynamic
memory, leaving 2039 bytes for local variables.
Maximum is 2048 bytes.
```

If the verification fails, the IDE will display information about any errors and reference the sketch line number where the error was found. You'll need to fix any errors before continuing to the next step.

Finally, click the Upload button; the IDE will repeat the verification step, then deploy the compiled sketch to the connected Arduino device. When the upload process completes, the Arduino device will immediately reset, then begin executing the new sketch. In this example, the Arduino will turn its on-board LED on and off repeatedly until power is removed from the board or a different sketch is uploaded.

Now it's time to play around with the code. If you remember from earlier, the sketch uses delay statements to control the amount of time the LED is on and off. Right now, they're coded to pause 1 second (1000 milliseconds); modify the code so the LED stays on for half a second (500 milliseconds) and pauses for two seconds (2000 milliseconds) in between. Upload the modified code to the board and see what happens. □

> **"** To program an Arduino device, you'll code applications in a language similar to **an old language called C;** these applications are called sketches **"**

NEXT STEPS

We've only lightly brushed the surface of what you can do with the Arduino platform. To make it easier for Arduino developers to get started, the IDE includes a whole catalogue of example applications you can study and use to expand your skills. To access these examples, in the Arduino IDE, open the File menu, select Examples, then look for a sketch category that appeals to you. The Basics category offers some simple sketches you can use to expand from where we've started here. There's a simple sketch to fade the on-board LED up and down (instead of turning it on and off, as in the Blink example). There are also sketches for reading analogue or digital signals; you'd use these with the appropriate analogue or digital output device connected to the Arduino. The other sketch categories offer more sophisticated sketches that work with different hardware devices and more.

SCHOOL OF MAKING

Reading digital data on the Arduino platform

Learn how to read external data in an Arduino project

John Wargo

🐦 @johnwargo

John is a professional software developer, writer, presenter, father, husband, and geek. He is currently a Program Manager at Microsoft, working on Visual Studio Mobile Center. You can find him at **johnwargo.com**

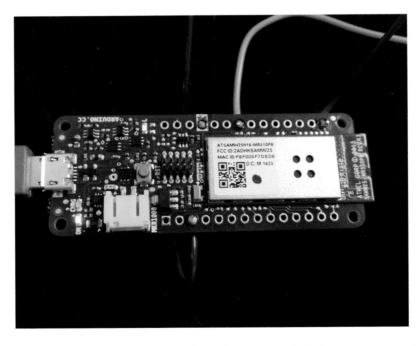

Left ◤
The Arduino development environment includes code highlighting, to help you spot typos in your code

n the previous tutorial, we showed you how to blink the built-in LED on an Arduino device. Here, we'll show you how to use a push-button to toggle the LED on and off. This article illustrates one way to read digital data using an Arduino.

Arduino boards offer several ways to interact with external hardware components, in all cases this means sending a signal to, or reading data from, an external device. Those inputs and outputs, coupled with the logic you've coded in your project's sketch, are the meat of any Arduino project. Arduino inputs come in two formats: analogue and digital, in this article, we'll cover one way to use digital inputs.

Each digital input on the Arduino can read two values: LOW and HIGH. LOW is a constant defined within the Arduino IDE that essentially means zero (or very little) voltage. A value of HIGH references the highest voltage value the Arduino can support (typically 3 V (volts) on an Arduino operating at 3 V, and 5 V on an Arduino operating at 5 V).

Note: Any Arduino device you use for your projects will have one or more digital inputs; these usually double as digital outputs as well. You learned how to use a digital output in the series' previous article.

You might be saying to yourself: "How useful is a digital input if it's only either on or off? That's only one bit, right?" On the Arduino, digital inputs are used in two different ways: to read point-in-time input values, such as the status of a button, or to read a stream of binary digits (bits) values which an application converts into more useful data such as bytes, or numbers. In this article, you'll find out how to use a digital input to read the status of a push-button.

DIGITAL INPUTS CAN READ SINGLE VALUES OR STREAMS OF DATA

In the previous article in this series, we showed you how to use the default Arduino Blink sketch to turn an Arduino's on-board LED on and off on a specific interval. In this tutorial, we'll extend that project and use a button to turn on and toggle the status of the LED. When the push-button is depressed (pushed), the LED turns on. When the push-button is up (open), the LED turns off.

Before we wire up the circuit, let's take a look at the code (you can find the complete code for the example at **hsmag.cc/KTioNX**).

The sketch defines the **BTNPIN** constant used to identify the Arduino digital input pin to which the button is connected. Following a common convention, we created the constant name in all capital letters, making it easy to distinguish constants from variables in a sketch. You'll populate this constant value with the pin number for your particular hardware implementation.

Next, the sketch defines the **btnState** variable, which is used to store the current state of the button; this value is used to determine whether to turn the LED on or off. Notice how we initialised the variable to **LOW**; this isn't required, but gives the sketch a fallback in case it can't read the button, setting the LED to off by default the first time through the loop.

```
// BTNPIN defines the Arduino input pin to which the
// button is connected
const int BTNPIN = 2;

// btnState stores the current button state (HIGH
or LOW)
// initialize it to LOW so the LED stays off until
the sketch
// reads a HIGH state for the button input
int btnState = LOW;
```

In the sketch's **setup** function, the code sets the mode for the Arduino I/O (input/output) pins used by the sketch. The sketch calls **pinMode** to set the default LED pin (defined in the Arduino IDE's constant **LED_BUILTIN**) to output mode, then calling **pinMode** again to set the push-button pin to input mode. Finally, the function turns the LED off, through a call to **digitalWrite**, just to make sure we start with the LED in a known state before the first loop begins.

```
// The setup function runs once every time the
Arduino
// powers up or resets (after a sketch update, for
example)
```

STAYING CONSTANT

A good practice for developers is to use constants to store values used in multiple places in a sketch. The **BTNPIN** constant is a good example for this; by pulling the value into a constant defined at the beginning of the sketch, you make it easy to change this value if the hardware configuration changes (if you connect the button to another digital input pin, for example). You could skip this step, but if you later changed the input pin for your project, you'd have to locate every place in the sketch where it's used, then change each instance. For this small sketch it's not that big of an issue, but for larger sketches it's much easier to do it this way and make one change that affects the whole sketch instead of many little edits, and potentially missing one.

```
void setup() {
// initialize digital pin LED_BUILTIN as an
output.
pinMode(LED_BUILTIN, OUTPUT);
// initialize the push button pin as an input:
pinMode(BTNPIN, INPUT);
// set the initial state of the LED (off)
digitalWrite(LED_BUILTIN, btnState);
}
```

In the sketch's **loop** function, the code reads the button status through a call to **digitalRead** and stores the result in the **btnState** variable. Next, the code →

Figure 1 ◈
The Fritzing tool (fritzing.org) can be a great way of desiging your circuits before starting on your breadboard

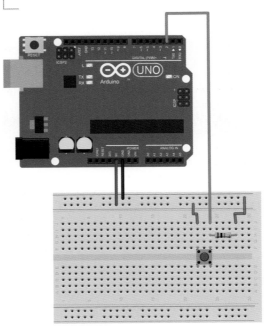

QUICK TIP

The resistor is used in this circuit to help force consistency of digital input values. Without the shunted circuit to ground, there's no clear definition of LOW vs. HIGH, and the input could 'float' at an indeterminate value without an input value applied. With the resistor in place, there's a clear definition of LOW when the button is open through the connection to ground. With the button pushed, the 'slower' path (through the resistor) is ignored because it's a more expensive route than the direct route to the digital input.

BOUNCING ALONG

Bouncing and debouncing are terms used when describing interactions with electrical connections like the one we have in the push-button used in this project. As a button or switch begins a connection or disconnection, there's an uncertainty in the connection as the contacts move. A button potentially makes multiple intermittent connections until the button contacts connect solidly; this is called bouncing. To mitigate bouncing, Arduino developers implement debouncing, a mechanism used to force a single signal from the button through some extra code. In this example, the code debounces the button connection by forcing the application to wait a minimum amount of time with a connection before considering it to be accurate.

uses the value in **btnState** to set the LED status using a call to **digitalWrite**. When **btnState** is **LOW**, the code turns the LED off; when **HIGH**, it turns it on.

```
// The loop function runs repeatedly as long as a sketch is
// loaded and the Arduino has power.
void loop() {
 // Read the state of the button; it's a digital input,
 // so possible returned values are HIGH or LOW.
 btnState = digitalRead(BTNPIN);
 // Use the measured value to set the LED state
 digitalWrite(LED_BUILTIN, btnState);
 // This whole function can be simplified to the following
 // single line of code:
 // digitalWrite(LED_BUILTIN, digitalRead(BTNPIN));
}
```

Below ⬏
The complete circuit assembled and running with an Arduino Uno

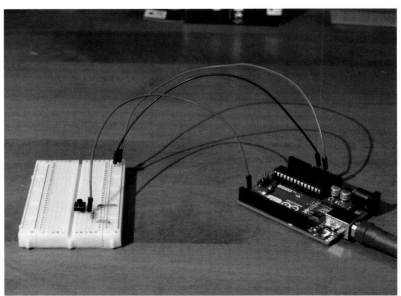

The code, as shown, breaks that action into two steps: reading the value from the input pin into a variable, then using that variable value to set the output on the default LED pin. That's a great way to do it when you're illustrating how to do something, but you'll use less memory and get better performance in your sketch if you consolidate the two steps into one, as shown in the commented line in the code (shown here uncommented):

```
digitalWrite(LED_BUILTIN, digitalRead(BTNPIN));
```

Here, the result from the call to **digitalRead** is passed as an input to **digitalWrite**. You won't get tremendous performance benefit doing this here but, for larger sketches, especially when you're bumping up against memory limits on the Arduino device, it's a useful approach.

PUSH TO START

Push-buttons are mechanical devices, and as you're pushing or releasing the button, there's no guarantee that the Arduino can get a solid reading every time the button is pushed or released. To accommodate this, you can adjust your sketch so it debounces the button connection, ensuring that the button has been pressed for a minimum number of time before triggering a change in LED status.

In the following example, we've enhanced the previous example to include debouncing; you can find the complete code for the following example at **hsmag.cc/pEzXyu**.

At the beginning of the code, the sketch defines the same **BTNPIN** constant and **btnState** variable used in the previous example. We've also added the **prevBtnState** variable to keep track of the previous state of the button, and the **ledState** to track the current state of the LED. The **lastToggle** variable keeps track of the time the button state changed. Finally, the **DEBOUNCE_DELTA** constant defines the number of milliseconds the sketch waits before it believes in a reading from the button. You'll see all of these in action later in the sketch.

```
// BTNPIN defines the Arduino input pin to which the
// button is connected
const int BTNPIN = 2;
// btnState stores the current button state (HIGH or LOW)
// initialize it to LOW so the LED stays off until the sketch
// reads a HIGH state for the button input
```

```
int btnState = LOW;
// A place to store the previous loop's button
state
int prevBtnState = LOW;
// Used to track the current state of the LED
int ledState = LOW;
// Stores the last time the status of the button
changed
unsigned long lastToggle = 0;
// Specifies the amount of time the button must
stay pushed for it
// to trigger the LED on or off. Increase this
value if your LED
// flickers
const unsigned long DEBOUNCE_DELTA = 100;   //
milliseconds
```

The **setup** function is precisely the same as the previous example.

```
void setup() {
  // initialize digital pin LED_BUILTIN as an
output.
  pinMode(LED_BUILTIN, OUTPUT);
  // initialize the push button pin as an input:
  pinMode(BTNPIN, INPUT);
  // set the initial state of the LED
  digitalWrite(LED_BUILTIN, ledState);
}
```

In the **loop** function, the code reads the button using **digitalRead**, just like the previous example. Next, the code checks to see if the current state of the button is the same as it was the previous time the loop executed. If it isn't, the code stores the current time in the **lastToggle** variable.

AROUND AGAIN
The next time through the loop, if the button state hasn't changed, the sketch checks to see how long its been since the last toggle (by subtracting the value in **lastToggle** from the current time). If the button state hasn't changed in more than **DEBOUNCE_DELTA** milliseconds **(if ((millis() - lastToggle) > DEBOUNCE_DELTA))**, then the sketch knows it has an accurate button reading, and it toggles the LED.

```
void loop() {
  // Read the current state of the button
  btnState = digitalRead(BTNPIN);

  // Is the button in the same state as the last
time
  // we came through the loop? No? Then we need
```

```
to record
  // the current time (in milliseconds)
  if (btnState != prevBtnState) {
    // store the current time in milliseconds
    //It doesn't matter what the actual time is,
all we need
    // to know is how long did the button stay in
this state
    lastToggle = millis();
    //Reset our previous state, so this check
skips next time
    prevBtnState = btnState;
  } else {
    // OK, the button states (current and
previous) are the same
    // Lets see if they've been the same for
DEBOUNCE_DELTA
    // milliseconds
    if ((millis() - lastToggle) > DEBOUNCE_DELTA)
{
      // the button's been pushed (or not pushed)
for at
      // least debounceDelta milliseconds, so its
time to
      // toggle the LED if needed
      //Is the LED at the same state as the button?
      if (ledState != btnState) {
      // No? Then toggle it
      digitalWrite(LED_BUILTIN, btnState);
      //Then reset the LED status
      ledState = btnState;
    }
   }
  }
}
```

To test either of these sketches, wire a button into an Arduino (see **Figure 1**, page 21). On one side of the button, the connection shunts from the 5 V connection through the 10 kΩ resistor to ground (GND). The other button connection routes to the digital input pin 2. With the button pushed, a connection is made from the 5 V source to the digital input, bypassing the resistor and forcing the circuit to **HIGH**. When the button is released, the connection to the digital input pin disappears, and the voltage runs through the resistor to ground, making it **LOW**.

Using the Arduino IDE, upload the code to the Arduino device and try pushing the button to toggle the LED on and off. Play around with the value in the **DEBOUNCE_DELTA** constant to see how it affects the sketch's reaction to the button.

Don't forget, all of the project source code is available at **hsmag.cc/dMDWFx**. □

QUICK TIP
The Arduino's `millis()` method retrieves the current time in milliseconds since the Arduino started running the current sketch; it doesn't give the sketch an accurate time, but does let the sketch track how long it has been since a previous measurement.

BIG DELTA
`lastToggle` and `DEBOUNCE_DELTA` are both long integers because the sketch uses them to calculate time deltas, and time values are very large integers. Even though `DEBOUNCE_DELTA` is a small number (comparatively), since the sketch will be doing arithmetic using those values, we made them the same type to avoid any conversion issues.

SCHOOL OF MAKING

Arduino programming:
Seven-segment displays and multidimensional arrays

Get meaningful output out of your projects and master interdimensional data storage

Graham Morrison

🐦 @degville

Graham is a veteran Linux journalist who is on a life-long quest to find music in the perfect arrangement of silicon

YOU'LL NEED

- **Kingbright SC10-EWA**
- **Arduino Uno**
- **7 × 220 Ω resistors**
- **Breadboard**
- **Connectors**

Left ⬉
You can get RGB seven-segment displays that have separate pins for the red, green, and blue LEDs in each segment

W hen it comes to programming the Arduino, one of the most important skills to master is taking a physical problem and then constructing a solution that can be expressed efficiently in code. This gets easier with hardware and code experience, but it's important to note that whether you're an expert or a complete beginner, your first solution is highly unlikely to be the best, and in most cases a project may be completely rewritten once, twice, thrice, even four times. Each successive rewrite will incorporate the experience learned from the previous version, as you begin to better understand how to make your solution work.

This is what makes variable types, and the related subject of data structures, so important. Not only do they enable you to write code that makes the most efficient use of your hardware, they allow you to more accurately define your solutions in code. For example, it's perfectly acceptable to use an 'int' type to store which Arduino digital pin to use for an LED. But, as the typical Arduino only has around 14 digital pins, using a variable capable of holding any whole number between -32 768 and +32 767 is considerable, especially when Arduinos have so little RAM. And there's a variable type that works the same and takes less space: the 'byte' type holds an 8-bit unsigned number and, if you can remember your binary mathematics, this works out to be a number between 0 and 255. It's not perfect, but it's more memory-efficient and easier for readers of your code to understand and modify because you've set limits on how the variable should be used. Creating structures that have limits is one of the cornerstones of object-oriented programming.

To put this idea into practice, and explore further how variables are used in a working example, we're going to create a simple foundation project that can be used at the heart of many more ambitious projects. The reason why this project can be used in so many others is because it takes the simple idea behind every basic Arduino LED example and expands upon this to build a fully fledged output device capable of representing many different alphanumeric characters. The simple component used to perform this magic is the humble seven-segment display, as used on the Apollo spacecraft, pinball machines, and microwave ovens. With a seven-segment display, your devices can communicate with the outside world, whether that's a temperature or volume reading, or the radiation level on your Geiger counter. In fact, a seven-segment display would be the perfect upgrade to the temperature sensor project described in HackSpace issue 3 (**hsmag/issue3**)

A seven-segment display is really little more than seven LEDs in a single package, or eight if you include a decimal point. Pins alongside two edges will correspond to either the negative or positive input pins for each LED, dependent on whether your display uses a common anode or common cathode path. This type difference dictates whether a segment/LED is lit by either grounding the pin, or by providing it with 5 volts (respectively). In our example, we'll be using the more usual 'common cathode' type, but the wiring can be simply inverted if you find yourself with the opposite kind of display.

> A seven-segment display is really little more than seven LEDs in a single package, **or eight if you include a decimal point**

WIRING UP

Getting the polarity of an LED correct is vital, and the same is true with a seven-segment display. The only real difference is that with a seven-segment display, all seven of those LEDs are fused into either common anode or common cathode, and you need to get this correct for the whole thing to work. Only the specification of your displays will tell you which way around you'll need to wire the display and which pins are used for common ground or power, but it should still be a very simple circuit to wire. With our specific hardware, one pin connects to ground (GND) on the Arduino while the majority of the remaining pins connect to Arduino →

Below ◈
For a common cathode display, Arduino digital pins 2,3,4,5,6, and 7 should connect with segments a,b,c,d, e,f,g respectively, plus ground

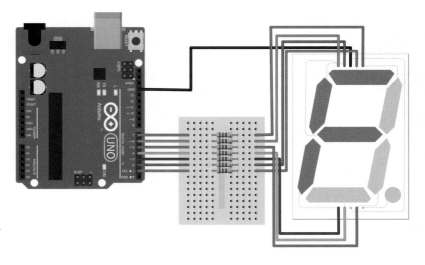

SCHOOL OF MAKING

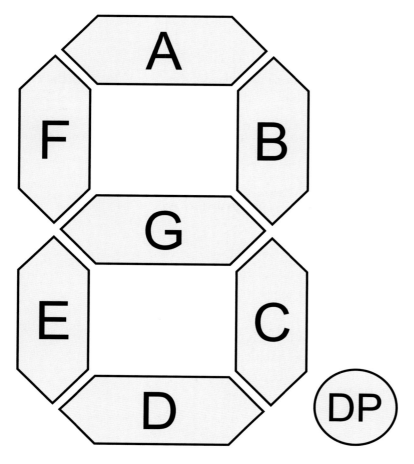

Right ◈
Defining all your data at the start of an Arduino sketch makes it easy to find and update if your hardware changes

We'll start off by introducing an array. The good news is that if you've done any kind of programming before, you'll already be familiar with arrays. An array is a series of values, all of the same type, encapsulated into a single variable. By defining an array, you don't have to go through the lengthy process of creating and assigning values separately, plus the compiler that turns your code into a binary file can usually make more efficient use of an array. It can ask for ten consecutive chunks of memory, all of the same size, for example, rather than ten individual requests that may be scattered about in memory. The consecutive nature of data stored within an array is often reflected in the way a programming language will let you automatically step through one, or access values within an array via an offset.

ARRAY WE GO

You define an array just like any other variable, except you need to specify the size of the array (so that the memory can be reserved for the correct number of values), and the values for each position within the array.

For example, the following creates an array called **segPin** that holds seven values, each of the type 'byte':

```
const int segPin[7]={1,7,5,4,3,2,6};
```

As you can guess, **segPin** holds the number of each Arduino digital pin that's connected to the seven-segment display, following the clockwise wiring of the segment order. Pin 1, for instance, is connected to the pin that activates the segment labelled 'a'. The reason why our example isn't a sequential set of numbers is

digital outputs 2–7 via 220 ohm resistors (that prevent too much current flowing through the LEDs). The usual configuration sees the pins wired clockwise from the top, but this should also be described in your display's specification document. Don't worry if you can't make sense of which pin is responsible for which segment – see the 'Which segment is which?' box on page 29 for how to work this out manually.

Which leaves us with the code. Writing the code for lighting an LED connected to a digital pin on the Arduino has been covered many times before, and specifically in HackSpace #3. A single variable holds the pin number which is used as an argument within a function called **digitalWrite** to send either an on or off signal to the pin. We could approach a seven-segment display in exactly the same way, creating seven separate variables to hold the pin numbers and then writing seven different function calls to either turn on or turn off the specific elements within the display. And this is where both knowledge of the programming language and experience with design comes in, because computers and their programming languages are developed to solve this exact type of repetitive problem.

```
7seg-working | Arduino 1.8.5
File Edit Sketch Tools Help

7seg-working §

// Code for HackSpace magazine
// Displays hexadecimal numbers on a seven segment display

// DISPLAY ORDER: a,b,c,d,e,f,g
const byte segPin[7] = {1, 7, 5, 4, 3, 2, 6};

// Characters 0,1,2,3,4,5,6,7,8,9,a,b,c,d,e,f
bool segNum[16][7] = {
  {1, 1, 1, 1, 1, 1, 0}, {0, 1, 1, 0, 0, 0, 0},
  {1, 1, 0, 1, 1, 0, 1}, {1, 1, 1, 1, 0, 0, 1},
  {0, 1, 1, 0, 0, 1, 1}, {1, 0, 1, 1, 0, 1, 1},
  {1, 0, 1, 1, 1, 1, 1}, {1, 1, 1, 0, 0, 0, 0},
  {1, 1, 1, 1, 1, 1, 1}, {1, 1, 1, 1, 0, 1, 1},
  {1, 1, 1, 0, 1, 1, 1}, {0, 0, 1, 1, 1, 1, 1},
  {1, 0, 0, 1, 1, 1, 0}, {0, 1, 1, 1, 1, 0, 1},
  {1, 0, 0, 1, 1, 1, 1}, {1, 0, 0, 0, 1, 1, 1},
};

//// useful for testing
//bool segNum[10][7]={
//{1,0,0,0,0,0,0}, {0,1,0,0,0,0,0},
//{0,0,1,0,0,0,0}, {0,0,0,1,0,0,0},
//{0,0,0,0,1,0,0}, {0,0,0,0,0,1,0},
//{0,0,0,0,0,0,1}, {0,0,0,0,0,0,0},
//{1,1,1,1,1,1,1}, {0,0,0,0,0,0,0},
//};
```

Left ◧
Multiple seven-segment displays may be multiplexed, and this allows them to run on fewer pins at the expense of more complex code

purely to do with the way we wired the circuit, and more organised builders would surely connect 1 to a, 2 to b, and so on. We, however, got our cables crossed at some point and this is reflected in the order of the array. If you wire them in order, simply replace the array with {1,2,3,4,5,6,7}. And because these pin assignments aren't going to change while the code is running, we've made the type 'constant', as covered in HackSpace #4.

An array can be used just like any other variable except that rather than using the name of the array alone, you need to also target a specific element within the array within square brackets. To set the pin mode of the first element within the array to 'OUTPUT', for instance, you'd use this:

```
pinMode(segPin[0], OUTPUT);
```

Infamously, arrays and lots of other sequential programming elements start at zero rather than one, so the above code is setting the pin mode of the first element (coincidentally, digital pin 1) to OUTPUT. So far, this is no different to using a regular variable. We could copy this line seven times and update the array reference number to run through the list of pins, just as we would with variables. But the array reference number is a clue. By making this a reference to another variable which we then increment to step through every element of the array, we can construct a much smaller and more efficient loop. Here's the code that does exactly that:

```
void setup(){
  for (int i=0; i<=7; i++){
    pinMode(segPin[i], OUTPUT);
  }
}
```

We've tucked the above code within the **setup()** function, as this is called automatically when your sketch starts. It's perfect for doing initialisation, such as setting pin modes, which is exactly what we're doing here. We've replaced the specific element value of the array, 0, with a variable called **i**. This variable is initialised within the arguments of the **for** command, which is probably one of the most common logical constructs of any programming languages. The **for** statement will simply repeat through the code that follows within the curly braces for as many times as defined by an increment counter initialised within the brackets. This initialiser always seems a little arcane, but regardless of language, it's only ever really saying, "take this variable, check it doesn't meet these requirements, and increment (or decrement) until it hopefully does."

In our example, we're creating the variable **i** with an initial value of 0. The **for** loop will then run while **i** remains less than 8 (our array holds elements 0 to 7, so the loop will stop before **i** gets to 8) and after each run will increment **i** by 1. This is what **i++** means; **++** and **--** are special kinds of operators, known →

QUICK TIP

A seven-segment display is actually capable of representing 127 different patterns – enough to create your own alphanumeric code!

Right ◈
Seven segments not enough? You can display a full range of alphanumeric characters on a 14-segment display

> A seven-segment display is capable of generating lots of recognisable output, **easily showing the numbers 0–9 and the characters a–f**

as compound operators, that take a single operand and either increment or decrement the value by 1. They're almost shorthand for `i = i + 1` or `i = i - 1` with one exception: if the `++` is placed after the variable, the variable is incremented after any evaluation. If the `++` comes before the variable, the variable is incremented before any evaluation. The following code should make this clearer:

```
1. i = 1;
2. j = i++;
3. j = ++i;
```

On line 2 above, `j` is assigned the value of `i` before `i` is incremented, making `j` equal to 1 while `i` equals 2. On line 3, `i` is incremented before any evaluation and then assigned to `j`, making both `i` and `j` equal 3.

The only code executed within the curly braces after the **for** definition is a single line, almost identical to the line we used earlier to set the mode of pin 0. The difference is an individual character where we've replaced the absolute value of 0 for

the first element in the array with `i`. It shouldn't take much to guess that as **for** loops over each iteration of `i`, this value will step through 0,1,2,3,4,5,6, and 7, assigning all the Arduino pins we've configured to output with a single line. That's why arrays can be so powerful and why, as your projects become more complex, you can save yourself a lot of time and pain by simply choosing the best data structures. Such as the one in our next step – two-dimensional arrays!

THE SECOND DIMENSION

So far, we have used an array to store the pin allocation for the connections to the seven-segment display. The next step is to send on and off signals to the various elements within the display to create some meaningful output. As you will already know, despite being only a grouping of LEDs, the layout and design of these means a seven-segment display is capable of generating lots of recognisable output, easily showing the numbers 0–9 and the characters a–f. This perfectly corresponds to the base 16 or hexadecimal numeral system, with characters (a–f) representing the values (10–15) respectively, and this is what we're going to code our display to show.

We could easily use an array to store each of these 16 characters. For example, the following creates an array of type 'bool' to hold either an on (1) or off (0) value for each pin connected to the display:

```
bool segNum[7]={1,1,1,1,1,1,0};
```

If you were to display the above using a **for** loop similar to the one we created earlier, you would see the number 0, which you can guess because there's only one element not lit – the middle element of the seven-segment display.

We could go on and create arrays for every character we want to display along with **for** loops and functions to handle them. But this would be horribly inefficient and tedious to implement and maintain. You might think that we've already played the array card, but they have the answer once again. Just like a line on a single axis is said to have a single dimension, an array has a single dimension if it only has one set of elements. But like a line with two dimensions, x and y co-ordinates for example, an array can have two dimensions and even more.

Here is the code for an array with two dimensions, the first for the 16 characters we want the array to store and the second for the seven on/off pin configurations for each character:

```
bool segNum[16][7]={
{1,1,1,1,1,1,0}, {0,1,1,0,0,0,0},
{1,1,0,1,1,0,1}, {1,1,1,1,0,0,1},
{0,1,1,0,0,1,1}, {1,0,1,1,0,1,1},
{1,0,1,1,1,1,1}, {1,1,1,0,0,0,0},
{1,1,1,1,1,1,1}, {1,1,1,1,0,1,1},
{1,1,1,0,1,1,1}, {0,0,1,1,1,1,1},
{1,0,0,1,1,1,0}, {0,1,1,1,1,0,1},
{1,0,0,1,1,1,1}, {1,0,0,0,1,1,1},
};
```

As you can see if you follow the curly braces, the first set holds the outside array of 16 elements, each held within its own smaller seven-element array. You can even add more dimensions to an array, but like multidimensional space-time, these arrays become very difficult to conceptualise.

The only problem we now have left to solve is augmenting our **for** loop to handle all this interdimensional space. This is easy if we put the whole thing into its own function:

```
void displayNum (int number) {
  for (int i = 0; i < 8; i++) {
    if (segNum[number][i]) {
      digitalWrite(segPin[i], HIGH);
    } else {
      digitalWrite(segPin[i], LOW);
} } }
```

The above code expands on the earlier **for** loop in several ways. Firstly, it's encapsulated the logic within a function. This means we can call **displayNum(4)**

whenever we need the number 4 displayed, rather than repeating the same old code. Within the function, the **for** loop steps through a counter for each pin, only this time there's an extra **if** and **else** command. These reference our two-dimensional **segPin** array to check whether a pin should be set to on (HIGH) or off (LOW), and they do this using the two sets of the same square brackets used to create the array. Only this time, rather than setting the size of the array, they're used to reference a specific element. Keeping with our two-dimensional line theory, this is equivalent to a specific x and y location. The trick is that this location is defined by the number passed to the function, used to point at the character we want to draw, and the value of **i** which is being incremented by the **for** loop so that each pin can be set separately.

All that is now left to do is write the central **loop** function that the sketch calls automatically and use this to call the new **displayNum** function, ideally stepping through all the characters we can now step through on our seven-segment display:

```
void loop() {
  for (int i = 0; i <= 15; i++) {
    displayNum(i);
    delay(500);
} }
```

WHICH SEGMENT IS WHICH?

The schematics for elements like a seven-segment display can be difficult to follow. For this reason, you might find it easier to work out which pin goes where with a brute force approach. This is actually what we had to do and why the array that holds the order of pin connections is in a strange order.

The easiest way to do this is to take the code from this tutorial and replace the two-dimensional array holding the characters with the following:

```
bool segNum[10][7]={
{1,0,0,0,0,0,0}, {0,1,0,0,0,0,0},
{0,0,1,0,0,0,0}, {0,0,0,1,0,0,0},
{0,0,0,0,1,0,0}, {0,0,0,0,0,1,0},
{0,0,0,0,0,0,1}, {0,0,0,0,0,0,0},
{1,1,1,1,1,1,1}, {0,0,0,0,0,0,0},
};
```

When you run this code, the seven-segment display should light up each element in order, a–f. You just need to change the pin array variable so that what you see follows the same order and then everything else will work automatically.

QUICK TIP

The code for this project can be found at the following URL: **git.io/vAS8Y**

SCHOOL OF MAKING ━━━━━━━━━━━━━━━━━━━━━━━━━━━━━━━━━━━━

Arduino programming:
multiplexing, operators, and four seven-segments

Use the simple power of operators to multiply your project's capabilities without adding code

Graham Morrison

🐦 @degville

Graham is a veteran Linux journalist who is on a life-long quest to find music in the perfect arrangement of silicon

I**n the previous tutorial, we had fun getting a seven-segment display to work and writing the code to make it show something useful.** This time we're going to expand on those foundations to build something four times better. Four times better exactly, in fact, as we're going to upgrade our hardware from a single digit to four, transforming the humble seven-segment into something capable of far more – numbers up to 9999 in base ten, and even a few words.

The first thing that likely crossed your mind with this plan, apart from trying to work out which swear words can be shown, is how this is all going to be wired to a humble Arduino. If you followed our tutorial last time,

you'll know that we needed to use a total of eight pins on the Arduino to control the display, exactly as we would if we were driving seven LEDs separately, which is all a seven-segment display really is. With eight pins taken, there aren't enough remaining on a normal Arduino to handle another seven-segment display, let alone another three. So how is it going to be done? The answer to this is multiplexing (see the 'Multiplexing' box on the next page for details of how this works).

Below ◈
With multiplexing, you can light up more LEDs than you've got pins for. Bring on the blinkenlights!

The main problem with multiplexing is that you can only turn on one segment at a time. Turn on any more and other segments on other digits will also light up. The solution to this is to light each LED briefly as part of a cycle through the LEDs that need to be lit. It may seem remarkable in an age where computers take seconds to boot and webpages minutes to load, but the Arduino can do this quickly enough that the persistence of vision effect, where your eyes still see an object for a brief moment after the object is no longer visible, makes them appear solid.

The specific unit we're using is a 3461BS four-digit seven-segment display, although each digit also has a decimal point. This unit has twelve pins, six on the top edge and six on the lower edge, and while other four-digit displays may place these pins in different locations, the physical configuration will be the same after you've identified (from the unit's specification sheet) which pin does what. The specification for our display uses pins 1,2,3,4,5,7,10, and 11 for segments E, D, decimal point, C, G, B, F, and A respectively, and pins 6, 8, 9, and 12 for the common cathode

MULTIPLEXING

Multiplexing allows you to drive multiple LEDs, ergo multiple seven-segment displays, by taking advantage of the way LEDs use a potential difference in voltages to activate rather than just simply being 'on'. This dependence on a differential means that if the two pins connected to a segment are set the same, such as both being set to HIGH or LOW, the LED won't light, whereas any difference in the two connections, such as LOW and HIGH or HIGH and LOW, will light the LED. This behaviour can be exploited by wiring multiple LEDs or segments to a grid of crossing connections. As long as each pair of connections is unique, such as (A,B), (A,C), (B,C), the specific LED using those connections can be targeted. This saves your breadboard doubling as a tapestry loom, but it also means you can drive many more LEDs with the Arduino's humble allotment of digital I/O pins. However, there's one significant caveat: only one element or segment can be lit at any one time. Try to turn on more than one and the crosstalk in the wiring matrix will light other segments too.

or anode. Those last four connections are going to be used to multiplex the limited digital connections from the Arduino to the display. See the Wiring box (overleaf) for more details on how to connect these to the pins on your Arduino.

CODE WORDS

With everything wired up, we can finally start playing with some new code. Rather than start from scratch, we're going to augment the code from the previous tutorial, both to avoid repetition and to provide some continuity, but the code can be grabbed from **git.io/vAS8Y**.

With the old code loaded into the Arduino IDE, we're going to start at the top of the file with something we should have added initially – code to automatically handle whether your seven-segment display uses a common anode or common cathode configuration, as explained last time. As programmers, we should be making as few assumptions about the people using our code as possible, and that often means making things that could be specific more generic. In this case, we start by setting a global true of false value for whether a common anode display is being used:

```
const bool ANODE = true;
```

This line does nothing on its own but, like the array we used to hold the pin order for the connections, it's used by later logic to change the behaviour of the code. If we were using old-school C, we'd typically use a #DEFINE statement to declare a global constant value like this. The compiler then effectively swaps a defined value whenever it is referenced within the code. But for Arduino's Processing language, **const** is recommended as it better obeys the rules of variable scoping, which means they're far safer when working with multiple files.

BITWISE OPERATORS

The only part of the code that cares whether the display we're using is common anode or cathode is the part that sets the HIGH or LOW values for the segments. This is because a common anode display requires the opposite signals to the common cathode. The behaviour can be described using something called a 'truth table', which is a very useful tool for understanding your hardware requirements and how they might best be implemented in code. In our case, a truth table can be used to show how we want to reverse the output depending on whether we're using a common anode configuration or not. Using 0 for off and 1 for on, the table would look like the following: →

QUICK TIP

While we definitely recommend the use of resistors to keep your displays and Arduino safe, segments are only turned on for milliseconds, which means you could get away without them.

WIRING

To wire this up, connect the following Arduino pins to those segments indicated on the display, via a 330 Ω resistor. These aren't required for the common anode/cathode pins 10–13:

```
2 -> A
3 -> B
4 -> C
5 -> D
6 -> E
7 -> F
8 -> G

10 -> D1
11 -> D2
12 -> D3
13 -> D4
```

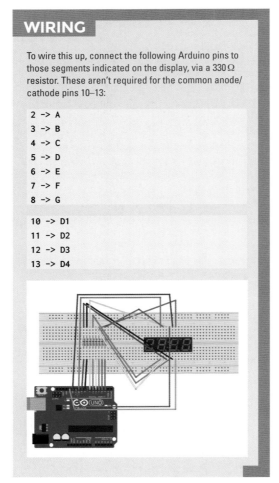

Right ◈
The exact wiring will depend on the specification and pin configuration of your specific display

	A B	Output
1.	0 0	LOW
2.	0 1	HIGH
3.	1 0	HIGH
4.	1 1	LOW

1. If the segment is off (A=0) and the display isn't common anode (B=0), output is LOW.
2. If the segment is off (A=0) and the display is common anode (B=1), output is HIGH.
3. If the segment is on (A=1) and the display isn't common anode (B=0), output is HIGH.
4. If the segment is on (A=1) and the display is common anode (B=1), output is LOW.

The reason for mapping everything out like this is that the simple behaviour described in truth tables can be mapped to special logical operators in code. You're likely already familiar with the logical operators AND and OR – they turn on output depending on where

input 1 AND input 2 are on, or they turn on output if either input 1 OR input 2 are on, including both inputs. Their truth tables look like the following:

```
A B AND        A B OR
0 0 0          0 0 0
0 1 0          0 1 1
1 0 0          1 0 1
1 1 1          1 1 1
```

In Arduino C, the operators that process this simple input are looking at individual bits, the true and false values, and these actually correlate to low-level gates and low-level code. This makes these operators incredibly efficient, which is why it's always worth attempting to refactor your code into these simple computational terms.

Going back to our example and the requirement we have to reverse the input for common anode displays, the first truth table correlates exactly to an operator called XOR, or exclusive 'or'. The X differentiates this operator from the ordinary OR above by not including a positive output when both the inputs values are on (or 1 in the truth table).

We're going to use this operator in a new function that isolates the `digitalWrite` commands:

```
void setSegment(int pin, bool state) {
  if (state ^ ANODE) {
    digitalWrite(pin, HIGH);
  } else {
    digitalWrite(pin, LOW);
  }
}
```

The XOR operator appears on the second line as the circumflex symbol (^). The function itself is called with two arguments: the pin to send the signal to and whether that pin needs to be HIGH or LOW. The efficiency comes because we can question both the requested state and whether the values need inverting with the XOR command, which is going to act exactly like the first truth table.

FOUR TIMES SEVEN

We now need to augment our original routines to handle both the new digits and what will be our method of rendering them. This starts with a new array to hold the pin numbers for the connections to the common anode or cathode. This array will be called `digPin` and the backwards order we've used – 13, 12, 11, and 10 – is intentional as these are connected from least to most significant digits respectively, which will help when we write the program logic. Also, we're updating the pin values we used in the **segPin** array as we've reorganised our circuit to use sequential pin ordering rather than the random plug and pray approach used last time:

```
const byte segPin[8] = {2, 3, 4, 5, 6, 7, 8, 9};
const byte digPin[4]  = {13, 12, 11, 10};
```

The **setup** function also needs to be updated to initialise the new pins we're using. To do this we just add another **for** loop to handle the pins used to target the separate digits:

```
void setup() {
  for (int i = 0; i < 8; i++) {
    pinMode(segPin[i], OUTPUT);
  }
  for (int i = 0; i < 4; i++) {
    pinMode(digPin[i], OUTPUT);
  }
}
```

The next new functions we're going to add will be used to display a number on one of the four displays, rather than displaying a number on the single display we coded last time. The big difference in this implementation is the multiplexing, and this is accomplished by first making the common pin for the digit 'HIGH', writing the number to the seven-segment display, waiting a period for the number to remain visible, and then setting the common pin to LOW to terminate the drawing process.

Here's the code:

```
void displayDigit(int digit, int number) {
  digitalWrite(digPin[digit], HIGH);
  for (int i = 0; i < 8; i++) {
    setSegment(segPin[i], segNum[number][i]);
  }
  delay(5);
  digitalWrite(digPin[digit], LOW);
}
```

The **delay** function pauses execution of the code, allowing the character on the display to linger for a set number of milliseconds. The 5 milliseconds we're using is virtually imperceptible to the human eye, but if you wanted to see how the multiplexing works, set this to something like 200 (a fifth of a second) and watch each seven-segment display update with each different number.

The final piece of this puzzle is to transform the **displayNum** function we used last time to adapt to the four digits rather than a single one. The main job of the new additions will be to split a four-digit number, such as 2543, into its constituent digits, which can then be sent individually to each display.

Above ⬉
We've used the cheap and readily available 3461BS for this project, but almost any other quad seven-segment display will work

To do this, we're going to rely on another incredibly useful operator, the modulo, which uses the percent character (**%**). Modulo will return the remainder of a division, rather than the number of times one number goes into another. This makes it useful in loops as a zero is often interpreted as false, but it's also perfect for peeling off digits. 1234 % 10, for example, will return the last digit, 4. If we then divide the number by 10 and run the modulo again, we'll get the next digit. And that's exactly what we do in this function:

```
void displayNum (int number) {
  int tens = 0;
  while (tens < 4) {
    displayDigit(tens++, number % 10);
    number /= 10;
  }
}
```

The above code includes one last new operator, the **/=** operator. This is closely related to the iterative operators we looked at last time, but instead of incrementing a value, here we divide **number** by 10 and assign the result to **number** in a single command.

All that's now left to do is update the main loop to remove the delay and count to an appropriately large number. This is as simple as changing it to the following:

```
void loop() {
  for (int i = 0; i <= 9999; i++) {
    displayNum(i);
  }
}
```

With that done, upload the code to your Arduino and pretend you've got the ultimate Geiger counter. The code can be found here: **git.io/vxMZ6**. ☐

QUICK TIP

If you connect the segment pins to the same Arduino pins we used last time, you won't need to modify your character or pin order code.

SCHOOL OF MAKING

Arduino programming:
Temperature, humidity, and libraries

Add temperature and humidity readings by summoning external expertise
and knowledge, with just a few lines of your own code

Graham Morrison

🐦 @degville

Graham is a veteran
Linux journalist who is
on a life-long quest to
find music in the perfect
arrangement of silicon

n the previous tutorial, we applied our
nascent C programming skills to extend
what we'd learnt about seven-segment
displays into controlling four seven-
segment displays concurrently, all from
the same Arduino Uno. We finished with
the display counting from 0 to 9999 over and over,
like a 5 volt Sisyphus. This means we now have the
ability to display a four-digit number. Or maybe two
smaller ones side by side...

For the first time, rather than simply using the
Arduino to manage a fancy set of LEDs, we're going
to use it to measure something and then display the
product of those measurements. And to do that,

we're going to turn our seven-segment displays into
both a temperature gauge and a humidity monitor.
The hardware component we're building this project
around is a DHT11 sensor module. These are cheap
and readily available, and the concepts we use to
interface one with the Arduino are almost universal.

The module itself combines both temperature
and humidity sensors, and the great thing about
this module is that it's incredibly easy to use.
They're pre-calibrated, for instance, which means

Below ◈
The exact wiring will depend on the specification and pin
configuration of your specific display

> **The module itself combines both temperature and humidity sensors,** and the great thing about this module is that it's incredibly easy to use

we don't need to worry about the validity of the values we receive, and they send the values when asked correctly. Connecting one to your own projects couldn't be easier either, as there's only a single digital pin that needs to be connected to the Arduino. This pin handles all the communication between the modules and the Arduino, with the only other connections being 3V to 5V VCC for power and GND for a ground connection, both of which can be supplied by the Arduino. A four-pin variant is also available, but the extra pin can be ignored. The specification also recommends the use of a 5 kΩ pull-up resistor connected to the data wire.

HARDWARE

The reason why we've chosen the DHT11 rather than one of its more capable siblings, such as the DHT22, is that the DHT11 returns only integer →

WIRING IT ALL UP

The data line to the sensor can be up to 20 metres long, which may be useful for garden readings!

The circuit for this project builds on the one from the previous tutorial, adding a DHT11 temperature and humidity sensor. The three pins of this sensor need to connect to the 5 V and GND provided by the Arduino, with the data pin connected to digital pin 2 on the Arduino. The specification for our sensor also needed a 5 kΩ resistor between the 5V and data wires, with an optional 100 nF capacitor between power and GND for power filtering.

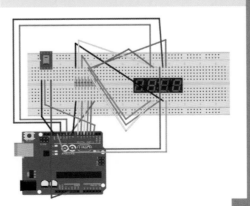

Above ◪
See the temperature and humidity changes in real time on your seven-segment display

SCHOOL OF MAKING

Right ◈
The DHT11 contains a calibrated temperature and humidity sensor, and can operate over 20 metres from your Arduino

temperature and humidity values. This would be limiting if you need a monitor with more precision, such as a temperature sensor attached to a beer fermenter, but it's accurate enough for our needs. In fact, as we're intending to connect the sensor output to four seven-segment displays, we only have four digits to play with – we'll put the temperature on one side and the humidity on the other. This makes the DHT11 perfect for our needs. But you can easily extend its capabilities by swapping out the sensor and just using the temperature value across four digits, or even setting up a line of LEDs to act as a bar graph for today's temperature.

We're now going to dive into the code to get this project to work. Normally, at this point, we'd need to deconstruct exactly what's happening with our circuit. In the previous tutorial, we covered multiplexing; for example, as a way to connect the multiple segments in the display with the limited number of digital pins on the Arduino. Similarly, we would ordinarily need to understand exactly how to communicate with the DHT11 and interpret any data the sensor sends back. This would itself be a complex job, even for a simple sensor like the DHT11. It uses a single pin – a 1-Wire data bus – to both receive signals and to send the data, which would require us to understand the protocol it uses.

If you're lucky, the protocol is well defined and even supplied by the manufacturer, leaving you to implement the code in whatever way works best for you. But often, these protocols aren't documented and will need to be reverse-engineered, either through experimentation or by analysing the input and outputs of a sensor in a working configuration.

> **❝**
> Fortunately, most manufacturers of the DHT11 **also provide a very informative datasheet ❞**

Fortunately, most manufacturers of the DHT11 also provide a very informative datasheet that not only covers the hardware specification and tolerances, but also the details of communicating with the sensor across the 1-Wire data bus. By reading this specification, you find out that the sensor needs a whole second with no signal to pass an initial 'unstable' status, and then you can send a signal to the bus lasting more than 18 ms in order to instantiate a request. The response signal is a 40-bit

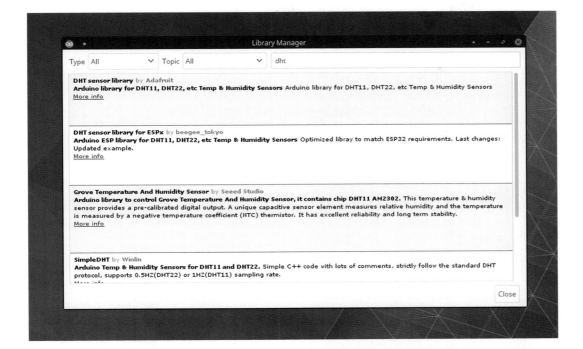

Left ◈
Libraries can be
added manually or
through the Arduino
IDE. They're brilliant
for making complex
hardware easy to use

packet that contains both the relative humidity and
the temperature. But we don't have to worry about
any of this, thanks to what are known as libraries.

LIBRARIES

Previously, we've broken our code into functions
that act as self-contained units that we call
whenever convenient. We call function `displayNum`
to show a number on the seven-segment display,
for instance. We don't need to worry about how
the LEDs are triggered, or how the numbers are
displayed or sorted, or even how the delays are
handled for multiplexing – we simply call the
function with a single argument to pass the number
we want shown. We could extrapolate this function
into its own file by making sure that file contains
all the information and variables it needs. We could
then reuse the file in other projects, or share it with
programmers who want the same functionality
without wanting to constantly reinvent the wheel.
You can see where this is going. C includes (hint)
a way to import the contents of an external file so
that you can access those external functions from
within your code. And that's exactly what a library
is. In fact, you add a library to your project using the
special `#include` keyword, usually at the very top of
your source file.

A library is usually a group of functions bundled
with all the necessary definitions, structures,
and variables to make those functions work as a
self-contained piece of code. To keep these parts
isolated from your own code, and to stop parts of
your code falling into the scope of the library → →

FLICKERING DISPLAY

One thing you may notice when running this code in this
project, depending on your sensitivity, is that the seven-
segment displays start to flicker. The cause of this is the
processing and waiting delays of our code waiting for
the data from the sensor, and it's an incredibly common
problem. There's a direct trade-off in the number of
jobs you ask your Arduino to perform and its ability to
keep up a constant rate of updates with something
like a display. This is why buffers were invented, so
that the buffers can be filled in quiet periods and read
from when the system is busy, and there are certainly
designs that could update the displays from a buffer.
But we can also do a lot in code, and while we'll look
into more advanced options, such as using interrupts,
in future tutorials, there is one area of our project that
can be improved now, and it's the `delay()` call in the
`displayDigit()` function. This delay was required
to create enough persistence in the display for the
characters to be easily visible, but as there's now more
processing going on in the body of the code, the delay
can be reduced. We've had best results by reducing
this delay to 2 ms, so the code looks like the following:

```
void displayDigit(int digit, int number) {
  digitalWrite(digPin[digit], HIGH);
  for (int i = 0; i < 8; i++) {
    setSegment(segPin[i], segNum[number]
[i]);
  }
  delay(2);
  digitalWrite(digPin[digit], LOW);
```

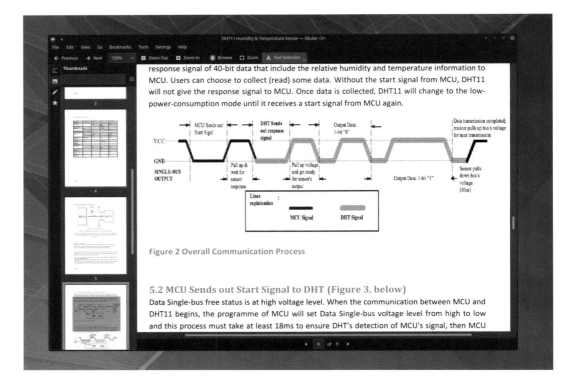

Right ⬀
The specification for the DHT11 includes analysis of the single-wire protocol. Checking this against the library implementation is a great way to learn new skills

QUICK TIP

Another advantage of the 1-Wire data bus used by the DHT11, apart from cost, is that it can run across huge distances, with even 20 metres being feasible. Great for outside applications.

and vice versa – a library is split into two files. The code that does the work is written in the '.cpp' file, analogous to the '.ino' files created by the Arduino IDE. But the part you import into your own project using the `#include` keyword is known as the interface, and is written in a 'header' file that has the '.h' suffix. It's called the header because the include command basically pastes its contents into wherever the command is implanted, which is nearly always in the header of your source file. The header itself doesn't include any functionality at all, but it does include template definitions for the structure and any functions and variables that you're going to use. This is how the compiler is taught about their existence and capabilities without including the functionality in your own code. The '.cpp' will also 'include' its own header file as it fleshes out the template with the implementation.

You can browse and download libraries automatically with the Arduino IDE. This feature is accessed by selecting Use Library > Manage Libraries from the Sketch menu, and you search for what you're looking for, such as DHT11, and click Install on the result. However, we feel it's worth doing this manually the first time so you can see how it works. Due to the popularity of the hardware, there are several libraries that make accessing the

DHT11 easy. The one we're going to use is called 'DHT Library', and is has the advantage of being compatible with the DHT11, 21, 22, 33, and 44 sensors, so you can upgrade the hardware in your project without having to change large chunks of the code logic.

Grab the latest **dht.cpp** and **dht.h** files from the GitHub repository: **git.io/vpudX**.

There are numerous ways to include these files in your project. You can, for example, create your own interface and implementation files and place them in the same directory as your project file. You can then use the include command with double quotes to add the library from the current location:

```
#include "dht.h"
```

> **The brilliant thing about using a library** like this is that now have 'ourDHT' created via the definition in the library

The Arduino build environment will also look in the **libraries** folder just under where your projects live, and this is where you'll find any libraries installed via the Arduino IDE. This is also where we've put our downloaded **dht.cpp** and **dht.h** files, tucked away within a folder called **DHT**. As this location is part of the build environment path, you can include any libraries stored within the **libraries** system folder using the greater than/less than symbols around the library name, and this is what we're going to do with our project, adding the following to the end results of the code from our previous Arduino tutorial:

```
#include <dht.h>
```

OBJECTS

Just as you look at hardware specifications to understand how to use your components, you can use a header file to understand the capabilities of a library and how its features have been implemented. In particular, **dht.h** places almost everything within a 'class'. We've yet to discuss classes like these in our programming adventure, but we have discussed all the various components that go into them to make them useful. A class is a set of functions and variables all grouped together into something that operates a lot like its own type. Unlike a header file, a class is created to be directly assignable within your own code, allowing values to be set within its type and operations to be run against its state without the scope of your own code affecting that of the class. To add this type to our own project, we need to add the following:

```
dht ourDHT;
```

If you look at the header file for the library, you'll see the name given to the class is **dht**, which we use in our own code just as we might **int** or **float**. The brilliant thing about using a library like this is that now have **ourDHT** created via the definition in the library, we can very nearly start using our sensor. All that's needed, if you read the library documentation, is a **#define** statement to tell the class which pin we're using for the data line:

```
#define DHT11_PIN 2
```

As we've discussed previously, a 'define' statement is really just a global definition to replace the string with the value assigned to it, which made digital pin 2 on the Arduino Uno. That definition will percolate into the functions with the class so that everything works correctly. If you've got a brilliant memory, you'll have already noticed that the same

pin is already being used to drive our seven-segment display. In fact, we only have one pin free, and that's pin 9. We could simply attach the DHT11 data pin to this and change the define, but we found it easier to move the wire from pin 2 to pin 9 of the seven-segment display, followed by updating our array of pins to reflect this change:

```
const byte segPin[8] = {9, 3, 4, 5, 6, 7, 8};
```

 A class is a set of functions and variables all grouped together into something that operates **a lot like its own type**

We now get to the part where we deal with all the complexity of working out temperature variations and connection protocols. Except we don't. All we need to do is wait for a ready signal from the sensor before reading the temperature and humidity values from the class that's dealing with all the complexity on our behalf. To get the temperature, for example, you could simply use **float newtemp = ourDHT.temperature;**. The dot after our class name means that **temperature** is a member of the class, as described by the header. We don't need to worry about how this value was placed in **ourDHT. temperature**, just that it was assigned to temperature which we're now assigning to **newtemp**. That's what's so brilliant about using libraries. But we don't even need to do this, because if we multiply the temperature by 100 to move it left by two digits, and then add this to the humidity reading, we can perform the entire step in the same command that sends the values to the display.

This means our entire **loop()** function need only be two lines long:

```
void loop() {
    int chk = ourDHT.read11(DHT11_PIN);
    displayNum((ourDHT.temperature*100)+ourDHT.
humidity);
}
```

And that's it. As usual, and for brevity, we've omitted any code to error-check the sensor, but this should really be added as homework. Otherwise, send the code to your Arduino and we're done. You can download the updated source for this project from **git.io/vpzvg**. ▫

QUICK TIP

A class will be composed of public and private elements. As their names suggest, public elements can be manipulated by your code, while private elements are intended only for the internal workings of the class.

SCHOOL OF MAKING

Arduino programming:
Stacks, classes, and scrolling displays

Learn new code skills and impress your friends with the coolest looking thermometer in the land

Graham Morrison

🐦 @degville

Graham is a veteran Linux journalist who is on a life-long quest to find music in the perfect arrangement of silicon

Right ◈
The completed project shows both temperature and humidity, alongside a chart for recent temperature changes

YOU'LL NEED

◈ **SSD1306 monochrome 0.96" 128 × 64 OLED graphic display**

◈ **DHT11 digital temperature and humidity sensor**

In our previous Arduino tutorial, we expanded both our C programming knowledge and our data visualisation potential by using a library – we stood on the metaphorical shoulders of giants and imported code written by other developers. Rather than being a cheat or a lazy option, this is how nearly every project is developed. Libraries, and their close relation, the API, allow programmers to utilise all kinds of advanced functionality without having to constantly reinvent the wheel. Not only that, but you also benefit from the programming wisdom that goes into the development of a library, wisdom that can sometimes stretch generations when dealing with old system libraries, more true when programming with C than many modern languages.

We're going to use a couple of new libraries in this tutorial to do some magical stuff that would otherwise take a year's worth of tutorials. We'll use the same temperature and humidity sensor from before, but we're moving on from the hipster austerity of seven-segment displays to a whole new world of usefulness – a real bona fide screen. The screen we're using is known as an SSD1306. It's commonly available and costs very little, and yet has a bright OLED display with a resolution of 128 × 64. It's also tiny, making it perfect for embedded projects where you need to output a few more details than a couple of numbers. In fact, we're going to use this display to create a real-time side-scrolling histogram, so you can see changes in temperature over time with a simple glance.

CODE

We're going to use two new libraries. The first is the equivalent of the DHT library, only for the screen. This allows us to easily access the hardware without needing to understand or reverse-engineer the protocol it uses to speak to the Arduino. The wonderful Adafruit provides this library, and it's called Adafruit_SSD1306. The second library is also from Adafruit, Adafruit_GFX, and provides a collection of graphics 'primitives' for drawing things like lines, rectangles, and text without needing to write the algorithms ourselves. Both libraries can be installed by opening the library dialogue from the Arduino IDE (Sketch > Include Library > Manage Libraries…), searching for the library names, and clicking 'Install' from the correct result.

> **"** We're going to use a couple of new libraries in this tutorial to do some magical stuff that would otherwise take **a year's worth of tutorials "**

Before we dive into writing our own code, we need to edit the header files of the Adafruit_SSD1306 library. Without this edit, our screen would only display every other line, and this is because the header is hard-coded to use a display resolution of 128 × 32 rather than 128 × 64. To change this, open **Adafruit_SSD1306.h** (usually found in **Arduino/libraries/Adafruit_SSD1306**) and uncomment `#define SSD1306_128_64` by removing the first two forward slashes (on line 73 in our version). Add two slashes to the beginning of the `#define SSD1306_128_32` line to comment out the old resolution and save the file. Your code should look like the following:

```
#define SSD1306_128_64
//    #define SSD1306_128_32
//    #define SSD1306_96_16
```

With that out of the way, let's start our own new project. Although the skeleton of the code is similar to the previous tutorial, we're going to be changing most of the implementation. At the top of the file, →

WIRING

One of the nice things about the SSD1306 display we're using, and many of its derivatives, is that it pushes straight into your breadboard without requiring any additional jumpers. The signal carried by each of its four pins is annotated across the top of the screen, and this means you can still see which pin does what, even with the board plugged in. This is particularly important because you need to pay attention to which pin carries the power (usually labelled VCC) and which is for ground (GND). Get these the wrong way round and you may break the screen, your Arduino, or both. You also need to check that power requirements for your board match the Arduino – ours is 3 V ~ 5 V DC. Power needs to be connected directly to 5 V on the Arduino and ground to the GND adjacent to this on the Arduino.

However, we also need to connect the temperature and humidity sensor to the same power pins. The best way of doing this is to use the power and ground 'rails' on a typical breadboard.

Two are usually found on the outer edge of each long side of the breadboard, and connecting 5 V from the Arduino to one of these and GND to the other will deliver the power and ground to any pin connected across the length of the rail. With those connections in place, it's then as simple as making one connection from the 5 V rail to VDD on the screen and another from the 5 V rail to VCC on the sensor, and the same must be done for both GND pins.

The screen and the Arduino talk to each other using the I²C protocol, and this requires the use of specific pins on the Arduino. These two pins, normally labelled SCL and SCA on the screen, need to be connected to the corresponding pins on your Arduino, and these can be different depending on which Arduino you're using. As we're using an Uno R3, SCL is analogue pin 5 and SCA is analogue pin 4. Finally, the data pin on the temperature and humidity sensor is connected to digital pin 2 on the Arduino, as it was in the previous tutorial.

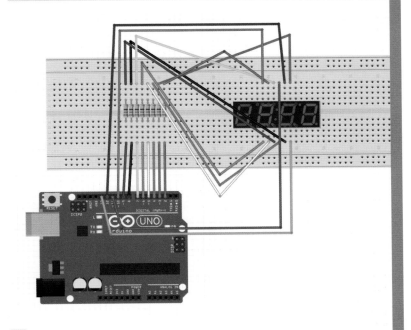

Above ◈
The screen and sensor share the same 5 V and GND rails on the breadboard

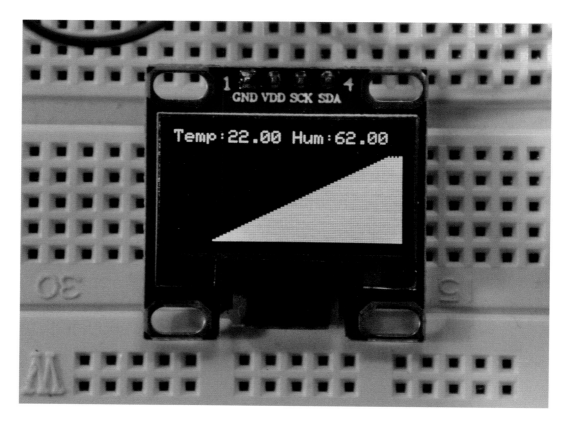

Right ◩
The display we're using is less than an inch across, which is ideal for tiny IoT installations and self-contained devices

we want to include the two new library header files alongside **dht.h** for the sensor:

```
#include <dht.h>
#include <Adafruit_SSD1306.h>
#include <Adafruit_GFX.h>
```

Beneath these lines, we're going to use three **#define** statements to bake-in system-wide values that save us from changing the actual code to accommodate hardware differences:

```
#define DHT11_PIN 2
#define SCREENADR 0x3C
#define MAXSTACK 128
```

The first line sets the pin connected to the temperature and humidity sensor, the same as in the previous tutorial. The second line is the I²C address of the screen. The screen and the Arduino talk to each other using the I²C protocol, and because you can connect multiple devices over I²C, each is differentiated with an address. Ours is 0x3C. This should be included in your screen documentation, or even burnt into the PCB, but you can also run a script to probe any connected I²C devices and return the address of each device if you need to (**hsmag.cc/kigPeT**).

The third statement in the above code is a precursor to a new and important concept we're going to introduce in this tutorial, and that's

something called a 'stack'. We're going to use a simplified stack to hold 128 separate temperature measurements, so that we can draw a histogram of changes in temperature over time. You might wonder why we don't use a simple array to hold these values, but this is because we want the histogram to scroll in real time as temperatures are added. If we were to simply update the values in an array sequentially, the histogram would draw itself across the screen, left to right, and then simply reset to the left border of the screen again, as you see in many such implementations. But a stack allows us to have a sliding window of values that follow a leading edge, effectively creating a scrolling histogram of temperature data. This all sounds more complicated than the actual code, so let's take a look:

```
class Stack
{
  private:
    int ourList[MAXSTACK];
    int top;
  public:
    Stack() {
      top = 0;
      for (int i = 0; i <= MAXSTACK; i++)
        ourList[i] = 0;
    }
```

QUICK TIP

Using the text function requires a foreground and background colour. Without a background colour, when the text updates it will look corrupted, but it's because old text pixels are still there in the background.

```
    void push(int item) {
      if (top == MAXSTACK)
        top = 0;
      ourList[top++] = item;
    }
    int peek(int x) {
      return ourList[(top + x) % MAXSTACK];
    }
};
```

This stack is a list of data that we can keep pushing data to, and peeking at data in. It will always hold the most recent 128 datapoints pushed into the stack.

Our stack is implemented within a class. We discussed classes in the previous tutorial when we used one to access the DHT11, but in the above code we're creating our own. Classes, a little like stacks, are a huge subject that can even dictate the design of an entire programming language, but they're basically just a way of co-locating data with the functions that use the data. In our case, that means the data is the value for each temperature reading, and the functions add and read values from the stack. If the data and functions are solely for the use of the class, they're defined beneath a 'private' specifier, and won't be accessible outside the class – this helps hide the complexity and avoids erroneous access from outside the class. Conversely, for data and functions intended to be accessed by you, the programmer, we use the 'public' specifier. In our above class, the **push**

and **peek** functions are all public, as we'll be using these to create and view our stack. The array that holds the temperature readings, **ourList**, is private, as too is an integer that holds the current top array position of the stack.

There are three functions that are members of this class. The first is special because it takes the name of the class itself – **Stack()**. This is the constructor, and like **setup()** in an Arduino project, it runs automatically when a class is instantiated. We use this instantiation to set the internal values to zero, including every element of the array. This safeguards against wayward values being left over in memory or a previous execution. Although we've not used it here, the opposite function to the constructor is the destructor, written as **~Stack()** in a class definition, and this function is run when a class is deleted. As our code only quits when the Arduino is reset or powered off, we're saving space and not →

Above ◈
SSD1306-compatible screens are cheap and readily available, and can even be found in different colours and in multiple colour configurations

Left ◩
The OLED display and temperature sensor in situ on the breadboard

QUICK TIP

If you experience display problems, you may need to use an external 5V power source for the screen, connecting the common ground to the Arduino.

QUICK TIP

The term 'stack overflow' actually refers to when you try to write to the stack and the stack is full. Fortunately, as ours is fixed in size, this won't happen.

Right ◈
Libraries can be downloaded and installed manually, as discussed last time, but it's much easier to just use the Arduino IDE

adding a destructor, but a good programmer uses the destructor to free up any allocated memory and generally clean up after themselves.

The **push** function simply checks to make sure the top isn't yet at the maximum stack size value, and enters the **item** value at the current top position before incrementing **top** to the next array location. We haven't implemented **pop** because it's not needed – we're simply overwriting previous values in the array. Instead, we have **peek** to return the

> **The module itself combines both temperature and humidity sensors,** and the great thing about this module is that it's incredibly easy to use

item value at **x**. The tricky part is that because **top** is always changing, **x** is an offset from the value of **top**, which we modulo against the maximum stack size, to make sure it's both within range and loops over when higher. Modulo is very useful for such a simple operator!

DRAWING LINES

The next chunk of code instantiates three types for the sensor, our new **Stack** class and for the screen, before filling out the Arduino's **setup** function. This

STACK OVERFLOW

A stack is a data structure, and that just means it holds data in a specific way. The most common stack holds data in the same way you create a deck of cards, putting one card on top of the next and removing cards from the top of the pile. In stack terminology, this is a LIFO stack – the card that was last in is first out. FIFO (first in, first out) is another common variant, and this operates as a basic queue. Alan Turing even coined the terms 'bury' and 'unbury' in 1946 to describe the process of adding and removing data from a stack, but we now use the terms 'push' and 'pop' for the same thing. Additionally, 'peek' is often used when you want to take a look at the top card, rather than remove it, or examine another card in the pack. Just like in 1946, however, stacks are ideal when you only have a limited amount of memory.

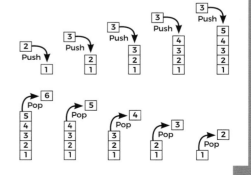

initiates the display and runs a function to clear the display of the noise that typically accompanies the display turning on:

```
dht ourDHT;
Stack temperature_stack;
Adafruit_SSD1306 display(4);

void setup() {
  display.begin(SSD1306_SWITCHCAPVCC, SCREENADR);
  display.clearDisplay();
}
```

The next piece of code is all that's needed to draw the histogram. Thanks to Adafruit's graphics library, we call its `display.drawLine` function to draw a line from one set of coordinates to another, and we do this to first black out a column (the same x value) and then to draw a white line up to the temperature value in that column. We get the value from our stack using our `peek` function.

```
void displayChart() {
  for (int x = 0; x < MAXSTACK; x++) {
    display.drawLine(x, display.height(), x,
display.height(), BLACK);
    display.drawLine(x, display.height(), x,
display.height() - temperature_stack.peek(x),
WHITE);
  }}
```

For good measure, we're also going to add text to show the current temperature and humidity readings. This is just as easy as drawing a line, although we do pull the readings directly from the sensor rather than our stack:

```
// Function to display a character
void displayNum() {
  display.setTextSize(1);
  display.setTextColor(WHITE, BLACK);
  display.setCursor(0, 0);
  display.println("Temp:" + String(ourDHT.
temperature) + " Hum:" + String(ourDHT.
humidity));
}
```

All that's now left to do is write the main `loop` function. This simply pushes a new temperature value onto the stack, runs both the text and histogram generation functions, and finishes up with the `display.display()` function to update the display. We then add a delay in milliseconds to wait until we repeat the sequence. Changing this will affect the duration between each reading, altering the scroll speed from seconds to hours if you so wish,

which is great if you want to monitor the change in temperature over an entire day – try **delay(86400000)**.

```
void loop() {
  int chk = ourDHT.read11(DHT11_PIN);
  temperature_stack.push(ourDHT.temperature);
  displayChart();
  displayNum();
  display.display();
  delay(100);
}
```

The code for this tutorial can be found at **git.io/vh4x9**. □

Above
You need to edit the screen driver header to make sure it uses the correct resolution for your display

Below
A rear view of the mini OLED display, showing its four pins

Arduino programming:
pointers and linked lists

Upgrade your skills and demystify two of the most arcane aspects of Arduino and C

Graham Morrison

🐦 @degville

Graham is a veteran Linux journalist who is on a life-long quest to find music in the perfect arrangement of silicon

W

e were ambitious in our previous tutorial, creating a scrolling histogram of temperature data on a simple display with less than 80 lines of code. In the process, we also introduced two fundamental programming concepts: classes and stacks. We used classes to abstract both data and functions into a single object, and stacks as a kind of data structure where you can push values onto the top and pop them back off again. In this tutorial, we'll be revisiting these ideas and the same code, but introducing a couple of new fundamental concepts that are equally important – and one you've likely heard about if you've read or seen anything about C programming: pointers and linked lists.

Pointers, especially, are a little more theoretical than the practical nature of classes and stacks, especially on the Arduino platform. But they're important because they're closer to how the hardware works. They're also a fundamental part of the C programming canon. But there's a serious caveat. Most – if not all – programs can be written without them, and there's a good argument for avoiding them completely. They add a potentially catastrophic level of complexity to your code that most beginners don't need to contend with when they're just trying to get stuff done. They can cause your code to crash unpredictably, they can introduce subtle problems that are difficult to track down, and they can be difficult to predict. These are problems you avoid with 'static' types and data structures, such as a two-dimensional array.

Get Started With Arduino

In previous tutorials, we've been using types that implement static memory allocation. This means the compiler and the Arduino know exactly what the memory demands of our code are going to be before the code starts to run. In the `int ourList[MAXSTACK];` line, for instance, we're declaring exactly how many integers the `ourList` array is going to hold, which is a value defined by `MAXSTACK`. This is a very common approach with embedded systems, such as the Arduino, because the programmer needs to stay in absolute control of the resources being used, to make sure the hardware isn't asked to store data it doesn't have the memory for – a situation that would cause all kinds of unpredictable behaviour and, ultimately, cause your code to crash the Arduino.

But knowing what pointers are and what they're capable of is an essential step in any programmer's journey, and there are instances where they can be used to elegantly solve some specific problems. In particular, pointers can be a very effective way of passing large sets of values between functions without your program or hardware having to allocate extra memory or spending time copying that data. But they're also great at implementing something called a linked list.

POINTER SISTERS

Up until now, the inner operations of your hardware have been abstracted away by the programming language. Pointers pull the curtain away from this by making you think more like a CPU. To create a pointer, you simply insert an asterisk (*) symbol before the variable name:

```
int *example;
```

Without the asterisk, the compiler would make sure that enough space was allocated to hold an integer value referenced by the 'example' name. With the asterisk, however, we're now saying 'example' is a pointer to a memory location that holds an integer. 'Example' doesn't hold the integer value, but the memory location of where that value is stored. This is the key to understanding pointers, and it can take a little bit of time to get your head around. It means that, regardless of the value being held at the memory location, in our example an integer, the pointer will only ever hold the value of the memory location itself. On an Arduino, where every memory location can be addressed via a two-byte value, this means pointers use two bytes of storage, regardless of the data type or structure on the end of the dereferenced pointer.

 Knowing what pointers are and what they're capable of is an essential step in any programmer's journey

To prove this point, we're going to rewrite the stack class from the previous tutorial to use both pointers and a linked list to re-implement the class that surrounded the static array we originally used. A linked list is a very common form of dynamic data structure, and it can also be very simple. As a minimum, it's a structure that holds two elements: a value to be stored and a link to the structure that holds the next element in the list. The link is a pointer. The structure can obviously be augmented with many more components, such as holding a class value instead of a simple variable, and another pointer for the previous element in the list. But for our usage, we're going to keep it as basic as possible with just a pointer and an integer data value: →

Below
The SSD1306 display is tiny, requiring only four pins to connect, and yet is immensely useful for all kinds of output

QUICK TIP

The asterisk used by
a pointer is known
as the dereference
operator because it
returns the memory
location where a
variable is stored.

SCOPE RESOLUTION
OPERATORS

In the previous tutorial, we defined the functions that
belonged to the class within the { and } brackets that
delimited the class definition. Normally, these class
definitions would be separate to the implementation
code. This makes the class easier to understand at a
conceptual level without having to resort to the code,
and it's why you often get the class definition in the
header (.h). But you can do the same thing even when
you're working within the same file – you just need
to create your functions using the scope resolution
operator. Scope is a fundamental concept in many
languages. It allows you to have variables of the same
name in different classes, or global variables that
won't interfere with function variables with the same
name. Two colons are used to define the class you're
assigning the function to (or a variable, though that's
rarer). Here's the constructor function for our new
linked list method, using 'stackList::' to tell the compiler
it's a member of the stackList class even though it's
outside of the bracketed scope of that class:

```
stackList::stackList()
```

We've followed this new protocol for all the class-
bound functions in the code.

These pointers will allow the class to keep
track of the elements at the **beginning and
the end of the list**

```
struct stackNode {
  int value = 0;
  stackNode *next;
};
```

With the above 'struct', we've created our own
data structure holding the value we want to store
and the pointer to what will be the next element
in our linked list. This would have been the next
element in an array, if we were still using arrays. To
hold the functionality of our linked list, and to provide
the same transparent functionality of our class from
the previous tutorial, we're going to augment this
structure with a new class to do all the hard work
for us.

```
class stackList {
  protected:
    byte stacksize;
```

QUICK TIP

The arrow coupling
of '->' is really just a
short-cut to using an
asterisk. For example,
`ptrtmp->value =
item` is functionally
equivalent to
`(*ptrtmp).value`.

```
    stackNode *top;
    stackNode *tail;
  public:
    stackList();
    void push (int);
    int peek (int);
};
```

You'll see that the above code constructs a class
that's almost identical to the array-based class we
used last time, with the exception replacing the array
with pointers to two 'stackNode' types, as defined
by our new structure: top and tail. These pointers
will allow the class to keep track of the elements at
the beginning and the end of the list. Similarly, we'll
be using 'stacksize' to hold the number of elements
within the list. But the big difference between this
implementation and the implementation using the
array is that the class is no longer storing the values in
the stack, it's simply holding pointers to the beginning
and end elements. The values are going to be stored
somewhere in memory, and it's going to be our job
– and not the job of the compiler or the Arduino – to
keep track of where each of these elements are and
how many we've created.

CLASS ELEMENTS

```
stackList::stackList() {
    stacksize = 0;
    top = NULL;
    tail = NULL;
}
```

The above code is run whenever we create a
stackList within our code, and we use the constructor
to define default values and initialise variables. It's
identical to the constructor we created when working
with arrays, except we no longer need to run through
the array to define default values. Instead, we assign
the value of 'NULL' to the two pointers we create.
NULL is a special value that effectively makes sure
nothing is assigned as a value. Anything can be
assigned a NULL value, but it can be most useful
with pointers because there's always a possibility
that, without being initialised in this way, they contain
some random memory location that's a vestige of
a previous run cycle. Assigning a NULL value is the
pointer equivalent of setting a variable to 0.

PUSH AND PULL

We're now going to tackle the main function in our
new class, the push function. As before, this takes
an integer value and adds it to the stack that we're
constructing to hold the values that we're measuring.

The difference this time is that we're going to use pointers and a linked list. Here's the first part:

```
void stackList::push(int item) {
    stackNode *ptrtmp = new stackNode;
    ptrtmp->value = item;
    ptrtmp->next = NULL;
```

There are only three new lines of code above, but they encapsulate everything you need to know about pointers and linked lists, how they work, and how they can be used. Everything else we're going to add is basic maintenance of what we create above.

The first line after the function name (`stackNode *tmp = new stackNode;`) is creating a new node to hold

 This takes an integer value and adds it to the stack that we're constructing to hold the values that we're measuring

this new value, and we're calling this 'ptrtmp'. It's a pointer to the new node. But the most important part here is the 'new' keyword. Without this, the pointer would be created but there would be no memory allocated for the data we want stored. Using 'new' handles this for us automatically, setting aside memory for a 'stackNode' element and its contents. There a vital difference between this and creating a normal type, such as by using `stackNode tmp`. In our example, even when `ptrtmp` no longer

exists and we've left the scope of the function, the data it holds will still be in memory and reserved from anything overwriting it. As long as we've still got a handle on its location, which is what a pointer is, we can get at the data.

The use of the '->' characters is a short-cut to what the pointer is referencing, allowing you to change the value of what's being stored in the memory location the pointer is pointing at. The element that holds this pointer will be the previous element in the linked list, which is what the `ptrtmp` pointer holds. However, as we currently know nothing of what the next element might be, the pointer to the next element is created with a NULL assignment. We now deal with situation where the first element is added to the list:

```
if (tail == NULL)
        tail = ptrtmp;
    else
        top->next = ptrtmp;
top = ptrtmp;
```

The above illustrates the awesome power of pointers. Firstly, by asking whether the 'tail' pointer is still NULL, we're checking to see whether this is the first element we're adding to the list, as this needs special consideration. If it is, then we point the tail pointer at the new ptrtmp element we've just created. If it isn't, then we know there's at least one element already in the list and the previous element to be added will be pointed to from 'top'. Now we're adding a new element, top's 'next' pointer needs to point at the new one we're creating, which we can simply do with `top->next = ptrtmp;`. Remember, →

Below ⬈
The circuit and wiring for this tutorial is identical to the previous one, except you can forgo the temperature sensor if you update the graphics routine

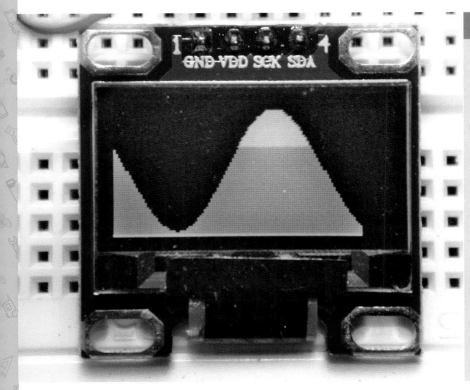

Above ◈
Replace the static
temperature reading
chart with a sine
wave – you could
even modulate its
frequency with
temperature changes!

GRAPHICS UPGRADE

It didn't seem fair to leave this project generating exactly the same output as the previous tutorial's one. As an added bonus, and to investigate mathematical functions a little, you can forgo the temperature sensor and replace the main loop code with the following:

```
void loop() {
  if (counter > 180)
    counter = -180;
  temp_stack.push((sin(counter * 3.14 /
180) + 1.1) * 29);
  counter = counter + 2;
  displayChart();
  display.display();
  delay(1);
}
```

You will also need to add `int counter = 0;` as a global variable outside the scope of the `loop()` function. The above uses `sin()` to generate the sine function for the angles between -180 and +180, as counted by `counter`. The output will be a regular sine wave drawn and scrolled along on the OLED display, but you can play with the numbers to change both its frequency and its amplitude.

these are just pointers – we're not moving the values they're storing, we're just assigning the memory location. The node holding the value we want to be stored isn't moving.

The next chunk of code stops our linked list expanding further than your Arduino has the capacity to store:

```
if (++stacksize > MAXSTACK) {
  ptrtmp = tail;
  tail = ptrtmp->next;
  delete tail;
  stacksize--;
  }
}
```

In the above code, we're checking to see whether there are now more elements in the list than we want, as defined by MAXSTACK. If there are, we store the memory location of the oldest node, the tail, in the ptrtmp pointer. This is so we can then make the new tail pointer point to the next item in the list while before deleting what was the oldest element linked to within the list. You will also need to reduce the value of MAXSTACK in your code too, typically to between 60–100 or you'll run out of RAM.

QUICK TIP

The code for this
project can be found
here: **git.io/fSGkD**

The **delete** command here is the opposite of the **new** command we used earlier, freeing up the memory that we allocated to hold the structure. We can now tackle the final function that returns a value for the node in the list we request. This is

> **This is more complex than the array equivalent** as we're unable to directly address the value stored by the list at location 'x'

more complex than the array equivalent as we're unable to directly address the value stored by the list at location 'x'. Instead, count through the positions until we reach the correct node and return the value it holds:

```
int stackList::peek(int x) {
  int pos = 0;
  stackNode* current = tail;
```

```
while ((pos < x) && (current != top)) {
  current = current->next;
  pos++;
}
if (x > pos)
  return -1;
else
  return current->value;
  }
};
```

The only other part of the code we're going to touch is the part that draws the graph. We're doing this because there's no longer enough RAM on an Arduino Uno to hold the entire linked list, so we're going to only map values to the screen when there's a node, and stop the redraw process when there are no more elements left to render. However, we'll keep the same sliding window logic from the previous tutorial as this looks rather good:

Below ◈
A linked list is a dynamic data structure where each element contains a link – using a pointer – to the next element in the list

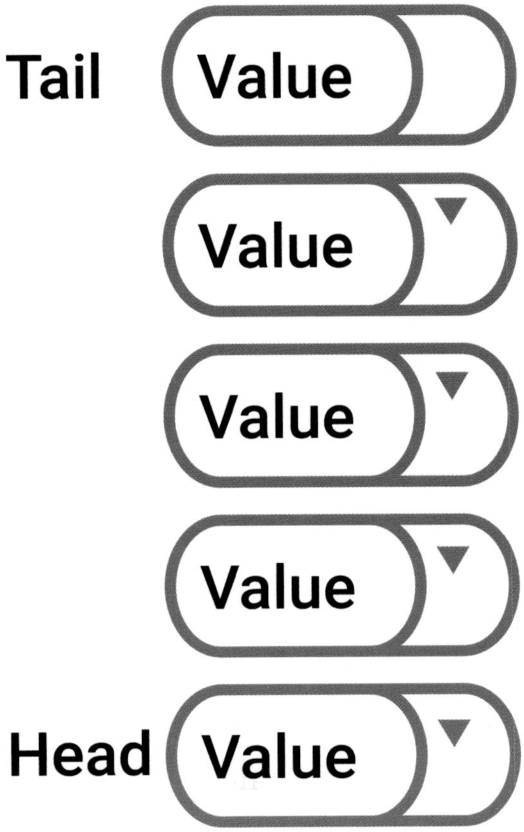

Tail (Value)

Value ▼

Value ▼

Value ▼

Head (Value ▼)

BEYOND **THE LIST**

Here, we've looked at a linked list because it's one of the simplest data structures (and serves the purpose we need), but there are lots of others that you can create, built on the same principle. Once you've mastered this technique of using pointers to link elements together, you can adapt it to make the others. In each case, you have a structure with a pointer showing the links to other nodes…
• **Trees:** In this data structure, a single root element has one or more children, and each child has children, and so on. Think of something like a family tree, but it can hold almost any sort of data. A common variation of this is the binary tree where each node has, at most, two children. This setup can be useful for searching as each node can represent a value and all left children can be lower, and all right ones can be higher.
• **Graphs:** In computer science, graphs have nothing to do with diagrams showing how a value changes over axes. Instead, they're collections of nodes that can be joined in any way. Think of it a bit like the linked list, but each node can be joined to many nodes, not just one. This can represent many things, particularly the structure of the internet, as this is made up of a large number of servers and data centres with various connections between them.
• **Heap:** These are similar to trees except that there's a heap property such that a parent node has to be either explicitly higher or lower than every node below it. One of the most common uses of a heap is a priority queue, where each node is more important than those below it.

QUICK TIP

Try changing `int` definitions to `byte` when you know the value it holds will be between 0 and 255. This will save a whole byte of valuable Arduino memory and give you a larger potential stack size.

```
void displayChart() {
  char x = 0;
  int value = 0;
  value = temp_stack.peek(x);
  while (value != -1) {
    display.drawLine(x, display.height(), x, 0,
BLACK);
    display.drawLine(x, display.height(), x,
display.height() - value, WHITE);
    value = temp_stack.peek(++x);
  }
}
```

With that done, you can run the code. With a bit of luck, you'll be rewarded by seeing absolutely no difference in the temperature mapping chart from last time – see the 'Graphics Upgrade' box to change this to a different rendering algorithm. But the way your code is working is now completely different – using pointers and a linked list rather than an array – and you've now mastered one of the most arcane and misunderstood aspects of the Arduino and C programming environments. □

SCHOOL OF MAKING ━━━━━━━━━━━━

Arduino programming:
Build a games console (part 1/2)

Put some of that hard-learnt theory into action. And we really mean action, with spaceships, analogue joysticks, and bitmap graphics

Graham Morrison

🐦 @degville

Graham is a veteran Linux journalist who is on a life-long quest to find music in the perfect arrangement of silicon

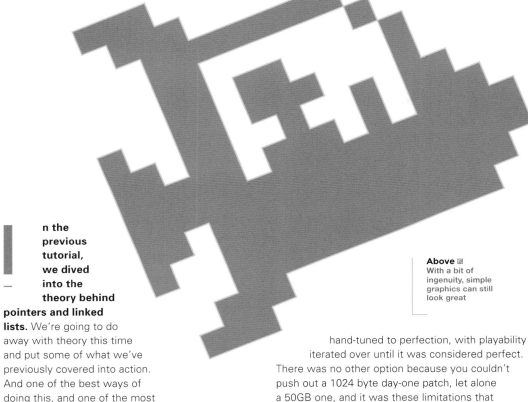

Above ◩
With a bit of ingenuity, simple graphics can still look great

QUICK TIP

You could replace the analogue joystick with five simple momentary buttons, but you'll lose the finer degree of control.

In the previous tutorial, we dived into the theory behind pointers and linked lists. We're going to do away with theory this time and put some of what we've previously covered into action. And one of the best ways of doing this, and one of the most entertaining, is to code a video game. The limited performance of the Arduino means writing any kind of modern game is impossible – we can't use anything like the libraries used by game developers to skip over the programming fundamentals, implement AI, and virtual reality reprojection. But we can write a game just as they did in golden era of 8-bit home computing. The limited hardware of those old machines forced the games designer's creativity, and that meant injecting games with as much simple, imaginative, and addictive gameplay as possible. Limited hardware also meant that every variable, function, sprite, and sound could be

hand-tuned to perfection, with playability iterated over until it was considered perfect. There was no other option because you couldn't push out a 1024 byte day-one patch, let alone a 50GB one, and it was these limitations that made so many of those old games playable today, decades later.

We're going to use the same setup we've been playing with in previous tutorials – mainly the same 128×64 I²C OLED display, but you can easily replace this with something larger than the 0.96″ model we're using. For input, we're going to use an analogue dual-axis joystick that includes a single momentary switch. These are cheaply and commonly available as a single module with the 'KY-023' label – and you may even have one left over from the joystick MIDI controller we featured previously. See the 'Get connected' box overleaf

PICKING A BOARD				
MEMORY	**ARDUINO TYPE**			
	Duemilanove (2009)	Uno Rev 3	Mega	Mega 2560
Flash	16 kBytes	32 kBytes	128 kBytes	256 kBytes
SRAM	1024 bytes	2048 bytes	8 kBytes	8 kBytes

Left ◈
One of the main differences between each version of the Arduino hardware is the amounts of both flash memory and SRAM available

for further details on how we put this together and connected it to the Arduino.

The inspiration for this project comes directly from our previous tutorials, where we used the screen to show a sideways-scrolling representation of changes in temperature over time. Sideways-scrolling backgrounds like this are a traditional game

> **Many of the earliest games used simple geometry to represent a spaceship.** One of the best known is Asteroids, which used an augmented triangle as the main craft

mechanic, used in classics like the original Defender from 1979/1980, and Super Mario Bros. But the game we're most inspired by for this project is called Scramble, from 1981. In Scramble you needed to fly your ship across a cityscape before entering a series of tunnels. These tunnels became a mini game in their own right as you tried to position your ship in the best part of the screen to navigate impossible turns and an ever-decreasing tunnel height. It's this part of Scramble we're going to loosely emulate with our own Arduino game, adapting the scrolling temperature chart we've already created into a tunnel. But to start with, we need to get the joystick controls working, and for that we need to be able see (and control) something on the screen.

SHIP SHAPE

Many of the earliest games used simple geometry to represent a spaceship. One of the best known is Asteroids, which used an augmented triangle as the

main craft for the player to control, with degrees of rotation and thrust. This was because the screen used a 'vector' display that could only draw lines from one point to another. We haven't suffered the same restrictions since raster-scanning cathode ray tubes became commonplace, and flatscreen modern technology made it all but a distant memory. But vectors like these are still used when you want an image to scale, or when you don't have the memory for more than two colours, and they're the basis for modern scalable graphics like SVG and 3D polygons. Thanks to the Adafruit graphics library, it only takes a single command to draw a triangle (or a rectangle, or a circle – filled or empty), and we'll revisit the idea when adding some stars to our game. But for now, we're going to use a bitmap for the ship, another →

Below ◈
The KY-023 module uses a joystick very similar to a PlayStation 2 controller joystick, which can also be extracted and used in the same way

QUICK TIP

Rather than using GIMP or similar to generate your Arduino bitmap code, use an online converter like **hsmag.cc/yGboIA**.

old term that still exists in places like the .bmp file extension and graphics programming.

The term 'bitmap' refers to an arrangement of 'bits', usually 1 for on and 0 for off, in series representing adjacent pixels on a screen. Different rows are represented by knowing the image width. If an image is 16 pixels wide, for instance, the 17th

> **Thanks to the sequential way memory is mapped to a display,** bitmaps remain an effective way of representing visual elements

bit in the sequence will represent the first pixel on the second row. It's really the most simplistic way of representing an image, although it can easily be extended to add 'bit depth'; for example, adding colour rather than on and off states. Thanks to the sequential way memory is mapped to a display, bitmaps remain an effective way of representing visual elements, especially when you consider this kind of structure is identical to an array we can use within our own code. Fortunately, the days when

Below
Our joystick includes a switch, triggered by pressing down, which we'll use to start the game

GET CONNECTED

Alongside the Arduino Uno and the 128×64 I²C OLED display we've connected for the previous couple of tutorials, we've added an analogue joystick labelled as KY-023, although almost any analogue joystick should work. We're using a version with a small breakout board, but nearly all joysticks of this type feature the same five connections: GND and 5 V that need to be connected to the corresponding outputs in the Arduino via the rails on your breadboard, VYx and VRy which we've connected to analogue inputs A0 and A1, and SW which we have connected to digital input pin 7. We then needed to update our project code to reflect these new inputs, using the following **const** global values:

```
// Analogue joystick connections for X
and Y
const int JOYY = A0;
const int JOYX = A1;
// Digital input for the Joystick switch
const int SWITCH_PIN = 7;
```

To make this project feel more like a games console and to make it more accessible to smaller fingers, we connected a long ribbon cable between the joystick and its connections. This allowed us to hold the joystick just as we would a games controller on a console, and also neatly side-stepped having to deal with horizontal pins connecting to the breadboard. Of course, if you end up keeping this configuration, there's no limit to how you connect and arrange the components – from a handheld in a mints tin, to a diminutive home entertainment system.

you needed to use cross-hatched mathematics paper, to pencil in your own designs and then translate these into a sequence of binary values, are gone and you can now draw your own bitmaps in your favourite image editor and convert them online or using GIMP – see the box overleaf for further details.

We converted a monochrome image we drew of a spaceship into the following array:

```
const unsigned char shipBMP [] PROGMEM = {
  // 'ship, 16x16px
  0x00, 0x00, 0x70, 0x00, 0x38, 0x00, 0x1f, 0xe0,
  0x18, 0x10, 0x1b, 0x08, 0x9b, 0x88, 0xd9, 0x2c,
  0xfb, 0xae, 0xff, 0xff, 0xdf, 0xff, 0x9f, 0xfe,
  0x1f, 0xfc, 0x38, 0x00, 0x70, 0x00, 0x00, 0x00
};
```

The above array contains 32 elements, but it represents a bitmap that's 16 pixels wide and 16 pixels high, or 256 on/off positions in total. The disparity between the number of elements and the number of bits we're representing is because we're using hexadecimal to describe the same data as 'char' rather than raw binary, and each element is equivalent to a byte/8 bits. Multiply the 32 elements by those 8 bits and you get 256, so we're not losing or compressing any data, only displaying them more efficiently. Efficiency is also why we use the 'PROGMEM' keyword when declaring the array. Arduino has different types of memory, and PROGMEM represents the flash storage rather than the SRAM used to store our program variables. As we saw in the previous tutorial that dealt with lists and pointers, SRAM quickly fills with any normal project, and each Arduino has much more flash storage than SRAM. Using PROGMEM instead of SRAM is perfect for larger arrays, such as the one we're using to hold a bitmap. The only limits are that PROGMEM variables must be global or defined as 'static'.

Thanks to the Adafruit graphics library we're already using to drive our screen, rendering the bitmap array to the screen is easy, taking just a single line, which we're putting within its own function that takes an x and y location for where we want the image drawn:

```
void displayShip(int x, int y) {
  display.drawBitmap(x, y, shipBMP, 16, 16, 1);
}
```

> **"** Thanks to the Adafruit graphics library, we're already using to drive our screen, **rendering the bitmap array to the screen is easy "**

Above ◈
An online bitmap converter, such as hsmag.cc/vfYQyz, can let you invert an image and preview the text output so you can make sure it will work with the screen

Left ◈
Playing your game is the best way of improving it, especially when it comes to fine-tuning the control system

SCHOOL OF MAKING

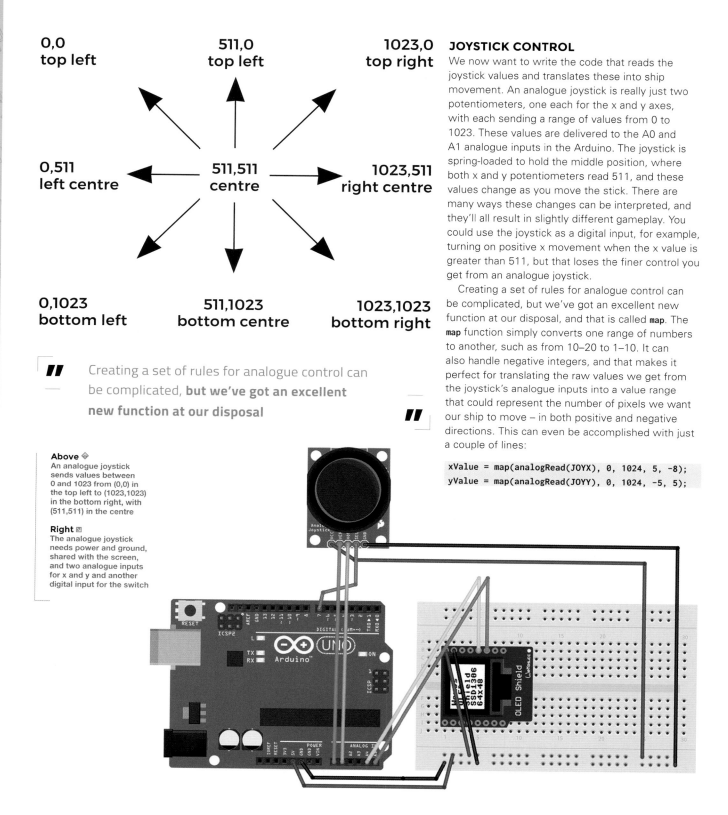

0,0
top left

511,0
top left

1023,0
top right

0,511
left centre

511,511
centre

1023,511
right centre

0,1023
bottom left

511,1023
bottom centre

1023,1023
bottom right

JOYSTICK CONTROL

We now want to write the code that reads the joystick values and translates these into ship movement. An analogue joystick is really just two potentiometers, one each for the x and y axes, with each sending a range of values from 0 to 1023. These values are delivered to the A0 and A1 analogue inputs in the Arduino. The joystick is spring-loaded to hold the middle position, where both x and y potentiometers read 511, and these values change as you move the stick. There are many ways these changes can be interpreted, and they'll all result in slightly different gameplay. You could use the joystick as a digital input, for example, turning on positive x movement when the x value is greater than 511, but that loses the finer control you get from an analogue joystick.

Creating a set of rules for analogue control can be complicated, but we've got an excellent new function at our disposal, and that is called **map**. The **map** function simply converts one range of numbers to another, such as from 10–20 to 1–10. It can also handle negative integers, and that makes it perfect for translating the raw values we get from the joystick's analogue inputs into a value range that could represent the number of pixels we want our ship to move – in both positive and negative directions. This can even be accomplished with just a couple of lines:

```
xValue = map(analogRead(JOYX), 0, 1024, 5, -8);
yValue = map(analogRead(JOYY), 0, 1024, -5, 5);
```

> Creating a set of rules for analogue control can be complicated, **but we've got an excellent new function at our disposal**

Above ◈
An analogue joystick sends values between 0 and 1023 from (0,0) in the top left to (1023,1023) in the bottom right, with (511,511) in the centre

Right ◙
The analogue joystick needs power and ground, shared with the screen, and two analogue inputs for x and y and another digital input for the switch

The `analogRead()` functions read the Arduino inputs from the joystick. All we're then doing is mapping the far left to 5 on the x axis and the far right to -8. The negative is because this axis is inverted, with the controls being opposite to what you'd expect. All the points in between will correspond to the degree the joystick is being moved, but the centre point isn't going to be 0, it's going to be -1. This is a gameplay trick that will move the ship back to the left edge of the screen when the player isn't controlling the ship. The y axis, by comparison, is a straight translation, with 0 as

> **The further the stick is from the centre,** the greater the jump in the number of pixels, which means the ship will travel faster across the screen

the centre point and no automatic movement. These values can then be added to the ship's current position to generate movement when we update the ship's location. The further the stick is from the centre, the greater the jump in the number of pixels, which means the ship will travel faster across the screen.

The only checks we need to add are for when the ship hits any of the edges of the screen, which we can accomplish with simple `if` statements. Placing all of this in single a function will look like the following:

```
void updateShip() {
  int xValue, yValue;
  xValue = map(analogRead(JOYX), 0, 1024, 5, -8);
// 5, -6 for no move backwards movement
  yValue = map(analogRead(JOYY), 0, 1024, -5, 5);
  shipx = shipx + xValue;
  shipy = shipy + yValue;
  if (shipx < 1)
    shipx = 1;
  if (shipy < 1)
    shipy = 1;
  if (shipx > display.width() - 12)
    shipx = display.width() - 12;
  if (shipy > display.height() - 12)
    shipy = display.height() - 12; }
```

All that's now left to do is to add the two ship location variables as global, and update the main loop function to call both the `updateShip()` function and the `displayShip()` function:

CREATE BITMAPS WITH GIMP

The easiest way to create a bitmap is with a pixel editor such as GIMP (**gimp.org**). Create a new image with File > New menu, and set the size to 16×16 with a type of 'px' for pixels. This makes sure there's no background scaling. Click on Advanced Options and make sure 'Fill with' is set to Transparency, so that only the pixels you draw will be in the output. Click on OK and then zoom into your new tiny canvas by either holding down the **CTRL** key and using the mouse wheel, or selecting Zoom from the view menu. To draw your image, select the pencil tool from the

tools palette, and from the 'Tool options' pane, set its size to 1 – this is equivalent to a single pixel. Finally, make sure the foreground colour is white. You can now start drawing your design.

When you're happy with your art, select Export As from the File menu and use the drop-down Type menu to set the output format to 'X BitMap image (*.xbm, *.icon, *.bitmap). Give your image a name and click Export. The file you've just generated is actually a text file you can use within your code, just as we have done in the main project.

Above ◈
GIMP is a good choice for editing large pixels, because you can easily set the size of the canvas and zoom in

```
int shipx, shipy;
void loop() {
  updateShip();
  displayShip(shipx, shipy);
  display.display();
  delay(1);
  display.fillScreen(BLACK); }
```

We now have the framework for a fully fledged game, which we'll build in the next tutorial. Until then, the code for this one can be downloaded from: **git.io/fNXzp**. □

Arduino programming:
build a games console (part 2/2)

Tackle all the main gameplay elements, from terrain generation to collision detection, and combine them into an addictive, easily modifiable game

Graham Morrison

🐦 @degville

Graham is a veteran Linux journalist who is on a life-long quest to find music in the perfect arrangement of silicon

Below ◩
Using a ribbon cable to separate the joystick from the Arduino and the screen makes it much easier for anyone to play the game without pulling everything apart

In the previous tutorial, we started on our adventure of turning a humble Arduino Uno into a games console, albeit one that plays only a single game that we've yet to write **(read on).** We ended last time with a joystick-controlled movement system and custom-drawn bitmap that we could move across the screen. In this tutorial, we're going to flesh out these ideas with the remainder of the code to create a fully fledged game, starting with the modifications that we need to make to our scrolling temperature chart to turn it into an endless tunnel for our ship to navigate. In the original code, we pushed temperature values onto a

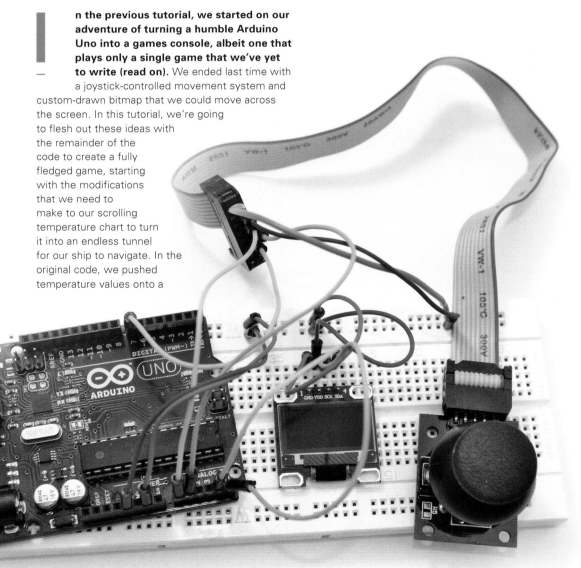

Left ◣
The aim of the game
is to steer your ship
for as long as you
can through a tunnel
whose dimensions
are ever decreasing

stack and read back those values into each column
of the screen. These values were held in a stack
and as we added a new value, the oldest one was
removed. This created a sliding window of the last
128 values. The screen is also 128 columns wide,
and drawing these values (one position per column)
has the effect of creating a scrolling display of values
that move from the right to the left.

We're going to subvert this effect to turn
those values into a cross-section of a cave for our
spaceship to fly through, and the first step is to
replace the temperature readings with something
we can generate indefinitely as a kind of landscape
generator. There are many creative ways of doing
this, but we've settled on using a couple of `sin()`
(sine wave) generated values that change according
to two counters. The first `sin()` value will be used
to generate the height, while the second counter
is used to adjust the angle jump for the next value.
The result is a modulated sine waveform that looks
almost natural, while providing enough unpredictable
variation to be a challenge. The following code does
the job, and it needs to replace the old stack code in
the `loop()` function:

```
void loop() {
  if (playstate) {
```

> **Adding values to our stack is only half of the
> solution.** The other half is how we render those
> values to the screen

```
    if (counter > 180)
      counter = -180;
    if (second_counter > 120)
      second_counter = -90;
    land_stack.push((sin(counter * 3.1 / 180) +
1.1) * (4 * difficulty));
    counter = counter + sin((second_counter++ *
3.1 / 180) + 1.1) * difficulty;
```

One addition in the above we've not yet
mentioned is the `difficulty` variable. We're going
to scatter these throughout our code to act as
multipliers that make calculations more extreme.
The idea is that we can increase the difficulty
in the game by increasing the value held in the
`difficulty` variable.

Adding values to our stack is only half of
the solution. The other half is how we render
those values to the screen, and because we
want to turn those values into a scrolling tunnel
rather than a scrolling histogram, we need to →

QUICK TIP

If you want to save
yourself the bother
of putting all the
code together, the
code for the entire
project can be found
here: **git.io/fNXzh**

ADD A STARFIELD

Even though it's not necessary for a game where a spacecraft flies through an imaginary cave, there's one simple and old visual effect that adds depth and movement. And that's the starfield. A starfield shows 'stars' of pixels scrolling alongside the player, with some moving faster, and some moving slower. This creates an impression of parallax, where the slower-moving stars seem further away, especially if you make those stars smaller. You still find a starfield used in many games, and even realistic space simulators, like Elite Dangerous, find an excuse to drop moving pixels into what would otherwise be empty space. A fully three-dimensional starfield is slightly more complex, as would be a properly calculated two-dimensional starfield, but you can create a realistic approximation of a starfield using an array of a simple structure that holds the x, y, and speed values for each star:

```
struct stars {
  int x, y, speed, size; };
stars starfield[MAXSTARS];
```

We've defined **const int MAXSTARS = 10;** as a global value for the amount of stars to draw, but you can actually increase this to whichever value suits you best, depending on your Arduino memory. We've also added a **size** variable to give ourselves more rendering options. To draw the starfield, we'll create a separate function:

```
void displayStars() {
  for (int i = 0; i < MAXSTARS;
i++) {
```

```
    display.
fillCircle((starfield[i].x / 10),
starfield[i].y, starfield[i].
size, WHITE);
    starfield[i].x =
(starfield[i].x - starfield[i].
speed);
```

You can see how this is a simple hack to place the stars, drawn as circles with a radius that equals the star size, at their x and y co-ordinates on the screen. We then subtract the speed value from the x position to move the star along for next time. One slightly unintuitive part is that we're dividing the x value by 10, and that's because we intend to initialise this value with a random number that could be ten times the width of the screen. By doing this, we allow stars to move at a rate slower than one x value per iteration, so that the further stars move slower.

When the star hits the left border, we regenerate it by assigning random values to everything except x, as we now want it to appear on the right screen border. This is where we give it the **display.width() * 10** value just mentioned:

```
    if (starfield[i].x < 0) {
      starfield[i].x = (display.
width() * 10);
      starfield[i].y = random(0,
display.height());
      starfield[i].speed =
random(1, 50);
      starfield[i].size =
random(1, difficulty - 2);
    }}}
```

modify the **displayChart()** function, which we've renamed **displayTunnel()**.

TUNNEL VISION
The principle behind drawing the tunnel is simple. We take the height values that we've pushed onto the stack and use them as both the floor height from the bottom of the screen and for the roof height from the top with a value in the middle to define the level of separation between the two. This creates a tunnel effect that will go up and down with the roof and floor moving in parallel. On its own, this wouldn't be very interesting, so we're going to add two modifiers. The first will move the entire tunnel

> **We're also adding the 'difficulty' variable here to** make things harder or easier depending on its size, and we assign all of this to a single integer called 'height'

up and down, forcing the player to also move up and down, while the second will make the tunnel smaller and progressively harder to navigate.

To tackle the first, we're going to use another **sin()** to modify the height level we've pushed onto the stack, unless that value is zero. We'll link this to the global counter that's already counting through the radians when generating the original height to save creating another counter. We're also adding the **difficulty** variable here to make things harder or easier depending on its size, and we assign all of this to a single integer called **height**:

```
void displayTunnel() {
  int height;
  for (int x = 0; x < MAXSTACK; x++) {
    if (land_stack.peek(x) != 0) {
      height = display.height() - ((land_
stack.peek(x) + sin(counter * 3.1 / 180) *
difficulty));
```

We can now draw both the roof and floor by using the height to either draw down from the top of the screen or up from the bottom of the screen. We're using a global integer called **tunnel_size** to set the number of pixels high we want the tunnel to be, and we subtract half of the value it will hold from roof and floor heights to carve out a space for our ship:

```
display.drawLine(x, height - (tunnel_size / 2), x,
-1, WHITE);
display.drawLine(x, display.height(), x, height +
(tunnel_size / 2) , WHITE);
}}}
```

That's all there is to the tunnel generation code, although we'll be revisiting the function to add a simple collision detection, as we'll now see.

COLLISION DETECTION

There are now just two functions left to write or update, and these updates are both going to manage keeping a score for the player. We've decided to go with a simple timer that will reward the player for surviving, and that needs a way of ending the game, which we're making an event when the ship crashes into the cave wall. There are many ways to do this. For the ultimate in accuracy, for example, you'd save the state of what the ship could collide with into an array and then check those locations against the pixels you know are part of the ship bitmap. This solution is complex and will steal considerable resources, and just like those original games designers of the 1980s, we need to cut corners. Our solution is to use a global true/false (Boolean) variable called `playstate` to store whether the game is still in progress. If the game is still in progress, we run through the functions that update the ship location and the tunnel, then increase a counter that holds the score. If the game isn't in progress, then show a 'Game Over' message.

We're going to insert the collision detection into the `displayTunnel()` function we've just updated. After the two `drawLine` lines, add the following: →

Below
Once you've got everything working, you might want to consider a more permanent setup

> " We've decided to go with a simple timer that will reward the player for surviving, **and that needs a way of ending the game** "

```
if (x == shipx) {
    if ( (shipy < (height - (tunnel_size / 2) ))
|| ((shipy + 12) > (height + (tunnel_size / 2) ))
) {
        playstate = false;          }}
```

All the above code is doing is checking to see whether the ship is in the vicinity of the current 'x' position where the tunnel is being drawn. If this is true, see whether its edges are likely to hit the roof and floor heights we've just calculated. If we detect a collision, we set the **playstate** to false, triggering the end of the game section in the **loop()** function. And that's where we turn our attention to next:

10 ESSENTIAL IMPROVEMENTS

The great thing about games like this, and our simple implementation, is that it offers all kinds of opportunities to make it better, and those improvements are perfect challenges if you're learning how to code. With that in mind, here's our hit list of new things we'd love to see added to our game to make it even better:

1. Increase the score multiplier the further to the right of the screen your ship is, adding to the risk reward and difficulty.

2. Add the score and high score to the play window so you can see how you're doing.

3. Make the collision detection more accurate.

4. Use the **difficulty** variable to increase the difficulty the more time you spend playing, and even add levels and level markers.

5. Find a way to reduce the tunnel size off screen, rather than showing the transition while you're playing.

6. Give the player more than one life and show these on the screen.

7. Animate the ship by using more than one bitmap, and add rocket pixels that appear only when you're moving to the right.

8. Use collision detection for the stars, and start off with fewer stars, making the player dodge these as they fly through the tunnel.

9. Add gravity so that the ship starts falling to the floor when you're not directly thrusting up.

10. Add aliens and use the switch to fire a laser to destroy them.

QUICK TIP

The joystick scaling is currently linear, but you can make the controls more interesting by playing with the input and output values so there's finer control at the joystick's extremes, for example.

```
void loop() {
  if (playstate) {
  /// counter code
    updateShip();
    displayTunnel();
    displayShip(shipx, shipy);
    // displayStars(); uncomment for starfield
    if (score_counter++ == 100) {
      tunnel_size--;
      score_counter = 0;
      current_score++;
    }  } else {
    displayStars();
    displayScore();
    switchstate = digitalRead(SWITCH_PIN);
    if (switchstate == LOW) {
      initGame();
      playstate = true;
    } }
  display.display();
  delay(1);
  display.fillScreen(BLACK); }
```

With the exception of the radian counter and stack code covered earlier, this is our new **loop()** function in its entirety. While the **playstate** is true, it runs through drawing the ship, the tunnel, and the stars (see 'Add a starfield' box on page 60), increasing the score. After every 100 iterations,

 If the playstate changes to false, we display the score (and the starfield!) and wait for the player to press the joystick switch to start the game

we reduce the size of the tunnel, making the game harder. If the **playstate** changes to false, we display the score (and starfield!) and wait for the player to press the joystick switch to begin the game. This is also the default state when you start the game. We then update the display and blank it after a delay, ready for the next frame. There are two new functions referenced in this code we need to write: **displayScore()** and **initGame()**. The first simply checks if you've got a new high score, and prints both values to the screen:

```
void displayScore() {
```

Above ◈
A simple setup like
this could easily be
battery-powered and
placed into a portable
console of some kind

```
if (current_score > high_score)
  high_score = current_score;
display.setTextSize(1);
display.setTextColor(WHITE, BLACK);
display.setCursor(0, 0);
display.println("Score:" + String(current_
score) + "    High:" + String(high_score));
display.setCursor(10, 28);
display.setTextSize(2);
display.println("Game Over");}
```

The second initialises all the values we use in the
game for the player to start afresh:

```
void initGame() {
  counter = 45;
  second_counter = 45;
  difficulty = 5;
  shipspeed = 10;
  shipx = 10;
  shipy = 10;
  switchstate = 0;
  tunnel_size = 80;
  current_score = 0;
```

```
for (int i = 0; i < MAXSTARS; i++) {
    starfield[i].x = random(0, (display.width()
* 10));
    starfield[i].y = random(0, display.height());
    starfield[i].speed = random(1, 50);
    starfield[i].size = random(1, difficulty -
2);   }
  for (int x = 0; x < MAXSTACK; x++) {
    land_stack.push(0); }}
```

All that's left to do is declare the global variables
we've littered throughout our code, giving them
default values as necessary. With this done, you can
send the game to your Arduino and start trying to
beat my high score of 32:

```
Stack land_stack;
int counter, second_counter;
int difficulty;
int shipspeed, shipx, shipy;
int switchstate;
int tunnel_size;
int current_score, high_score, score_counter;
bool playstate = false;
```

QUICK TIP

Get other people,
especially from your
target audience,
to try your game
(and thanks to
Elliott, Kaitlyn,
Eden, and Ingrid for
testing ours!).

SCHOOL OF MAKING ━━━━━━━━━━━━━━━━━━━━━━

Arduino programming: Sound, envelopes, and interrupts

Build a simple sound generator that allows you to control the pitch or timbre of the sound over time

Graham Morrison

🐦 @degville

Graham is a veteran Linux journalist who is on a life-long quest to find music in the perfect arrangement of silicon.

We spent the previous couple of tutorials putting some of our programming theory into action, creating a simple game where the player flew a craft through an ever-decreasing tunnel. In this tutorial, we're returning to practical theory, but we're going to explore some ideas that could be used to expand a game, and generally make your programming life easier. These ideas are going to be based on generating sounds using something we've not yet covered – interrupts.

Sound is obviously important, not just for games, but for all kinds of different projects. Audio feedback can replace the need for a visual element, such as a screen, and sound can be more intuitive and accessible. You don't need to explain the UI of an audible alert or alarm, for example, and if the sound is annoying enough, it can demand your attention in ways an on-screen notification can't. But the best thing about sound is that it's incredibly cheap and easy to implement. Even a basic Arduino with no specific

Right ◈
You can use almost anything you have around to generate sound from some input trigger with an Arduino

Left
Speakers are
remarkably resilient,
and can sound good
even when in a poor
state of repair

audio hardware, like the Uno we're using for our projects, can generate sound, because sound is generated by moving a speaker coil using nothing more than fluctuations in current.

The trigger to start the sound could be almost anything. An in-game event, for example. But for our purposes, and to make this project standalone, we're going to use an equally simple momentary switch or button. When the button is depressed, we'll generate the sound. When it's released, we'll stop the sound. Two things are going to make this different to how you might expect. The first is that we're going to use an interrupt to automatically wait for the button state to change, and the second is that we're going to modify the sound as it's being played. This is called 'modulation', and it's essential if you want your sound to be more interesting than a simple beep.

INTERRUPTS

Up until now, we've used the ever-running `loop()` function to look for changes in the state of things we wanted to monitor. If a button is pressed, or a joystick pushed, a variable would change and we could safely assume an event had taken place. This approach is typically called 'polling', because we're constantly waiting and watching, looking for

 An interrupt allows the programmer to define a function to **run when there's a change in state without manually waiting for it**

a value to change. Polling is a great solution on an Arduino because the device is always on, always running at full speed, and always iterating through `loop()`. Adding extra checks, or polls, shouldn't add to the overall processing burden. And if it does, it's something the programmer can manage by carefully prioritising those checks, or reducing the frequency of less important checks.

But there are strong use cases for not continually checking for changes in state, and instead waiting to be informed that something has changed. This is what an interrupt does. An interrupt allows the programmer to define a function to run when there's a change in state without manually waiting for it. Just like tapping someone on the shoulder, an interrupt is often triggered faster than the equivalent polling code, and the amount of time it takes to respond to an interrupt is more predictable. Polling response times can be unpredictable. It could be that you check for changes in state just as →

QUICK TIP

As you might imagine, one thing you can't do within the function triggered by the interrupt is wait. `delay()` won't work because the function is being executed outside of the main loop, and `millis()` won't be incremented either.

Below ◩
Momentary switches only stay connected as long as the user presses the button

Below ◈
We salvaged our speaker from an old PC, but they're easy to find by taking apart almost anything that used to make a sound

something has changed, and the response will be fast. Or something changed just after the previous check and won't now be serviced for a longer duration. This induces jitter, which is variations in the delay between when something happens and when your code can respond to it. Of course, we're talking about differences in milliseconds, but it can make a difference in time-critical situations, or when jitter can be easily detected such as with strobing lights or audio playback.

Let's get started by writing the code for the interrupt:

```
const int interruptPin = 2;
const int piezoPin = 3;
unsigned long note_time;
bool trigger = false;
void setup() {
  attachInterrupt
(digitalPinToInterrupt(interruptPin),
triggerSound,
CHANGE);
}
```

All we're doing in the above chunk is first declaring a global constant variable to hold the value of the pin connected to our button, and then using this value within **setup()**. We also create an 'unsigned long' variable to hold up to 4 bytes of data with

> **'attachInterrupt' is the important part,** as this is the Arduino magic that tells your hardware to automatically launch a function

no negative numbers, which we'll use to hold a timestamp, and a **bool** to hold the press state of the button. **attachInterrupt** is the important part, as this is the Arduino magic that tells your hardware to automatically launch a function, **triggerSound**, when it receives a signal corresponding to the final argument in the **attachInterrupt** function call. We've gone for **CHANGE**, as this triggers the interrupt when the button is being pressed and released. We could also have used **RISING** to trigger the interrupt when the button is pressed and **FALLING** when the button is released, but we can handle both of those states with **CHANGE** without using our one remaining interrupt, as we'll show. There's also **LOW** (and **HIGH** on selected

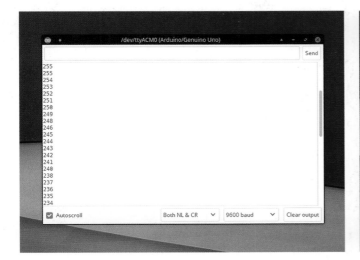

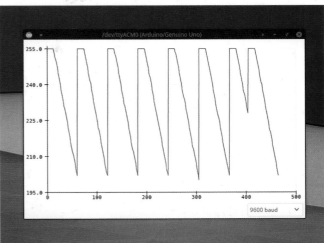

boards) to trigger the interrupt when the input changes to that particular state.

The **triggerSound** function that's called by the interrupt is actually very simple:

```
void triggerSound() {
  if (trigger = !trigger) {
    note_time = millis();
}}
```

As we're detecting a change in the button state, and not whether it's being turned on or off, we use a Boolean called **trigger** to flip between **true** when the button is pressed and **false** when the button is released. This isn't obvious in the above code, and we're perhaps guilty of needless obfuscation here, but the **if (trigger = !trigger)** line is both the assignment and the comparison. This isn't a comparison, using **==** or **!=**, as you'd usually expect to see with an **if** statement, it's actually an assignment. We're assigning the **not** value of trigger to trigger because the exclamation is the **not** operator. This makes **not true = false** and **not false = true**. If **trigger** is true after the assignment, the **if** statement will see the expression resolve as true and **note_time = millis();** will be executed. This line adds another new command, **millis()**, which assigns the number of milliseconds the Arduino has been powered on to **note_time**, the unsigned long variable we created earlier.

PLAYING A SOUND

Playing a sound on an Arduino is remarkably easy, partly because there's a built-in function, **tone()**, so you don't need to worry about pitch and partly because all the Arduino has to do is send pulses of →

HARDWARE

The great thing about this project is that you likely already have everything you need. You can use almost any old speaker, for example, although the better the speaker, the better the quality of sound – we took one from an old PC. You could also use a small piezo buzzer, often found in component kits. The sound output isn't so good, but the Arduino isn't exactly capable of high quality anyway. It's connected to pin 3 of the Arduino and ground, but if you find the output is too loud, place a resistor between the positive connection and the Arduino. The higher the resistance, the lower the volume.

Similarly, we plundered an old component box to find a momentary switch to use. One side of this switch is connected to both digital pin 2 on the Arduino and a 10 kΩ resistor, which is itself connected to ground. The other side of the switch is connected to the 5 V pin or rail from the Arduino. And that's all there is to this circuit.

Below ◩
All the components for this project should be easy to find

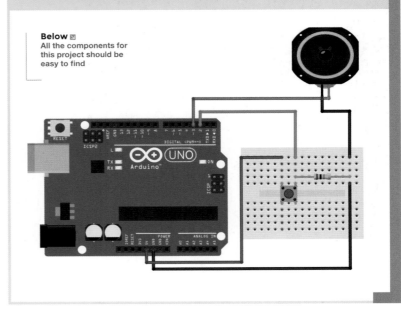

current to the pin connected to the speaker. It can all be done with a single line, which we'll place within its own function:

```
void playSound(int pitch) {
  tone (piezoPin, pitch);
}
```

We'll pair the above function with another to turn the sound off:

```
void stopSound(){
  noTone(piezoPin);
}
```

All we now need to do is write the simple **loop()** function to trigger either the **playSound** function or the **stopSound** function depending on the state of the **trigger** Boolean:

```
void loop()
{
```

```
  if (trigger) {
    playSound(261);
  } else {
    stopSound();
}}
```

If you now run all the code we've just written, you should find that your Arduino generates a tone at pitch equivalent to a middle 'C' on a piano keyboard. But this is only part of the project, because a simple tone isn't all that exciting. To solve this, we're going to change the sound during playback using something called an 'envelope' to modulate the playback pitch.

An audio envelope describes how much a sound changes over time, from the moment it's triggered to when it's released. Envelopes are typically used to change the amplitude and pitch of a sound over the duration of a note, and the most common envelope type consists of four stages: attack, decay, sustain, and release, also written as ADSR. Attack, decay, and release are time durations that indicate how fast or slowly the audio changes, whereas sustain is a level that is held while the note is being triggered.

ENVELOPE GENERATOR

Before we start creating our own envelope, we need to add a few global variables:

```
const int pitchEnv[] = {500, 250, 200};
const int pitchMax = 255;
```

The array is going to hold the attack, decay, and sustain values, with the first two being durations and the final element being level value. As we're going to use this

> **Envelopes are typically used to** change the amplitude and pitch of a sound over the duration of a note

envelope to vary the pitch of our sound, we've called it **pitchEnv**, along with **pitchMax** to hold the maximum value (amplitude) we want the envelope to reach on the initial attack. Apart from its name, though, there's no reason why the envelope can't be used to control any other audio-related value to modulate the sound. Before we write the envelope generator code itself, we need to patch the envelope effect into our current code. This is as simple as adding the following to the beginning of the **playSound** function:

HARDWARE INTERRUPTS

ARDUINO	INTERRUPT PINS
328-based, Uno, Nano, Mini	2, 3
32u4-based, Micro, Leonardo	0, 1, 2, 3, 7
Due	all digital inputs
Uno WiFi v2	all digital inputs
Zero	all digital inputs except 4
Mega, Mega2560, MegaADK	2, 3, 18, 19, 20, 21
MKR boards	0, 1, 4, 5, 6, 7, 8, 9, A1, A2

Arduino interrupts work at the hardware level and can respond to detected changes on specific pins, such as the rising or falling signal you get by pressing a button, but which pins you can use is restricted, and different Arduinos support different numbers of pins. On our Uno (and other 328-based Arduinos), pins 2 and 3 are the only two capable of generating interrupts, and we've settled on pin 3 for the button connection. But to get pin 3 to generate interrupts requires an extra step we wouldn't ordinarily take, and that's to convert this pin number into an 'interrupt number'. This is because most Arduinos support a restricted number of interrupts, just two on the Uno, and the number for each interrupt won't necessarily align with the pin being used to generate the input. If your project needs more interrupts, the best thing to do is upgrade your Arduino.

```
pitch += envMod();
```

The above operator is adding the value returned from the **envMod()** function we're about to write to the current value of **pitch**.

```
int envMod() {
  unsigned long current_dur = millis() - note_
time;
  if (current_dur <= pitchEnv[0]) {  // Attack
    return ((pitchMax * (100 * current_dur) /
pitchEnv[0]) / 100);
  } else if (current_dur <= (pitchEnv[0] +
pitchEnv[1])) { //Decay
 pitchEnv[1]) / 100);
    return (pitchMax - (pitchMax - pitchEnv[2])
* (100 * (current_dur - pitchEnv[0]) /
pitchEnv[1]) / 100);
  } else { // Sustain
    return (pitchEnv[2]);
}}
```

The above code is complicated, so we'll break it down into parts. It starts off by taking another timestamp for when the function is being run. By subtracting the note's start time, which we saved earlier, and by using the time values in the envelope array, we can calculate which stage of the envelope we should be in. This is what the **if** and **else** statements are doing, with the first simply checking to see whether the time is less than the time of

the attack stage, and the second whether the time frame is between the attack and the end of the decay. If it is, we have a long calculation that does the following:

1. Calculates current time frame as a percentage of the whole stage
2. Returns a percentage of changing value

We both multiply by 100 and divide by 100 in the expressions to keep the end values as integers and avoid floating point mathematics, which is a lot slower and resource hungry on an Arduino. With the attack stage finished, the next **if** deals with the release stage. Finally, if we're in the sustain stage, we simply return the sustain value from the array.

With that function written, you can now re-upload the project to your Arduino. When you press the button, the pitch of the sound will now change according to the durations and sustain level of the envelope, making the sound much more dynamic and interesting. You could even build this into a synthesizer, adding potentiometers to control the values for each stage of the envelope, or adding more modulation envelopes to control amplitude, or even pulse-width modulation. But that's another story.

The code for this project can be downloaded from **hsmag.cc/sEgZSN**. □

Arduino programming:
Copy and send
infrared signals

Build a secret infrared repeater to turn off Sky Sports
on the 65-inch screen in your local pub

Above ◈
While it's easy to
wire everything
together onto a
breadboard, you
might want to
consider working
this project into
a small battery-
powered container

We thought the humble
infrared remote would be
dead by 2019, the year of
Akira and *The Running Man*.
But infrared is still going,
and has yet to be replaced by
Bluetooth, WiFi, or Facebook. This means we still
invariably point a piece of plastic at an invisible
window on a television to change the channel.
However, simplicity in this case is a good thing,
because it means infrared is easy to subvert and
easy to harness for your own evil projects, whether
that's controlling your current equipment, or creating
a line-of-sight communication channel between any
of your own projects.

Despite being invisible to the human eye, infrared
light couldn't be any easier to generate and to play
around with. It behaves just like visible light, and
can be produced with circuits no more complex
than those using an LED, although infrared is usually
output from a photodiode rather than a light-emitting

diode. An infrared light has a light wavelength
between 700 nanometres and 1 micrometre,
whereas the human eye is sensitive to light between
380 and 750 nanometres, with the top of this range
being red (followed by infrared). A larger wavelength
means a lower frequency, which is why infrared has
a lower frequency than visible light; this is why the
term 'infra' – which means 'below' – is used.

We're going to create a super-flexible and generic
infrared recorder and retransmitter that you can use
to copy an infrared signal and resend it with many
different types of generic hardware. You can use
it as a single-button trigger for your own infrared
commands, or at the heart of an aggregating infrared
server you could use to send signals to multiple
pieces of hardware from a remote source – much
like Logitech's Harmony range of devices. It requires
just a few components: the transmitter and receiver,
a momentary button, an Arduino, and a smattering of
programming, and we'll be touching slightly on both
pointers and two-dimensional arrays.

HARDWARE

Even though you can get infrared LEDs to wire into your circuits, much like you would any LED, it's easier to use a pre-packaged module for both the transmitter element and the receiver. These packages are low-cost and help take some of the complexity out of the circuit, especially when it comes to decoding a signal. This is because the binary (digital) message that you send and receive

> **Other than the transmitter and the receiver,** we've added a simple momentary button

with light, or even sound, needs to be modulated into a meaningful signal the analogue hardware can work with. This is what modulation does. This is where old-school modems get their name – they 'mod'ulate and 'dem'odulate signals between the digital domain of computers across the analogue (at the time) telephone network. We need much the same function to send signals by modulating signals with infrared light. The signal is modulated for sending and demodulated for receiving, with the end result

being a string of binary digits appearing at one of your Arduino's pins. We then need to decode those bits into something we can understand, either by copying them and sending the same signal out on demand, or by looking for their meaning in a specification of a manufacturer's set of known infrared codes.

Both the receiver and the transmitter have three pins; two are connected to power and ground, which we connect to lines on a breadboard, and then data connections to pins on the Arduino. We've connected the receiver to pin 10 and the transmitter to pin 3. This is fixed because we're going to use a library to simplify sending and receiving signals, **IRremote.h**. This library requires the transmitter pin to be capable of pulse-width modulation, and is hard-coded to pin 3 for this purpose. The library will handle all the modulation complexity of sending and receiving infrared messages, as well as decoding them for lots of common equipment.

Other than the transmitter and the receiver, we've added a simple momentary button, the same we've already used in many projects. We're going to use this in two ways. First, by holding it down, we'll instantiate the 'receive and record' process for capturing an infrared message. And second, by pressing the button quickly, we'll send the message stored on the Arduino. Putting this into code is going to be an interesting challenge, so let's get started. →

Graham Morrison
🐦 @degville

Graham is a veteran Linux journalist who is on a life-long quest to find music in the perfect arrangement of silicon.

YOU'LL NEED

◆ **Arduino Uno**
◆ **Momentary push-button**
◆ **10 kΩ resistor**
◆ **IR receiver diode**
◆ **IR transmitter photodiode**

Left ◈
The receiver and the transmitter require only power and ground alongside a single data connection each to the Arduino

Above ⌷
There are several
different types
of receiver and
transmitter, but
they're all low-
cost, and mostly
work in the same
way as ours

Below ◈
Pre-made modules
can be a bit more
robust than just
soldering wires
to components

INFRARED LIBRARY

To a freshly created Arduino project in the IDE, the
first line of code we're going to add is the header
for the library we're using. We'll add this with the
constant integers that hold which input pins we're
using for the receiver and the button (remember,
the transmitter is hard-coded to be pin 3 within the
header files themselves);

```
#include <IRremote.h>
const int RECV_PIN = 10; // IR receiver input pin
const int BUTN_PIN = 7; // Button input pin
```

Don't forget that you need to first download and
install any external header you use in your own
project. This can be done easily from the Arduino
IDE by selecting Sketch > Include Library > Manage
Libraries from the menu and searching for 'irremote'.
You need the package built by 'shirriff', which is
nearly at the top of the search results. Click on Install
in this result to install it.

We now add two sets of global variables:

```
bool buttonActive = false;
bool longPressActive = false;
int msglen = 0;
int khz = 38;
unsigned int receivedData[RAWBUF];
```

The first Boolean on/off values are going to help
with the logic of the quick press/long press detection

> **Don't forget that you need
> to first download and install**
> any external header you use
> in your own project

of the button. Implementing this is more complicated
than it first appears, because simple momentary
buttons like this suffer from jitter and false positive
values during the transition from on to off and off to
on. These values become true as the button press
passes each state, so we know when a long press is
active and can run the appropriate code.

The following three global values start with
an integer for **msglen**. This will hold the size of a
message we receive so we can make sure we store
and send a message of the same length. After this
is an integer we've mysteriously called **khz**. We'll
be using **khz** when we transmit an infrared code
because it holds the modulation frequency for the
encoded data stream. The default is 38kHz, or
38,000 times a second, and is the most common
frequency used by equipment manufacturers. This
can obviously be changed if you need it to be. The
final variable, **receivedData**, is an array of integers
for the contents of the message. The size of this
array is defined by a constant called **RAWBUF** which is,
unusually, defined within **IRremote.h**.

We will now use three classes defined
within **IRremote**:

```
IRrecv irrecv(RECV_PIN);
IRsend irsend;
decode_results results; // decode_results class
is defined in IRremote.h
```

We use one class variable for communicating
with the receiver, one for communicating with
the transmitter, and one for processing any results.
This is a good example of using a class to hide,
or abstract, the functionality of what's happening,
such as the modulation and demodulation of a
message. The header simply presents to the
programmer an interface for controlling the
hardware. We'll be using **irrecv.enableIRIn();**,
for example, to initialise the receiver within the
setup(), alongside the usual pin configuration,
which is the next piece of code:

```
void setup() {
  pinMode(LED_BUILTIN, OUTPUT);
  pinMode(BUTN_PIN, INPUT);
  irrecv.enableIRIn();
}
```

PROGRAM LOGIC

With the boilerplate code out of the way, we're now
ready to tackle the logic of the code itself. First, we'll
cover the logic behind detecting both short and long
presses of the button. The main idea is that, as long
as we know the button isn't already being pressed,
we store the time when the first press is detected,
and we can use this to work out whether it's been a
long press or a short press. Here's the beginning of
the code that detects when the long press is active
(**longPressActive = true;**):

```
if (digitalRead(BUTN_PIN) == HIGH) {
  if (buttonActive == false) {
    buttonActive = true;
    buttonTimer = millis();
  }
  if ((millis() - buttonTimer > longPressTime)
&& (longPressActive == false)) {
    longPressActive = true;
  }
} else {  // EXECUTED ON RELEASE
```

We can only detect a short press when the button
is released, as it's only then we'll know the duration
of the press. This is why the release code comes
after the **else** statement above, indicating that →

REMOTE CONTROL DECODING

We've used a simple raw mode for recording and
playing back infrared signals, but IRrecord can
also decode and send signals to specific hardware
manufacturers, which is needed when they're using
their own protocols, or using a non-standard carrier
frequency. It can do this because it has a large
library of protocols from common manufacturers,
including Sony, JVC, Panasonic, and even Lego. If
you look at the header file for each manufacturer,
you also get hints on how to best communicate with
the equipment.

Using a function from each library, you can extract
the command code from the manufacturer-specific
code used as a container for the commands. This
means you can theoretically control elements
like volume or channel numbers using variables,
combining them with the code you know controls
volume when you send them from the Arduino. You
could even chain commands together for different
pieces of equipment, enabling you to set up a
home audio/video configuration for a movie, or for
music, for example, and then control playback from
something that can then talk to the Arduino.

QUICK TIP

Encoding signals by
varying the width
of a pulse (Pulse
Width Modulation) is
exactly how 'PWM'
audio synthesis
works, and also
how some audio
communication
protocols work.

Left ◈
Using one of the
manufacturer-
specific profiles in
the library can help
solve compatibility
issues. Panasonic,
for instance, uses
a carrier frequency
of 35

the button event is not setting the button to HIGH. We then reset the `longPressActive` variable if this event has already been detected as a long press. And if not, after another `else`, we finally get to play with some infrared code:

```
if (buttonActive == true) {
    if (longPressActive == true) {
      longPressActive = false;
    } else {
      if (msglen > 0) {
        irsend.sendRaw(receivedData, msglen,
khz);

        delay(50);
        irrecv.enableIRIn();
      }
    }
    buttonActive = false;
  }
```

INFRARED AND OSCILLOSCOPES

You can use an oscilloscope with an infrared receiver to calculate the frequency of the signal from an infrared source.

Despite being invisible to the naked eye, there are several ways to see an infrared signal (outside of joining the SAS and snagging some infrared night-vision goggles). The simplest is to use your smartphone camera. Looking at the real-time preview whilst pressing buttons on your remote should reveal flashes from the infrared LED. The front camera is usually best, as it's less likely to have an infrared filter because infrared is often used to help with motion detection and facial recognition. But if you happen to have an oscilloscope handy, you can study an infrared signal in much more detail. From the circuit we've created, just attach one of your oscilloscope probes to the output of the receiver – the same output that connected to pin 10 on the Arduino.

When you now fire a few infrared signals at the receiver, you should notice your oscilloscope come to life. In particular, if you set your update resolution to around 2 ms, you should see square waveforms with different widths. These changing widths are key to how different values are 'modulated' into the signal transmitted by the infrared LED. Notice, for example, that the 'off' width is always the same. This is the pause between transmissions, and it's constant. The actual data is carried in the variable widths of the on-time – hence, pulse-width modulation. Different widths hide different values, decoded automatically by any infrared receiver.

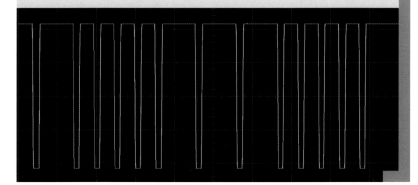

Thanks to **IRremote.h**, sending a signal is super-simple. First, we check to make sure there is a recorded message (`msglen > 0`), and then send the message with `irsend.sendRaw(receivedData, msglen, khz);`. The data we transmit is in `receivedData`, but you may notice something. We created this variable as an array, but we're not including any brackets, or targeting a specific element. This is called 'passing by reference', rather than the more common 'call by value'. This works because it's only a reference to the array that's being passed to the `sendRaw` function, and this reference is really the memory address where the first element of the array is being stored. The relative address of each element can then be calculated by generating an offset from the amount of space required to store an element of the array's type. If this sounds exactly like what a pointer does, you're right – by not including an element identifier, we're implicitly using the array variable name as a pointer.

The final piece of code is also the most functional because it's responsible for receiving the data and decoding it into something we can use. This code runs outside of all the previous code because this

 We can only detect a short press when the button is released, as it's only then we'll know the duration

improves the response time of our program when an infrared signal is received. This is how we start this block of code, quickly followed by a check to see whether the `longPressActive` Boolean is true. If so, this means the button is being held down and we can go ahead and record the infrared signal being received. If not, we can ignore the signal until next time.

```
if (irrecv.decode(&results)) {
    if (longPressActive) {
      msglen = results.rawlen - 1;
      for (int i = 1; i <= msglen; i++) {
        if (i % 2) {
          receivedData[i - 1] = results.rawbuf[i]
          * USECPERTICK - MARK_EXCESS;
        }
        else {
          // Space
          receivedData[i - 1] = results.rawbuf[i]
          * USECPERTICK + MARK_EXCESS;
```

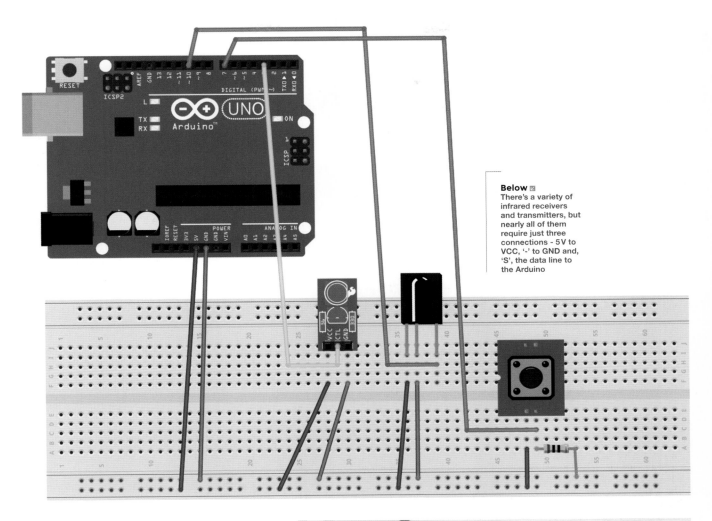

Below ☑
There's a variety of infrared receivers and transmitters, but nearly all of them require just three connections - 5V to VCC, '-' to GND and, 'S', the data line to the Arduino

```
      }
    }
  }
  irrecv.resume(); // resume receiver
 }
} // End bracket for project
```

The decoding code itself is taken from the IRremote library, using **%2** to work out whether we're receiving either an odd or even element for the array and then using this to tweak the gaps between the received elements to cancel out receiver distortion. The results are placed into the array and the size of the message stored in **msglen**, which is the message we can now send whenever we perform a short press on the button. And that's all there is to it. Build it and send it to your Arduino! □

Right ◈
Everything set up and running on a breadboard, but you might want to use protoboard to make this more permanent

SCHOOL OF MAKING ━━━━━━━━━━━━━━━

Arduino programming:
Debugging

Delve into the dark art of troubleshooting and work
out where things are going wrong

Graham Morrison

🐦 @degville

Graham is a veteran
Linux journalist who is
on a life-long quest to
find music in the perfect
arrangement of silicon.

Above ⬈
Creating a circuit
with a piezo sensor
couldn't be simpler.
Wire up positive to
an analogue pin,
negative to ground,
and bridge the two
with a 1 MΩ resistor

One aspect of Arduino
programming we've barely
touched on is the careful,
cautious, and necessary art
of debugging. Debugging is a
very general term that covers a
huge variety of processes that range from simply
trying to find out why your code doesn't work, or
why it's producing unexpected output, through to
performance monitoring, profiling, and optimisation.
The majority of modern development environments

and frameworks will offer tools to help with these
debugging processes, commonly allowing you to
step through your code line-for-line, while monitoring
the state of your hardware (as with a debugger such
as 'gdb'), or generating profile information from the
code execution, such as the length of time spent in
a function, or the amount of memory being used.
But we don't have the same level of luxury on
an Arduino.

With the Arduino, there's no graphical tool for
monitoring the memory, no performance profiling

or graphical debugger. In this way, debugging your Arduino project can feel very similar to debugging a 1980s-era home computer project, because you need to come up with your own tests, and write your own code directly into your projects. This isn't necessarily a bad thing because you're learning about your code and learning how best to avoid mistakes through trial and error. But there's a lot you can do to make the process easier, and a lot you can do to make your code faster – both of which we're going to tackle by using the serial monitor and some lovely piezo sensors.

SERIAL SCAFFOLDING

In writing any Arduino code, there's one element that's always required and yet nearly always cut prior to publication or release. This is the code used to debug the program, and it can be a little like the scaffolding around a building construction site. It performs an essential role that you seldom see

> Debugging your Arduino project can feel very similar **to debugging a 1980s-era home computer**

after the project is completed. You seldom (never!) get code working on the first write, and you often need to go back through what you've written and test your expectations against what is actually happening. The difficulty comes in trying to find out what is happening. This is actually very close to how professional development works, because you often have to write tests at the same time that measure those expectations against what can be shown to be happening. Those tests are then run whenever the code is updated, to make sure nothing added changes the behaviour of the older code; it's a process known as QA – quality assurance.

Programming for the Arduino presents several unique challenges. The biggest to overcome is that your code isn't running on the same system, or the same architecture, that you're writing your code on. An Arduino is really just a microcontroller. This is why there aren't any readily available native debugging tools, as these usually need to run and interpret the compiled output of your code on the system it's been built for. Instead, you only execute live Arduino code when it's been uploaded onto your device, and apart from a flashing LED, there's no →

BOOST SPEED WITH REGISTERS

The Arduino platform has been designed to be as broadly compatible as possible. This enables it to work across many different kinds of devices and in many different kinds of environments. But this flexibility sometimes comes at the cost of performance, especially for specific devices. And one of the best examples of this is the `digitalWrite` function, used by nearly every Arduino project to send a signal to a pin. The Arduino documentation admits the code for `digitalWrite` is a dozen lines long, compiled into a multiple of machine-specific instructions, one of which is executed per 16MHz clock cycle. This takes time. But it's possible to do without `digitalWrite` completely, and instead write directly to the pin in question using what is known as a 'register'. And what's more, it can be done with a single command:

```
PORTD &= ~_BV(PD2);
```

A register is a special kind of storage that's tied to a specific hardware location, which is then read directly by the hardware when a certain function is performed. The chips on an Arduino have three different kinds of registers to cover all the analogue and digital pins, including PORTD for read/write access to digital pins 0–7, as shown above. The `&=` chicanery is because we're working at a low hardware level, and this is a bitwise AND assignment operator. This is followed by a bitwise NOT for the tilde (~), effectively allowing you to switch the state pin 2 (PD2 on the Uno) with the `_BV` macro for convenience. A longer way to write the same thing is the equivalent of `PORTD = PORTD &(~_BV(0b00000100))`. But it doesn't need to make sense for it to just work. In our experiments, the above code takes around two CPU cycles, whereas `digitalWrite` takes around 36, at least on our Uno.

Below
The best thing about using the serial monitor is that you don't need any extra hardware, such as a screen, to get meaningful information back from your Arduino

```
/dev/ttyACM1 (Arduino/Genuino Uno)                          Send

Hello world.
Hello world.
Hello world.
Hello world.
Hello world.
Hello world.
Hello world.
Hello world.
Hello world.
Hello world.
Hello world.
Hello world.
Hello world.
Hello world.

☑ Autoscroll          Both NL & CR    9600 baud    Clear output
```

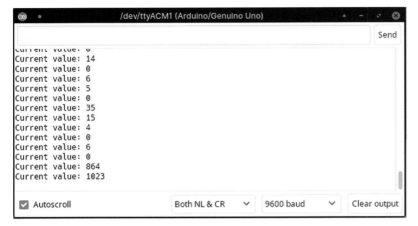

```
Current value: 0
Current value: 14
Current value: 0
Current value: 6
Current value: 5
Current value: 0
Current value: 35
Current value: 15
Current value: 4
Current value: 0
Current value: 6
Current value: 0
Current value: 864
Current value: 1023
```

Autoscroll   Both NL & CR   9600 baud   Clear output

Above
Without feedback, it's very difficult to tell which values occur when on a sensor, so you can then generate functions

Below
Most Arduinos have more than one serial connection, and this extra connection can be used to communicate with other hardware. The multiSerial example sketch shows how to do this

way for the device to communicate its running state, or whether it's encountered any problems, unless you specifically add that feedback into your code. What's more, while you can obviously create the code to send messages to attached LEDs, screen, and sound emitters, you can't then debug the output to those devices if even they don't work. The answer is to use the serial port.

The 'S' in the USB umbilical cord we use to upload our code to the Arduino is for 'serial', and even modern USB is descended from this very early form of cross-device communication, where bits bounce from one hardware pin to another, one bit at a time. These pins were simply for 'transmit' and 'receive', and even on many modern devices, such as Amazon's Echo or your ISP's router, hackers can often locate TX and RX pads or pins on the

motherboard. The Raspberry Pi also has these two pins and makes a convenient testing platform for working or hacking with other boards. These connections are more widely known as UART (universal asynchronous receiver/transmitter) when the pins are used for a serial connection in this way, which is reflected in the Linux device name on the Raspberry Pi. But UART is also widely on the Arduino too, both manually via its pin connection, and via the USB connection to send data back from your code to a host system.

For a serial connection to work, both the sender and the receiver need to know how quickly the data is travelling. This was the baud rate in old modem terminology, and it corresponds directly to the number of binary bits being sent across a wire per second. To set the baud rate for the serial connection to the Arduino, add `Serial.begin(9600);` to the `setup` function. With that done, you can now send data from your code running on the Arduino back to the host computer using the `Serial.println`:

```
void setup() {
Serial.begin(9600);
}

void loop()
{
Serial.println("Hello world.");
delay (500);

}
```

 Both the sender and the receiver need to know how quickly the data is travelling

115,200 bits per second is often the fastest serial speed you'll manage on Arduinos, and also with many devices using RX and TX pins. If you do experience problems, try slower speeds such as 57,600, 38,400, 19,200, or 9600. As the above code shows, we're starting at the slowest speed as this is always most likely to work. To test the above code, send it to your Arduino and open the 'Serial Monitor' from the IDE's 'Tools' window. This is the IDE's equivalent to those old pieces of terminal software that would help old computers connect to remote

```
MultiSerial | Arduino 1.8.5                    —   □   ×
File Edit Sketch Tools Help

[toolbar]

MultiSerial

void setup() {
  // initialize both serial ports:
  Serial.begin(9600);
  Serial1.begin(9600);
}

void loop() {
  // read from port 1, send to port 0:
  if (Serial1.available()) {
    int inByte = Serial1.read();
    Serial.write(inByte);
  }
}
```

bulletin board systems. The main window shows the output received from the connection, and the small 'Send' field lets you send data back across the serial connection. But before you can do that, you need to sync the monitor speed with the baud rate of the connection, which you can do with the drop-down 'baud' menu in the bottom right. If this is set wrong, you'll get a screen full of gibberish. When selected correctly, you should see a new 'Hello world' message every 500 milliseconds, or half a second.

DEBUGGING

Of course, printing out a single message is no help at all. But you can now use the serial connection to troubleshoot all kinds of otherwise difficult to solve problems by using the same `Serial.println` command to indicate when your code reaches a specific section, or to see the value of a specific variable, or when a specific event has triggered a function. And to give these examples more solidity by showing `Serial.println` in action, we're going to create a specific example using a single component – a piezoelectric knock or vibration sensor. They're cheap and incredibly versatile and, as their name suggests, they can be used to create anything from motion detectors and door monitors, to drum pads and pressure gauges.

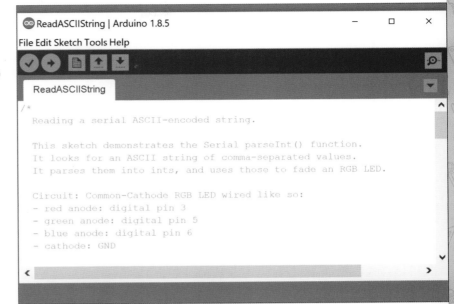

A piezoelectric knock sensor is closely related to the 'piezo' we used to generate sound in a previous tutorial, as well as the 'piezo' used within electric guitar pickups and, ultimately, many microphones. They generate voltages from bending forces and changes in pressure. They can be easily wired up to your Arduino with the positive (red wire) connected to analogue input 1 and the negative (black wire) to ground, with a 1 MΩ (megohm) resistor bridging the →

Above ◈
You can send data to your Arduino over serial as well. The example Communication > ReadASCIIString shows how to do this

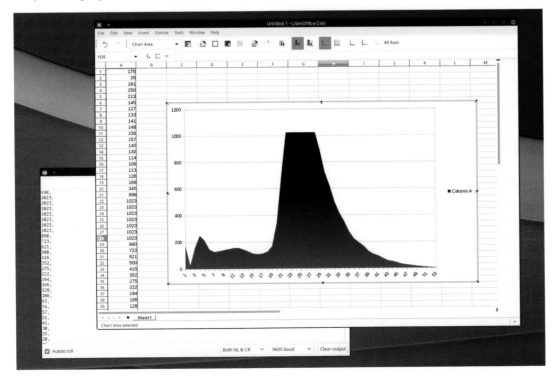

Left ◈
Generating CSV data from your sensors is a brilliant way to conduct experiments and visualise the output, such as the response curve from a piezo knock sensor

SCHOOL OF MAKING

Right ◺
Piezo sensors
are cheap, easy
to integrate, and
incredibly flexible. It's
always worth having
a few around

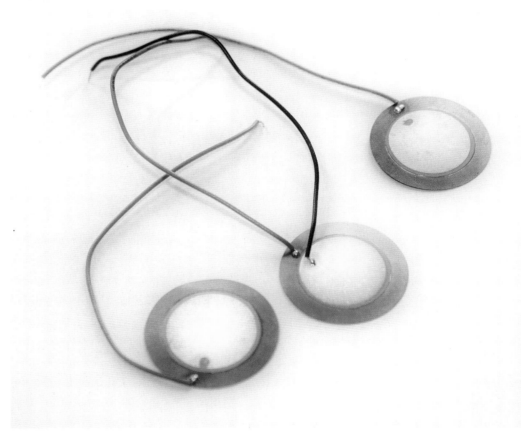

two to dampen potential voltage from the sensor. But these sensors are also unpredictable, and you often have no idea of what kind of analogue values they're going to generate until you start generating them. This is important if you want to trigger something at a certain threshold, for example, or make sure that the threshold doesn't change under different conditions. And that means you need to get the data back from your Arduino across the serial connection.

For this simple example, add the following to the top of your code to set the analogue pin we're using and the integer we'll use to store the reading:

```
const int PIEZO = A0;

int piezo_value = 0;
```

The main loop can then be updated with the following:

```
void loop()
{
piezo_value = analogRead(PIEZO);
Serial.print("Current value: ");
Serial.println(piezo_value);
delay (500);

}
```

There are two slight differences in the 'print' code above. The first is that we use `print`, as opposed to `println`, because we don't want a carriage return after the 'Current value: ' text, which is handled by the next `println` statement, although there are control codes that can do this within the text itself. But breaking this up into two lines makes it easy to see we're outputting the `piezo_value` with the second line.

When you now upload this, run the code, and open up the serial monitor as we did before, you should see the following output:

```
Current value: 0

Current value: 0
```

Now try pressing down on the piezo sensor. You should see this value jump, although not always in a predictable way. The maximum value for the analogue/digital converter on the input is 1023,

 You may wonder at which point you'd want the trigger to start, and this is a complicated problem

and this can sometimes be achieved with a soft press rather than a hard strike, but as long as the untriggered value is 0, you can work with the sensor as a trigger.

If you wanted to use the piezo as a drum trigger, you may wonder at which point you'd want the trigger to start, and this is a complicated problem. You could use the transition from zero to a non-zero value, for example, but devices like these and momentary buttons will often include multiple transitions from zero in a single hit, and it's not always easy to tell when the main trigger should occur. This is a great example of when you might want to look deeper into the debugging aspect of your code by mapping out the typical values a sensor has during the course of an event, such as a trigger. We can do this easily with our own code by making only a few modifications:

```
void loop()
{
  piezo_value = analogRead(PIEZO);
  if (piezo_value){
    Serial.print(piezo_value);
    Serial.println(", ");
  }
  delay (10);

}
```

The above code replaces the `loop` function with an `if` statement that's only triggered when the `piezo_value` isn't 0. It then prints out this value followed by a single comma, before waiting ten milliseconds and trying again. What this is actually doing is outputting a comma-separated list in the

format typically known as CSV (comma-separated values). This is a very simple format that's supported by many different types of visualisation tools, both online and offline, and you can copy and paste those values directly from the serial monitor window into one of these – such as LibreOffice Calc – and, from there, generate a chart of the values. You can then analyse the chart to see what the typical sensor response might be, especially if you combine multiple triggers. You should then be able to derive a series of values that constitute a proper event without bounce or repetition, and you can only do this because of the debugging output from the serial monitor. □

SERIAL **PLOTTER**

In the main text, we finish by outputting a CSV-formatted dataset that can be analysed from any one of the dozens of applications and web services that support CSV. But there's also a little-known feature in the Arduino IDE that lets you get real-time feedback from your sensors, without having to export your data at all. This feature is the 'Serial Plotter', found just beneath the 'Serial Monitor' in the Tools menu. It needs to be opened on its own, and it also requires the same baud rate setting as the monitor. But, most importantly, it requires a specific data format when sending values from your code. This is almost identical to the CSV format used in our original code, but replaces the comma with a single space. For example, our own code would look like the following:

```
if (piezo_value){
  Serial.print(piezo_value);
  Serial.println(" ");
}
```

With that small change and the code uploaded to your Arduino, you now simply have to open the plotter and start touching the piezo. You'll see the chart drawn almost in real-time in the plotter, which is a great way to both visualise sensors and the data they're generating, and create a model of how you might want to use specific value ranges within the data.

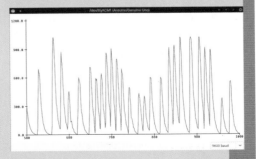

Project Tutorials

Expand your knowledge and skills by making these fun Arduino projects

118

126

84

WORK

HOME

Way Home Meter

Use an ESP8266 and some NeoPixels to let loved
ones know when you'll arrive back home

Brian Lough

🐦 @witnessmenow

Brian is a Maker from
Ireland who primarily
creates projects
and libraries for ESP
microcontrollers. Check
out his stuff on his
YouTube channel and
blough.ie

"**L**et me know what time you'll be home"– it's a common refrain in homes across the country.** We try to give good answers, but it's hard to know how traffic will affect us on the way. Rather than rely on guesswork, let's try to build something to let our families know when we'll make it back.

In this project we'll build a device that will give up-to-date home arrival times, based on the live traffic conditions. To make the device more useful for when it's not being used for that purpose, it works as a clock that automatically fetches its time from the internet and also automatically adjusts for daylight savings.

We've built this using an ESP8266, which is a surprisingly powerful microcontroller with built-in WiFi and can be programmed using the Arduino IDE.

The device makes use of a few different, free internet services:

- **Telegram:** an instant messaging service that allows for the creation of bots that users can interact with. It is a really good way of communicating with your ESP8266 or ESP32 projects from anywhere in the world, for free.

- **Google Maps API:** can be used to get travel time and traffic information between two places.

- **NTP servers:** Network Time Protocol, a way for network-connected devices to get the time. This saves the needs for a real-time clock, and also doesn't require the time to be set.

To use it, the person who is coming home uses Telegram on their phone to share their live location to a Telegram Bot that is running on the Way Home Meter. This will update the Way Home Meter with the person's GPS coordinates every 20 or 30 seconds.

The Way Home Meter takes these coordinates and sends a request to the Google Maps API to get the live travel time and distance between the person's location and home.

The Way Home Meter will then add the travel time onto the current time and display the estimated arrival time of the person and updates the dial and NeoPixels to represent what percentage of the journey (distance wise) has been completed.

CODE IT UP

The code for this project is available on GitHub. Go to the following URL, **hsmag.cc/ybAcHB**, and click the Clone or Download button on the right side of the page, and then Download Zip.

Left ◈
Screw terminals are useful for projects where components are separated from the PCB

YOU'LL NEED

◈ **An ESP8266 Wemos D1 mini microcontroller** (or equivalent e.g. Adafruit Feather Huzzah or NodeMCU etc.)

◈ **4-in-1 Max7219 dot matrix display**

◈ **A small servo** (sg90)

◈ **A 3D-printed dial for the servo** (optional, could be made from anything!)

◈ **11 × through-hole NeoPixel** (I used PL9823 LEDs)

◈ **220 pF capacitor**

◈ **Passive buzzer**

◈ **1 kΩ resistor**

◈ **NPN transistor**

◈ **Protoboard** (I used a prototype PCB I designed, but the project can easily be built with standard protoboard)

◈ **Screw terminals** (optional)

◈ **IKEA RIBBA frame**

◈ **A3 piece of 3 mm foam board**

◈ **Hot glue gun**

◈ **4 mm wood drill bit**

◈ **Sharp knife**

◈ **A metal ruler**

◈ **A compass and a protractor**

◈ **Micro USB phone charger** (for powering the project)

Extract the zip file. Inside the extracted folder, open up the **WayHomeMeter** folder and open the **WayHomeMeter.ino** file.

This sketch requires some additional Arduino libraries to be installed; start by opening the Arduino Library Manager by going to Sketch > Include Library > Manage Libraries.

You will need to add the following libraries:

- **Universal Arduino Telegram Bot** by Brian Lough – for creating a Telegram bot on the ESP8266.

- **Google Maps API** by Brian Lough – for getting the live traffic data.

- **Arduino JSON** by Benoît Blanchon – used by the libraries to parse the responses. Note: There is a breaking change in V6 of this library that

will cause it not to work with the Telegram and Google Maps library, so use the drop-down on the left of the window to change the version to V5.13.2.

- **MD_MAX72XX** by majicDesigns – for communicating with the dot matrix display.

- **MD_Parola** by majicDesigns – handles animations on the dot matrix display.

- **Adafruit NeoPixel** by Adafruit – for controlling the NeoPixels.

- **NTPClient** by Fabrice Weinberg – for getting the time from the internet.

- **Timezone** by Jack Christensen – for automatically switching the time for daylight savings. →

PROGRAMMING THE **ESP8266**

The standard Arduino IDE isn't set up to program the ESP8266, so before we can program the board, we need to set this up (you can skip this bit if you've already used the IDE with an ESP8266).

First, let's get the raw IDE. You can download this from the Arduino website and install it as you would any other software: **hsmag.cc/TAfEJp**.

Next, you will need to set up the IDE so it knows how to communicate with an ESP8266. Open the Arduino IDE, go to File > Preferences, and paste the following URL into the Additional Boards Manager URLs, then click OK:
http://arduino.esp8266.com/versions/2.4.2/package_esp8266com_index.json

Back on the main screen of the Arduino IDE, go to Tools > Board > Boards Manager. When this screen opens, search for 'ESP8266' and install it; this may take a few minutes depending on your internet connection.

After setting up a new board it is recommended to get the simple example blink sketch before trying anything more complicated; this can save a huge amount of headache down the line! You can find this in File > Examples > 01. Basics > Blink.

Upload this to your ESP8266 and you should see an LED blink on and off. If you get an error or don't get a blinking light, make sure you've got everything installed correctly and the ESP8266 is properly connected.

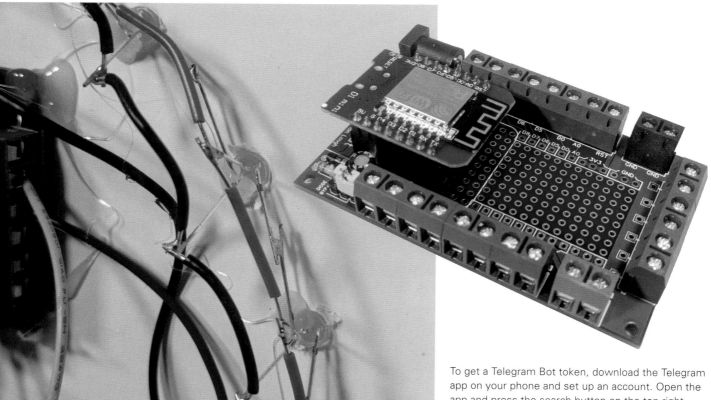

Above right 🗗
This is a custom
PCB that breaks out
all the pins of the
D1 Mini to screw
terminals, but it can
be easily recreated
with a standard
protoboard

Above ◈
The address pins of
the LEDs should be
able to reach each
other without the
need for extra wire.
The power pins need
to be joined by wire

After installing these libraries, you should click the 'verify' button (shaped like a tick) on the WayHomeMeter sketch to make sure that everything compiles fine.

SOME CONFIGURATION REQUIRED
You will need to make some configurations to get this sketch to work for you, but you will first need to get:

- Telegram Bot token
- Google Maps API token
- GPS coordinates of your home

GOOGLE BILLING

Google maps gives a free monthly allowance of credit – equivalent to 20,000 requests. That is just under what's required to send a request every two minutes in a month (about 22,000). This device only makes the request every two minutes that it is actively monitoring someone's home journey, so should stay under the limit if used occasionally. It's possible this limit will change in the future. How often it checks can be configured in the sketch by changing **delayBetweenGoogleMapsChecks**.

To get a Telegram Bot token, download the Telegram app on your phone and set up an account. Open the app and press the search button on the top-right of the screen. Search for 'botfather'. Type /newbot and follow the on-screen instructions. The botfather will provide you a link to the bot and an access token. The link is for the chat where people will share their location; the access token is used in the sketch to authenticate your ESP8266 as the bot you just created.

Next, you will need to get a Google Maps API key. Start by going to the following URL: **hsmag.cc/mPqFqh.**

Check the Routes option and click Continue. You will then be asked to create a project; you can give this any name. You will need to add a billing account, but this device will comfortably operate on the free allowance given by Google. You will then get an API token that can be used in the sketch.

And finally you will need to get your home's GPS location. A simple of way of doing this is using Google Maps. Using a web browser (not the app), navigate to your house on Google Maps and right-click and click 'Directions from here'. This will modify the URL, which will now contain the coordinates of your home; copy and paste these from the URL e.g. 51.5546466,-0.2794867.

You now have everything you need to configure the WayHomeMeter. Open up the WayHomeMeter sketch and click on the config.h tab. First thing you will need to enter is your WiFi details so that the ESP8266 is able to connect to your WiFi.

NEOPIXELS WITH A 3.3 V DEVICE

You can often have issues using NeoPixel LEDs with a 3.3 V logic level device such as an ESP8266 or Raspberry Pi. You can get around this issue by using a logic level shifter to convert the 3.3 V to 5 V for the Data In connection for the first LED. However, we've found that it works fine with just a small capacitor between Data In on the first LED and Ground (as seen in this project).

Next, you will need to add your Telegram Bot token, your Google Maps API key, and your home location. Finally, if you are not in the UK or Ireland, you will more than likely need to change your time zone. Uncomment the appropriate time zone and comment out the UK and Ireland time zone.

WHAT MAKES IT TICK

You'll need to wire everything together as shown in **Figure 1** (overleaf). The LEDs are addressable RGB LEDs, so they only require a single GPIO pin of your microcontroller and you can set the colour of each LED individually. The input of the first LED (the one over on the left when looking at it from the front) will be connected to the Wemos, and its output will be connected to the input of the second LED. For all subsequent LEDs, the input of the next

 Once you are happy everything is working correctly, **secure the components in place with some hot glue**

LED is connected to the output of the previous one. The output of the final LED will not be connected to anything. Soldering these LEDs should be left until the final assembly stage.

CREATING THE MOUNT

Take the back panel off the picture frame and use it to trace a square onto your foam board. Using a sharp blade, cut out the square.

Next, you'll need to separate the panels from the display, as you'll be placing the PCB on the back side of the foam and the panels on the front; this will hold the display in place and hide the cuts from view.

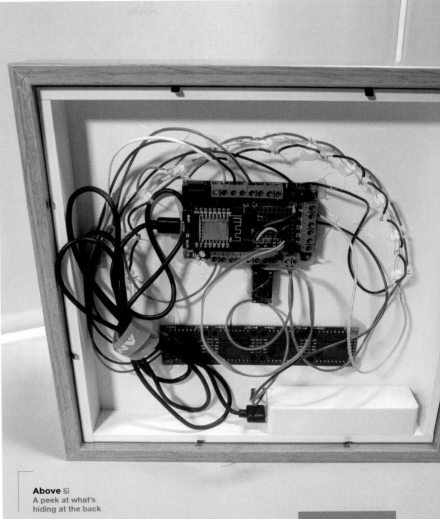

Above 🖾
A peek at what's hiding at the back

Carefully remove each of the dot matrix panels from the dot matrix display. There are markings on the side of each of the dot matrix panels; make a note of what direction they are facing in comparison to the PCB to ensure they are put back in the correct orientation.

If your PCB has header pins attached, desolder and remove them. Replacing these with wire will make the PCB fit flush to the foam board.

Measure the rectangle created by the pins and mark out that shape where you want to place it on the foam board. The objective is to cut out a shape that the pins of the PCB will fit through, but the PCB itself will be too big for.

The LEDs for this project are all on an arc around the centre point of the servo. Mark where you want the centre point of the servo arm to be and, using your compass, draw a semicircle lightly for where you want the LEDs to be. →

SHORT ON TIME?

If you are short on time, or just interested in quickly trying this project out, strip it back to be just the dot matrix display, the Wemos D1 Mini, and use DuPont cables to connect them together. The key piece of functionality, displaying the expected arrival time, uses only the display.

Place your protractor on the centre point and mark every 18 degrees. Then, using a ruler, line up the centre point and these new marks; where this line intersects with the semicircle is where each LED should be placed. Starting on the side that you want to be the front, use the 4 mm drill bit by hand (no power drill needed) to create a hole for each of the LEDs where you have marked.

Measure the dimensions of your servo and mark it on around the centre point. Remember that the part of the servo that rotates should be the centre point, so offset the servo shape to suit. Cut the shape out of the foam board and place the servo through from the front.

Finally, you will need to place the buzzer module. You can simply place the pins of the module into the foam to mark where the holes should be and, using a piece of wire, pierce the two holes so they go through the foam board.

ON THE FINAL STRETCH

Place all the LEDs into the foam board from the back. Bend the input pin of each LED back towards the previous LED, and bend the output pin of each

towards the input pin of the next LED, and solder them together. Slightly bend all the Ground pins of the LEDs towards the centre of the circle and all VCC pins away from the centre of the circle. Solder wire between all the Ground and VCC pins.

Place the dot matrix PCB in the cut-out, and put all the panels back in place. Pay careful attention

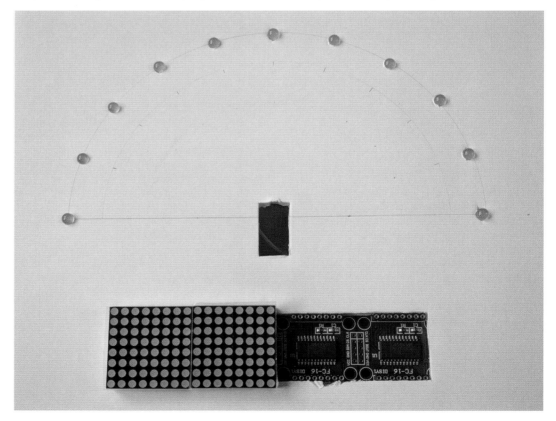

Right ◈
Foam board all cut and LEDs placed. The foam board will be clamped between the display module and the PCB

A POTENTIAL WEASLEY CLOCK?

A lot of people who saw early versions of this project mentioned that it reminded them of the Weasley Clock from Harry Potter, a clock that showed the current location of each of the members of the Weasley family. This Telegram-based solution could be used for a project like that, but it does require each of the users to actively enable the location sharing. A more passive solution might be better.

QUICK TIP

Always be generous with the lengths of wire you use, especially in a project where space is not an issue. If you need to make adjustments, it's easier to shorten them than lengthen them.

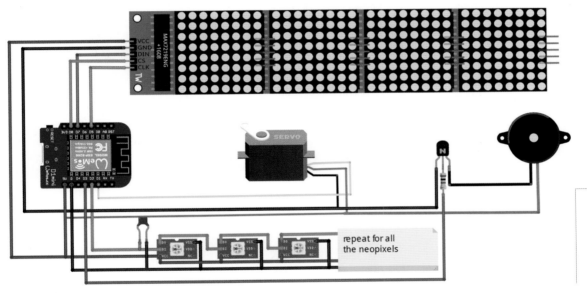

repeat for all the neopixels

Figure 1 ◈
The wiring diagram for our Way Home Meter

Below ◈
The name displayed comes from the user's Telegram name

to the orientation of the panels, as it is very difficult to remove these again without damaging the foam board.

You then want to thread the wire of the servo module through the hole for the servo, and then insert the servo. Glue the dial hand onto one of the connectors that comes with the servo, and attach it to the servo when dry. The 3D design used in this project can be downloaded from here: **hsmag.cc/iqOPiP**. However, you can use anything you want (and a model car could be substituted if you don't have access to a 3D printer).

Finally, solder wire to each pin of the buzzer module and push it through the front of the foam board.

Connect all the modules to the Wemos on the protoboard and test everything out. Once you are happy that everything is working correctly, secure the components in place with some hot glue. You are now ready to have super-accurate home arrival times! ▫

Desktop hydroponic gardening

Grow your own food with an Arduino and some rain guttering

Dr Andrew Lewis

🐦 @monkeysailor

Dr Andrew Lewis is the owner of **Shedlandia.com**, a restorer of old tools, a fabricator for hire, a research scientist, and a founder member of the Guild of Makers.

I n this project, you'll be making a scalable hydroponic growing system that uses easily sourced components to control the flow of water, light, and heat to your plants. Hydroponic systems use regular or constant flows of nutrient-enriched water to grow plants without soil, and are a great way to grow vegetables if you have restricted space or access to natural light.

This project represents a couple of years' worth of experimentation with homemade growing systems, and is a variation of a hydroponic technique called ebb-and-flow – where the water is tidal, and floods through the system several times a day. Plants are rooted into an absorbent substrate that holds water next to the roots of the plant when the flow of water stops.

If the pump in a constant flow system fails, the plants will die very quickly, while an ebb-and-flow system can survive for several hours in the event of a power failure.

GROW VERTICALLY TO SAVE SPACE

The hydroponic system described here has three main parts: the support system, the water system, and the control system. The support system is essentially a wooden box and a shelf unit, and is the easiest part to make.

Lay the smallest piece of plywood flat, and use some coins or hex nuts to raise it slightly from the surface it is resting on. Next, take the four planks, and arrange them to make a rectangular box around the smaller piece of plywood. Screw the planks together using corner brackets at the top and bottom of each corner, and then secure the plywood base to the planks using screws and glue. You should now have a simple box that you can use for the base of your hydroponic system.

You will use copper pipe to make shelf brackets. Measure 450 mm from the end of the 28 mm pipes, and drill a 15 mm hole right through. Drill a second

hole through the pipes, 750 mm from the end. The 15 mm pipe should slide through the hole in the 28 mm pipe and make a rudimentary shelf bracket. To figure out the length of the shelf brackets, measure the width of your guttering and add about

Hydroponics are a great way to grow vegetables **if you have restricted space**

40 mm. Cut four pieces of 15 mm pipe to this length, and add a copper elbow to the end of each pipe. If you have a blow-lamp and solder, you can use this to join the pipes and elbows; otherwise, you can just use hot glue.

Fix the 28 mm pipes 150 mm from the sides at the back of the box, using the 28 mm pipe clamps to hold each pipe in place vertically. You can now slide the 15 mm brackets into place, and fix them in position using solder or glue.

Next, you are going to extend the brackets to support LED lights above the guttering. Cut four pieces of copper pipe 250 mm long, and fit these

vertically into the elbows on the shelf brackets. Cut another four pieces of copper pipe slightly less than half of the width of your guttering, and connect them to the 250 mm verticals using elbows, so that they hang over the guttering. Cut two final pieces of copper pipe to join the left and right brackets together over the guttering.

The final piece of pipework will carry water from the pump to the top watering channel. The pipe is fitted vertically in the middle of the back of the box using 15 mm pipe clamps, and is approximately 800 mm long with a U-shaped section at the top to direct water into the guttering. It is much easier to use the copper pipe as a conduit for a length of narrow-bore, silicone pipe push-fitted to the pump than it is to connect to the copper pipe directly. Feed the silicone pipe through the 15 mm copper pipe and around the U-shape, leaving about 30 cm hanging out in the bottom of the box.

With the last of pipework done, you can complete the woodwork. Drill, or cut, a 10 mm hole through the back of the box at the right-hand side to accommodate your power cable, then drill a larger hole on both sides of the back to allow ventilation. To finish the box, cut slots in the larger piece of plywood so that it will fit onto the box as a lid without hitting the pipes. Mark the centre of the →

YOU'LL NEED

Electronics

- 12 V 20 A power supply
- Arduino Uno
- 60 W waterproof greenhouse tube heater
- 20×4 I²C LCD screen
- 4 × Momentary push buttons (normally open)
- 2 × TIP120 (or similar) transistors
- 1 × 10 A solid state relay
- 2 × 2.2 kΩ resistor
- 10 kΩ resistor
- 10 kΩ thermistor
- 5 m LED grow light strip (only 2 m needed)
- 12 V water pump
- 3m length of 240 3-core flex
- 13 A plug
- DuPont signal cables and 3 A rated cable

Other hardware

- 2 m length of flexible silicone tubing, approx. 6 mm bore
- 2 × 1 m lengths of 28 mm copper pipe
- 2 × 3 m lengths of 15 mm copper pipe
- 20 × 15 mm equal copper elbows
- 4 × 28 mm pipe clamps
- 2 × 15 mm pipe clamps

longest side of the plywood, and line this mark up with the centre of the box (where the water pipe goes up). Now use a square to mark the position of the pipes on the larger piece of plywood, and notch out the pieces using a jigsaw or fretsaw.

TIME TO GET YOUR FEET WET!

Water is pumped to the top of the system from the water tank, then drains down through a series of water channels under the force of gravity until it goes back down into the water tank. The tank is very simple to make from a 52 cm Stewart gravel tray. Apply double-sided tape or glue around the top of the gravel tray, and simply stick the polythene sheet to the top, so that the tray is completely covered. The tray is now a closed water tank.

Place the second Stewart gravel tray on the lid of the box, between the two 28 mm pipes. This tray will support larger potted plants, and will always have a few centimetres of water in it. Drill a 25 mm diameter hole through the slightly raised section at the bottom left-hand side of the tray, and continue the hole through the plywood lid of the box. This hole is where a water fitting will connect to the tank at the bottom, so there needs to be a hole in the water tank here.

> **This tray will support larger potted plants, and will always have a few centimetres of water in it**

Remove the tray and plywood lid from the box. Position the water tank at the left-hand side, and slit the polythene near the back of the tank. This slit is where the pump will draw water from. Replace the lid, and cut into the plastic through the hole you just made in the plywood. Glue the water tank into place with hot glue, and reinforce the polythene around the hole with a 15 mm washer or gaffer tape.

Screw the water pump into place near to the tank and connect the outlet to the silicone pipe, then use another length of silicone pipe to connect the pump's inlet to the water tank through the slit in the polythene. To make sure that the inlet pipe rests on the bottom of the tank, weigh it down or use rigid copper pipe to hold it in place. Use tape to seal the slit in the polythene.

Two pieces of guttering (with the end-caps fitted) make your high-level growing channels. Controlling the flow of water from one channel to another is critical for the proper operation of the hydroponics rig, and this project uses a special 3D-printed variation of a greedy cup (or Pythagoras cup) to do this. To make the greedy cups, you will need three small jam jars, three of the 3D-printed cup pieces, and three lengths of 15 mm copper pipe long enough to reach from slightly below the top of one channel to slightly above the top of the next channel.

Drill a 25 mm hole in each of the water channels, staggering the holes between the left and right side. Fit the 3D-printed cup pieces in the holes, and screw them on tightly with a little bit of waterproof sealant around the thread. Fit the third greedy cup into the hole in the Stewart tray, and use a short piece

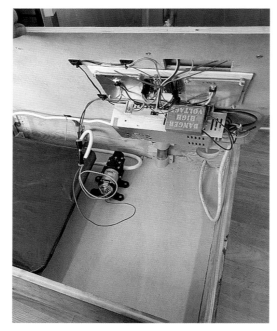

Right ◈
The inside of the base, showing the electronics mounted to the underside of the lid, and the water tank on the bottom-left of the box with the pump connected to it

Above ◈
Fitting the greedy cup into the hole in the water channel, with a little silicon rubber to ensure a waterproof seal

CURRENT STATUS
WATER: OFF
LIGHT: OFF
HEAT: ON   (19 C)

Above ◈
Keeping an eye on the status

Above ◈
The system under test, showing water flow from the outlet, and the greedy cup mechanism on the left of the photo

of 15 mm pipe to connect the tray and the water tank below.

All that remains is to develop a control system for the Arduino, and wire up the electronics. We've already written some commented code and a wiring diagram to make this step less complicated. The control system uses a 20×4 LCD and four buttons to navigate between pages, tab between items, and alter values up and down. Print out the panel for the LCD and buttons and the housing for mounting the panel onto the lid of the box, and then wire the buttons as shown in the diagram (**Figure 1**, overleaf).

Position the LCD housing on the lid of the box near to the front. Drill a hole through the plywood for the LCD wires, and screw or glue the mounting into place. Mount the Arduino and heat sinks to a plastic sheet, and screw the sheet to the underside of the

> **"** All that remains is to develop a control system for the Arduino, **and wire up the electronics "**

lid near to the hole for the LCD wires. Mount the TIP120 transistors to the heat sinks. Add the 12 V power supply to the underside of the lid near to the cable hole you drilled at the back. Make sure that all the electronics, but particularly the high voltage side is mounted so that it's protected against water. You also need to ensure that the high voltage cable is not at risk of coming loose, and make sure that anything →

QUICK TIP

Don't put both TIP120 transistors on the same heat sink. The mounting tab is connected to the transistor base.

TUTORIAL

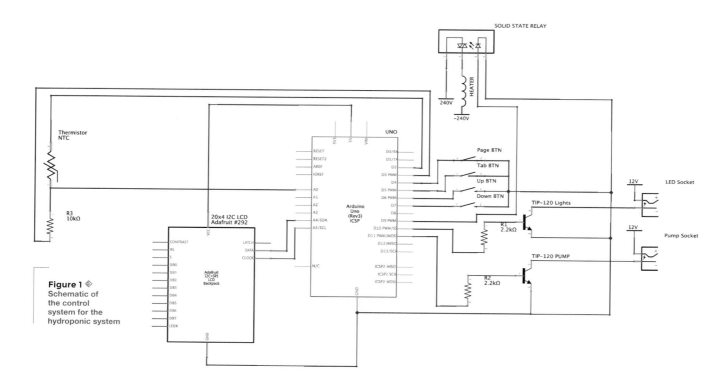

Figure 1 ◈
Schematic of the control system for the hydroponic system

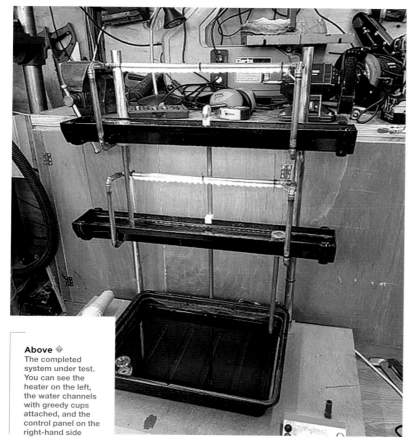

Above ◈
The completed system under test. You can see the heater on the left, the water channels with greedy cups attached, and the control panel on the right-hand side

that needs grounding is connected to ground. Working with mains voltage safely takes experience and if you're not experienced enough to work safely with mains voltage, seek advice from someone who is before proceeding with this build. Take your safety seriously as you don't always get a second chance! You can mount the PSU using four metal brackets.

Add the LED lights to the tubes above the water channels, and run the wires down to the box using cable ties to hold them in place. Position the thermistor about halfway up the right-hand pipe using cable ties, and connect the wires to the Arduino as shown in the diagram (**Figure 1**).

Add the heater to the left-hand side of the box, and drill a hole to pass the cable through to the underside of the lid. Run the cable along the underside of the lid to the PSU. Mount the solid-state relay to the side of the PSU by drilling into the case and using machine screws or bolts. Wire the electronics as shown in the circuit diagram, and ensure that any live contacts are well protected with insulating material. Cables should be routed using cable ties and clips. Flash the Arduino with the hydroponics sketch (from **hsmag.cc/issue20**), and test out the interface using just the USB power to make sure everything is working.

If the Arduino seems to be working, test the water channels by pouring water into the top channel and tracing its path back to the water tank. Watch for any leaks or blockages. If the water channels seem

Above ◈
Almost ready to harvest

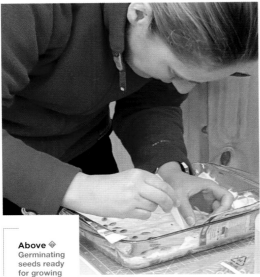

Above ◈
Germinating
seeds ready
for growing

SAFETY

This project combines electricity and water, which can be a tricky, and dangerous, combination. You need be knowledgeable enough to work with this combination before embarking on this build. You can reduce the safety issues by using an external power supply. We'd also recommend using a residual current device (RCD) for further protection.

OK, pour in a whole bucket of water to the Stewart tray. The water will drain into the tank, and you can reconnect the power once you're sure there are no leaks to worry about. Now you can test the pump by setting the water flows, and adjust your light settings. It's recommended to start the pump at a low setting (maybe 25% power). If you're planning on using the heater, you'll need to put the hydroponic unit inside a polythene tent to contain the heat. The tent can be made with a few garden canes or pieces of PVC pipe, and held together with bulldog clips. □

QUICK TIP

The thermistor only gets power just before a reading is taken, because supplying it with constant power can make it heat up over time.

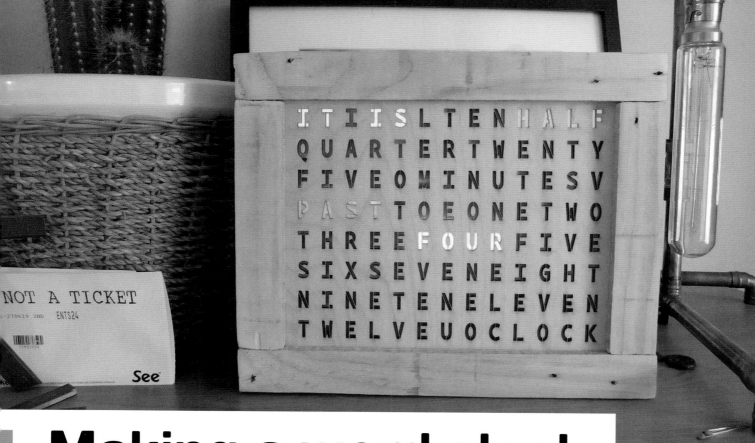

Making a word clock

Build your own attractive timepiece

Ben Everard

🐦 @ben_everard

Ben loves cutting stuff, any stuff. There's no longer a shelf to store these tools on (it's now two shelves), and the door's in danger.

K, settle in. This project turned out to be a bit more complex than expected. Actually, complex isn't quite the right word. There's nothing in here that's fundamentally hard, but it did test our skills in quite a few different areas of making, and each area posed its own little challenges that needed to be overcome. We'll guide you through it as best as we can.

In this project, we used quite a wide range of equipment and parts. These represent the tools and parts we had available, rather than a canonical set of things you actually need. There's no 'right' way of doing this, and you can find alternatives to almost everything we've used if you need to.

The basic way a word clock works is that it shines a light through letters spelling out the words to say the time. The heart of our clock, then, is these letters and the LEDs to make the light. We used laser-cut 3 mm plywood for our clock face, but other people have had success using printed acetate sheets (the sort used in overhead projectors that older – but not too old – readers will remember from their school days). Thinner laser-cut sheets would also work, but we'd recommend going no thicker than 3 mm as this will reduce your viewing angle.

You can grab our design from **hsmag.cc/issue20**, but it's fairly easy to create your own (or modify ours if you'd prefer). The crucial point for the lettering is that we need to use a stencil font – this ensures that there's a connection to any isolated parts of a letter (such as the middle of the letter O), so they don't fall out when laser-cut. It makes layout easier if the font is monospaced – we used BP Mono Stencil (**hsmag.cc/BPMonoStencil**).

The LEDs must be held in the appropriate place behind the letters. There are two approaches that you can take here – you can design your letters so that they line up with off-the-shelf LED strips, or you can use strings of LEDs to line up with whatever spacing you use for the letters. We opted for the latter, but the former would make a more

Left ⬥
The LED string inserted. We had to join three strings together to get 104 LEDs for the clock. In hindsight, only 100 are needed, as some letters are never lit

YOU'LL NEED

⬥ **WiFi-enabled microcontroller (such as the MKR1000)**

⬥ **String of 104 NeoPixels**

⬥ **1 A diode**

⬥ **9 mm plywood**

⬥ **3 mm laserply**

⬥ **Wood for frame**

⬥ **Laser cutter**

⬥ **Modelling foam**

straightforward build if you're less fussy about the size of the clock.

We then need a way of holding the LEDs in place behind the letters. There are a few parts to this – first, you need a way of holding the LEDs in place far enough behind the letters so that they illuminate them evenly; then you need a way of minimising the amount of 'bleed', where lighting one letter illuminates the letters either side of it; finally, you need something to diffuse the light.

Our setup used plywood with 7 mm holes drilled into it. This is just large enough for surface-mounted 5050 LEDs to be pushed in place and held with a drop of superglue. These shone through the holes in the plywood and into a square honeycomb made of modelling foam hot-glued together. Finally, it hit a double-layer of diffusion fabric before shining through the laser-cut face. All we needed was a frame to hold it in place. We made this from 4×1 inch reclaimed wood with routed grooves to hold the face and plywood LED panel in place.

Let's take a closer look at this process before diving into the microcontroller brains.

THE BUILD

First, you'll need to laser-cut your clock face – that's the easy bit of woodwork. Now on to the manual part…

As mentioned, we started building our frame with reclaimed 4×1 inch wood that cost just £1 from our local wood recycling project. We sanded this down to give it a smooth finish, but it lacks the hard corners of planed wood. There are also holes from old nails which combine with the rustic

joining technique to give the look we wanted for our clock.

If you're an experienced woodworker, you may choose a more elegant method for making the frame, but as we're not, we'll keep it simple. We've used butt joints in the corners which are held together with two screws each. First, we routed two grooves in one side of the wood – one to hold the 3 mm face, and one to hold the 9 mm

> **"** It hits a double-layer of diffusion fabric before shining through the laser-cut face **"**

plywood LED panel. 9 mm ply is overkill for such a frame, but we happened to have some spare from a previous project – you could easily get by with 3 mm or 6 mm plywood, and MDF would work just as well. We routed these grooves 3 mm deep into the wood. →

WIRING

The simplest wiring for the clock is to connect the 5 V and GND pins and one data point (we used pin 6) from the microcontroller to the 5 V, GND, and data input pins on the first LED. The LED chain will then propagate power and data along the strip. However, there are a few problems with this.

Firstly, this results in an out-of-spec power situation which you might, or might not get away with (see 'Power problems' box on page 101). Secondly, the jitter on the power line may cause problems – putting a capacitor between the 5 V and GND lines can smooth that. Thirdly, you should include a 470 Ω resistor between the Arduino pin and the data-in line. You might get away without this, but it will prevent any problems with too much current being drawn.

Above ◈
The two grooves
routed in our wooden
frame to hold the
clock face and the
LED board

If you've got a plunge router bit, you might choose to do this groove-cutting later, and not rout all the way to the edge of each section of frame as this will give a better finish.

We then needed to cut the wood into four appropriate length sections. You need two for the top and bottom that are:

length = width of face + (2 × width of frame wood) – (2 × depth of groove)
And two for the side that are:
length = height of face – (2 × depth of groove)

You should now be able to hold them all by hand and everything should fit together (don't screw or glue them together yet). If they don't fit, you'll need to make adjustments before moving on. This might entail routing the grooves a little deeper, or trimming down the wooden frame.

INNARDS

The quickest way to mark up the plywood LED holder is by eye. It needs to be the same size as the clock face, and you can pencil-mark the spots for the LEDs very quickly without the need for a tape measure (though measure and mark properly if you'd prefer).

As previously mentioned, we drilled these out with a 7 mm drill bit. The diagonal on a 5050 surface-mount part is just larger than 7 mm, so it's a tight fit. We used strings of WS2812 LEDs (often known as NeoPixels). Each LED is on a small, circular PCB. We applied a drop of superglue to the edge of each LED, then pushed it into the hole in the circuit board. They take a bit of force to get in, but be careful, as we pushed too hard on one and dislodged a resistor (if you do this, just cut out the LED in question and join the wires with solder).

TESTING

Your build will almost certainly be slightly different to ours, so rather than just following along by rote and hoping that the results are the same, now's a good

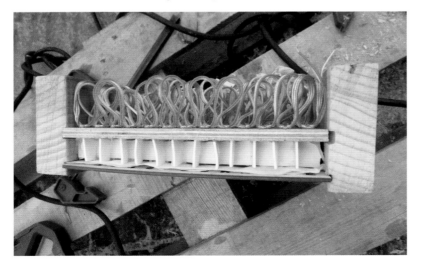

Left ◈
The foam honeycomb – if we'd made
this fit better, we'd have less bleed
between the different letters

point to pause and check that everything's working as you'd like.

Connect the microcontroller up to the NeoPixels (we used crocodile clips, but you can solder it up if you don't have these). See the 'Wiring' instructions box on page 97.

We used the test code from the Adafruit NeoPixel Überguide to make sure everything was working properly (**hsmag.cc/ArduinoLibraryUse**). Bear in mind that lighting up all the pixels at once will take quite a bit of current, so you will want to either use an external power supply or dial down the brightness (we tested ours with a colour of (10,10,10) and this worked with the on-board regulator on the MKR1000).

With this and a mess of wires in place, and everything working, let's move on with the assembly. Screw together three sides (one long side and two short sides) of the frame. To ensure that it is in the right place, it's a good idea to use an F-clamp to hold it together with the clock face and the plywood panel in place while drilling and screwing.

Leave one F-clamp in place, holding the two ends of the wood on the exposed side together while finishing the internal assembly.

We used 1 mm-thick white modelling foam for the square honeycomb inside the frame. You may want to consider laser-cutting this out using something like the tray insert pattern from **hsmag.cc/TrayInsert**; however, we didn't. We cut long strips the width of the frame and the height of the gap between the plywood and the back of the face, and small 'separator' strips to split it up vertically. Gluing this together was a bit more

challenging than we anticipated, but with the right technique it's not too hard.

First, anchor one end of one long strip to the frame and wait for the glue to harden. Then put a 'U' of glue in where you want one of the separators to go, and then slot the separator into this glue (don't try to hold it in place while you put the glue in). With practice, you can do several of these 'Us' of glue at a time (we found four or five was a good number), then insert all the separators in one go. Before you finish one row, anchor the next long row strip to the frame, as this gives it time for the glue to harden before starting that row.

Left ◈
We didn't have screws small enough for the mounting hole, so we used nails. In hindsight, this was a very risky move, and one we don't recommend you copy

> **Experiment with what you have** to see what creates the aesthetic that you want

DIFFUSION

The final thing to add before assembly is diffusion. This can be anything that's translucent and thin enough to fit in the space. We used photographer's diffusion fabric (essentially a thin, white nylon material), and we found that we needed two layers of this to get the look we wanted, but it's not standard fabric, so experiment with what you have to see what creates the aesthetic that you want.

We cut this to size and placed it over the square honeycomb. A few dabs of hot glue on the corners held it all in place (and this won't be visible once it's fully assembled). →

Below ◈
The Arduino code checks the time on the internet every minute and displays it on the clock

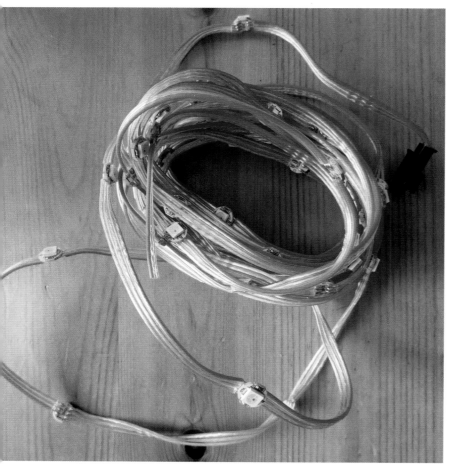

```xml
<?xml version="1.0" encoding="ISO-8859-1"?>
<result>
<status>OK</status>
<message/>
<formatted>2019-05-30 14:52:07</formatted>
</result>
```

There are two parts to getting and processing this in Arduino. First, we have to download this XML, and then we have to extract the time from it. The method of connecting to WiFi differs a little depending on what hardware you're using. We used the WiFi101 library, but if you're using different hardware (such as an ESP8266) you might need to do it slightly differently. Take a look at your board's example WiFi sketches for details.

Once connected, we have a client object linked to the **api.timezonedb.com** server (see the full code for more info on this). We can then extract the appropriate line in the response with the following:

```
    client.println("GET /v2/get-time-zone?key=YOUR
KEY&format=xml&fields=formatted&by=zone&zone=Euro
pe/London HTTP/1.1");
    client.println("Host: api.timezonedb.com");
    client.println("Connection: close");
    client.println();
    }
delay(10000);
payload = "";
    Serial.println("stand by for data");
    while (client.available()) {
    char c = client.read();
    Serial.write(c);
    if (c == '\n') {
    payload = "";
    }
    payload += c;
    if(payload.endsWith("</result>")) {
    parse_response();
    }
```

This reads the HTTP response character by character and builds up a string called **payload**. If it reaches a newline character, it empties **payload** as we only want one line. If it reaches the string **</result>**, it knows that it's got the data it needs, so it called the function **parse_response**.

The key parts of this function are as follows:

```
    int colon = payload.indexOf(':');
// Set the first colon in time as reference point
    nowday = payload.substring(colon - 5,
```

Once you're happy with the amount of diffusion, you can attach the final side of the frame, and that's the hardware setup complete. Now let's take a look at the software.

The full code for this is available from **hsmag.cc/ClockCode**, but let's take a look at the most pertinent bits.

Obviously, our clock needs to know what the time is. We could have used a real-time clock, but this would still necessitate setting the clock time manually and adjusting the time for daylight savings. Instead, we decided to grab the time from the internet – specifically, **timezonedb.com**.

You'll need to register for a free API key, but we'll be staying well within the limits of free use. Once you've got that, you can grab the current time in a particular location by pointing your web browser to **api.timezonedb.com/v2/get-time-zone?key=KEY HERE&format=xml&fields=formatted&by=zone& zone=Europe/London**.

You'll need to replace **KEYHERE** with your key, and if you're not in the UK you'll need to update the zone to your location. The result comes back in XML, and should be something like:

```
colon - 3);
    d = nowday.toInt();
    nowmonth = payload.substring(colon - 8,
colon - 6);
    mo = nowmonth.toInt();
    nowyear = payload.substring(colon - 13,
colon - 9);
    y = nowyear.toInt();
    nowhour = payload.substring(colon - 2, colon);
    h = nowhour.toInt();
    nowmin = payload.substring(colon + 1, c
olon + 3);
    mi = nowmin.toInt();
    nowsec = payload.substring(colon + 4,
colon + 6);
    s = nowsec.toInt();
```

POWER PROBLEMS

Once we wired up our clock, we found that it frequently glitched out and flashed strange colours. After unsoldering all the connections and rewiring it all up, we realised that the problem wasn't a cold joint, or even code problems, but a voltage mismatch.

We powered the LEDs from the 5 V pin on the microcontroller (we can keep the LED numbers and brightnesses sufficiently low to allow this to work); however, the data pins on the MKR1000 are 3.3 V. The input to the LEDs should be (according to their datasheet) at least 0.7 times the power voltage (3.5 V), so we're going out-of-spec by powering it at 3.3 V. Usually we can get away with this, but the particular LEDs we used proved to be particularly finickety about this.

There are two basic solutions to this – increase the input voltage or decrease the power voltage. We opted to do the latter by putting a diode with a forward voltage of 0.8 V on the power line. This diode has to be able to take the full current of the LEDs (we used a 1 A diode, which should give us plenty of leeway). Alternatively, you can use a level shifter (these are available in both module and IC form) to increase the voltage from the data signal to 5 V.

Since the time and date is in a specific format, we can locate the particular part we want relative to the first colon. This code pulls the string apart and converts the relevant segments into integer values for the hours, minutes, and seconds. It also extracts the date, but we don't use that. We adapted this code from Arduino forum user Aggertroll – thanks Aggertroll!

 This reads the HTTP response character by character and builds up a string called 'payload'

Now that we've got the time, we need a way of displaying it on the NeoPixel strip. This is done by first creating a series of arrays that hold the locations for the pixels in different words, such as:

```
int itis[] = {8,9,11,12};
int five[] = {35,36,37,38};
int ten[] = {4,5,6};
```

We also created a function that turns the LEDs in one of these arrays a specific colour:

```
void lightup(int letters[], int letters_len, int
red, int green, int blue) {
    for(int i = 0; i<letters_len; i++) {
    strip.setPixelColor(letters[i], red, green,
blue);
    }
    strip.show();
}
```

The final code for lighting up the correct time is as follows:

```
strip.fill();
lightup(itis, 4, 100,100,0);
int hour = h;
if (mi > 33) { hour+=1;}
 if (hour > 12) { hour -= 12;}
if (hour==1) { lightup(h_one, 3, hour_red, hour_
green, hour_blue); }
if (hour==2) { lightup(h_two, 3, hour_red, hour_
green, hour_blue); }
...
//past or to?
if (mi > 3 && mi < 34) { lightup(past, 4,0, 150,
0); }
if (mi > 33 && mi < 58) {lightup(to,2,0,150,0);}
if (mi > 57 || mi < 4) {lightup(oclock,6,50, 50,
100);}
// minutes
if (mi > 3 && mi < 8) {lightup(five, 4, mins_red,
mins_green, mins_blue); lightup(minutes, 7,mins_
red,mins_green, mins_blue);}
if (mi > 7 && mi < 14) {lightup(ten, 3, mins_red,
mins_green, mins_blue); lightup(minutes, 7,mins_
red,mins_green, mins_blue);}
...
```

The first line in this code blanks the whole strip, then the line **lightup(itis, 4, 100,100,0);** lights up the words 'it is'. We then have to find the first hour, bearing in mind that as soon as the minutes have gone past 34, it will switch to 'twenty-five to' the next hour. The code then ends with a series of **if** statements that find the correct letters. □

Polyphonic digital synthesizer **Part one**

Build a full-featured polyphonic digital synthesizer in our two-part guide

Matt Bradshaw

mattbradshawdesign.com

Matt Bradshaw is a programmer, maker, and musician from Oxford. He likes to build instruments to play with his band, Robot Swans. You can find more of his projects at **mattbradshawdesign.com**

Analogue synthesizers have made a big comeback in the last few years, but building a synth that can play multiple notes (i.e. chords) using only analogue circuitry is a big challenge. In this tutorial, you will see how to build a versatile synthesizer with a 'patchable' signal chain, but where the sound is generated digitally by code that you can write yourself. This is a two-part tutorial, but even by the end of part one you'll already be able to make some great sounds.

GOING DIGITAL

Modular synthesizers are awesome. They let you create your own signal chain by plugging cables into different points in the circuit, giving you the freedom to create any sound you can imagine. A true modular synth is basically a box which you

Above ◆
This design combines aspects of digital and analogue synthesizers, to give you a versatile, but cheap-to-make, instrument

populate with individual modules that you can either buy or build (see the feature starting on page 138 for an example). Some modules generate signals, while other modules take a signal and change it in some way.

This tutorial will show you how to create a miniature, digital version of an analogue modular synthesizer. The process of 'patching' different signals into each other will be done on the breadboard with jumper wires, and that information will be processed by the Teensy microcontroller.

Firstly, we need to set up our Teensy 3.2, which is a bit like an Arduino but powerful enough to process audio. When you buy a Teensy, it usually comes

Above ◈
The extra-long headers are soldered underneath the Teensy and the audio board

Above ◈
Here's how the Teensy and audio board should look on the breadboard – make sure that the pin numbers line up

YOU'LL NEED

◈ **Teensy 3**

◈ **Teensy audio adapter board**

◈ **4 × 14-pin stackable male/ female headers** (2 kits)

◈ **2 × breadboards**

◈ **Jumper wires**

◈ **2 × rotary potentiometers** (10 kΩ, linear)

◈ **5 × 4051 multiplexer chips**

◈ **8 × tactile buttons**

◈ **LED**

◈ **6N139 optocoupler chip**

◈ **MIDI socket**

◈ **Capacitor** (0.1 µF)

◈ **Resistors** (various)

◈ **USB micro cable**

◈ **Soldering equipment**

◈ **Headphones**

◈ **Computer**

without any headers, so you'll have to do a bit of soldering. The audio board, which sits either directly above or below the Teensy, also requires soldering. Using stackable headers is a good idea (female headers with long male pins on the other side), as these will make both the Teensy and the audio board compatible with a breadboard.

Once your Teensy is ready, download the Teensyduino software from **hsmag.cc/aRWmgD**,

> **The Teensy has its own library of code** for adding audio to projects

and try running an example audio sketch, such as File > Examples > Audio > Synthesis > PlaySynthMusic. You should then be able to hear music through the headphones jack.

START SMALL
Before we can connect lots of modules together, we should try a simple sketch to get the hang of writing code to produce audio. The Teensy has its own library of code for adding audio to projects, and it works a lot like a modular synthesizer.

For instance, in the **sine_wave** example sketch, an oscillator is connected to an output via two `AudioConnection` instances (one for each stereo channel), meaning that a sine wave is heard through the headphones. Download this sketch from **hsmag.cc/issue16**, and try it for yourself.

Our synth will consist of eight sockets, and we will need to know which sockets are connected to each other. For instance, if the oscillator socket is connected to the main output socket, the Teensy needs to be able to read this and then recreate the connection digitally, producing audio. On a 'real' synth, these sockets would be sturdy 3.5 mm connectors (basically headphone jacks), but for this synth we are simply going to use a row of breadboard sockets. For now, it doesn't really matter which socket corresponds to which input or output – we just want to know whether socket A is connected to socket B, and so on.

ONE THING AT A TIME
In order to test the connections between the sockets, we will use an integrated circuit called the 4051. This is an eight-channel multiplexer or demultiplexer; in layman's terms, eight 'things' are connected to the chip, and you can talk to them →

AVERTING THE **SPAGHETTI**

This synth, particularly once you complete part two, will involve a lot of wires in a relatively small space. If you use lots of standard-length jumper wires, you will quickly end up with an unmaintainable rat's nest (albeit a very pretty one). To alleviate this problem, it's worth making a batch of your own tiny jumper wires from single core wire, maybe 4 cm long each, with about 5 mm of insulation stripped away at each end.

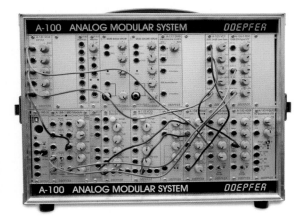

Left ◈
This is what a full modular synth looks like, with removable modules and patch cables

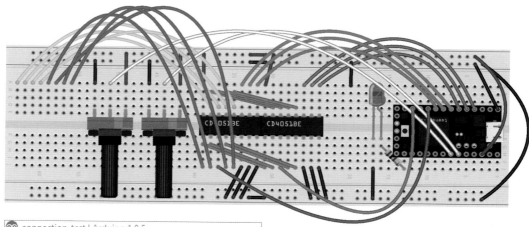

Figure 1 ◈
The full breadboard
layout, with the audio
board omitted for
clarity. Make sure to
connect the channels
of the two 4051 chips
(see orange wires)

Figure 2 ▨
In the 'connection_
test' sketch, you
can check that
your circuit is
working correctly

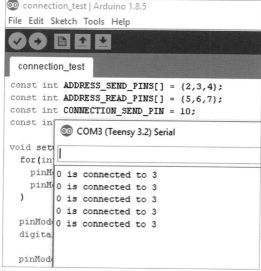

```
for(int b=0;b<8;b++) {
  setReadChannel(b);
  delayMicroseconds(10);
  if(a < b) {
    boolean connectionReading =
!digitalRead(CONNECTION_READ_PIN);
    if(connectionReading) {
      Serial.print(a);
      Serial.print(" is connected to ");
      Serial.print(b);
      Serial.print("\n"); }}}}
```

Upload the whole sketch to the Teensy and open
the serial monitor. Now try connecting two of the
sockets on the left end of the breadboard with a
jumper wire. If everything is working, the serial
monitor should report that a connection has been
detected (see **Figure 2**), and we're ready to move
onto the actual synth code.

THE INS AND OUTS
The 4051 gives us a maximum of eight sockets to
use, which are allocated as follows:

- Oscillator output #1 (square wave)
- Oscillator output #2 (sawtooth wave)
- Oscillator frequency modulation input
- Low-frequency oscillator output
- Filter input
- Filter modulation input
- Filter output
- Main output stage

These sockets are worth explaining in a bit more
detail, especially if you're not that familiar with
synthesizers. The two oscillator outputs are simply
tones with slightly different sounds (the sawtooth
is a bit more 'buzzy'). The oscillator modulation
input changes the pitch of the oscillator, meaning
that when you connect the low-frequency oscillator

one-at-a-time. Three pins are used to select which
'thing' you want to talk to (these are connected to the
Teensy), and eight pins are connected to the 'things'
(in our case, the sockets).

Start by building the breadboard circuit, as shown
in **Figure 1**. Notice that there are two 4051 chips,
both addressed separately, but with their channels
connected to common sockets. By using two 4051
chips in this way, you can send a test signal to each
channel in turn on the first chip, then listen for that
signal on each channel in turn on the second chip.
If a signal is sent to channel A on the first chip, for
example, and can be read on channel B of the second
chip, socket A must be connected to socket B.

To try this out, download the **connection_test**
sketch from **hsmag.cc/issue16**, and open it in the
Arduino IDE. You will see a nested **for** loop, with the
outer loop addressing the 'send' chip and the inner
loop addressing the 'read' chip.

```
for(int a=0;a<8;a++) {
  setSendChannel(a);
```

QUICK TIP

Once you've got
your Teensy and
audio board set up,
search the web for
'Teensy synth' for
more inspiration on
what to make.

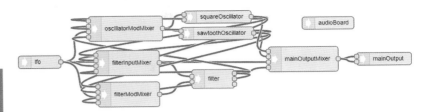

(LFO) into it, you'll hear a tone that rises and falls like an ambulance siren. The filter is an effect which restricts certain frequencies while boosting others, and can also be modulated by the LFO. Finally, the main output stage represents the final part of the signal chain – you won't hear anything until you plug something into it. Don't worry if you don't understand all the ins and outs – once you start playing around with the synth, it should all start to make sense.

MAKE SOME NOISE

The easiest way to start writing audio code for a Teensy is to use the online 'Audio System Design Tool' at: **hsmag.cc/OiKbYH**. It's a simple drag-and-drop interface for connecting audio modules together, and it's definitely worth getting familiar with. For this synth, however, you can just copy and paste the code directly to make things a bit easier. Download the main sketch code from: **hsmag.cc/issue16**.

It's a good idea to look through the code to understand what's going on. The sketch basically combines the two simpler sketches from earlier, and adds a few extra features. It begins by declaring the various audio objects and how they are connected – this code was generated in the online design tool. Next, we declare an array of references to the four input mixer objects, so that we can easily reference them by number later on.

In the `setup()` function, we initialise the various input and output pins, and set some initial parameters for our audio objects – feel free to tweak these numbers to produce different sounds. The `loop` function works much the same way as in the earlier example sketch, but instead of sending a serial message when a connection is made (or broken), the volume of a relevant mixer channel is set to either one (for a connection) or zero (for no connection).

At the end of the loop, the LED is lit if a bad connection (input-to-input or output-to-output) is

detected. Unlike on an analogue synth, making bad connections won't cause any harm in this design, but it's useful to know. Finally, the two potentiometers' values are read and used to control the LFO frequency and main oscillator frequency. Feel free to change this section of the code to customise your synth, by making the knobs control other parameters.

The last job is to label the patching area on the left of the breadboard. Either use a fine pen, or print a label from your computer in a small font, and use Blu Tack or tape to affix the label to the breadboard. Now you can start playing!

Try connecting different outputs to different inputs and see what happens. Turn the knobs up and down to control the sound. The synth is capable of dirty bass drones and *Doctor Who*-esque effects, but if you want to get really musical, you'll have to wait for part two! □

Above ◈
This is what the synth looks like in the online Teensy Audio System Design Tool – the lines represent possible audio connections

Left ◈
Playing with a simple but fun patch where the oscillator frequency is modulated by the LFO

QUICK TIP

If this synth has piqued your interest, try the free, open-source software 'VCV Rack', which is a virtual modular synth.

Below ◈
A sneak peek of what the synth will look like after part two, including a mini keyboard and MIDI input

NEXT TIME

In the second and final part of this tutorial, we'll be adding some features to really turn this project into a usable synthesizer. We'll be adding a second breadboard with a simple keyboard (allowing you to play melodies) and a MIDI input (allowing you to control the synth from another keyboard or a computer). We'll also double the number of connections you can make, and use a cunning trick to add polyphony to the synth, meaning you can play more complex music.

Polyphonic digital synthesizer **Part two**

The conclusion of our two-part guide to making a polyphonic digital synthesizer

Above ◥
The finished synth, featuring 16 patch points, two analogue controls, a miniature keyboard, and a MIDI input

Last time, we built a digital synthesizer on a breadboard. It could make some fun noises, but it wasn't very useful for playing music. This time, we're going to rectify that by adding a simple keyboard, as well as a 'MIDI input' port so that you can control the synth with an external keyboard. We're also going to double the number of patch points so you can create more complex sounds. Finally, we're going to edit the code to allow the synth to play multiple notes simultaneously.

If you haven't already read part one, go back and start there (page 102) – otherwise, let's get stuck in. We've already filled our first breadboard, so we need to add another one. We can leave a lot of our first synth in place: the Teensy, audio board, LED, resistor, and the two 4051 chips can remain untouched on the first breadboard. However, in order to make space for our awesome new features, you should remove the two potentiometers (and their wires), the row of eight

wires that connect the 'patch points' to the 4051 chips, and the label that showed what each patch point did.

The full new layout can be seen in **Figure 1** (overleaf). There is a 6N139 optocoupler (explained later) and three extra 4051 chips. Two of the 4051s perform the same function as in part one, detecting which patch points are connected to each other, but by adding another two chips, we are able to double the number of patch points.

The final (leftmost) 4051 chip acts as a multiplexer for the eight buttons of our mini-keyboard on the front breadboard. These eight buttons will play a simple major scale, although you can change this in the code if you'd prefer a more interesting set of notes.

The front breadboard also now contains the MIDI input, the 16 patch points, and the two potentiometers, so all of the 'hands-on' components (things you might want to access during a performance) are easily accessible.

WHAT'S NEW?

Before we assemble everything, let's look at what new 'modules' we're adding. The synth already has two oscillators, a low-frequency oscillator (LFO), and →

Matt Bradshaw

mattbradshawdesign.com

Matt Bradshaw is a programmer, maker, and musician from Oxford. He likes to build instruments to play with his band, Robot Swans. You can find more of his projects at **mattbradshawdesign.com**

Below ◈
Taking the synth for a test drive – playing with a proper keyboard via MIDI opens up a wider range of notes than the breadboard buttons

YOU'LL NEED

◈ **Teensy 3**

◈ **Teensy audio adapter board**

◈ **4 × 14-pin stackable male/ female headers** (2 kits)

◈ **2 × breadboards**

◈ **Jumper wires**

◈ **2 × rotary potentiometers** (10 kΩ, linear)

◈ **5 × 4051 multiplexer chips**

◈ **8 × tactile buttons**

◈ **LED**

◈ **6N139 optocoupler chip**

◈ **MIDI socket**

◈ **Capacitor** (0.1 µF)

◈ **Resistors** (various)

◈ **Micro USB cable**

◈ **Soldering equipment**

◈ **Headphones**

◈ **Computer**

◈ **1N4148 diode**

Polyphonic digital synthesizer (Part two)

—

Above ◈
Many MIDI devices
have three ports:
'in', 'out', and 'thru' –
make sure to connect
the MIDI out port of
your external device
to the MIDI in port on
the breadboard

WHAT CONNECTIONS
ARE ALLOWED?

In part one, we briefly discussed the 'bad
connection' LED, which lights up if you make a
connection other than input-to-output. This is a
useful feature for diagnosing why your patch might
not be working (perhaps you accidentally connected
an oscillator to the filter output instead of the input).
However, there are some valid patches which will
also trigger the LED. If, for instance, you connect
both the square and sawtooth oscillators to the main
output, the synth will happily mix the two signals, but
the LED will illuminate. This is because, electrically,
the two oscillator outputs are now connected
to each other in a circuit. If you would like an
interesting little programming challenge, you could
extend the LED code to detect valid connections
such as this and disregard them.

Finally, a MIDI-to-CV converter takes a MIDI signal
from an external keyboard and converts it to a CV
(control voltage) signal. This module outputs a 'note'
signal (which communicates the last note to have
been pressed), and a 'gate' signal (which is simply
high or low depending on whether a key is currently
being pressed).

Don't worry if these descriptions are new to you –
YouTube has plenty of videos detailing how different
synth modules work if you'd like to learn more, and
we've provided some patching examples to get
you started.

WE WILL REBUILD

Now we've got an idea of the new modules, let's add
some components. It makes sense to build the circuit
step by step, so we can check for errors at each
stage. Firstly, using **Figure 1** for reference, add the
two potentiometers, as well as the two 4051 chips
directly to the left of the existing ones, and wire them
up as shown.

Remember that the original synth required two
of these eight-channel chips to provide eight patch
points: one chip sends a test signal while the other
reads it. By adding another two chips, we can have
16 patch points.

You could patch directly between the chips but,
like last time, it's a lot easier if we run a jumper wire
from each patch point to a separate, labelled patching
area. These wires are omitted on the breadboard
diagram for clarity (there are already too many wires
on there!), but there is a separate zoomed-in diagram
(**Figure 2**) with the patch points labelled as follows:

A) LFO (out)
B) Sawtooth oscillator (out)
C) Square oscillator (out)
D) Filter (out)
E) Envelope generator (out)
F) Amplifier (out)
G) Keyboard CV (out)
H) Keyboard gate (out)
I) Sawtooth frequency (in)
J) Square frequency (in)
K) Filter (in)
L) Filter frequency (in)
M) Amplifier (in)
N) Amplifier CV (in)
O) Envelope gate (in)
P) Main output stage (in)

As before, make yourself a label and Blu Tack it to
the breadboard.

a filter. This time we will add an amplifier, an envelope
generator, and a MIDI-to-CV converter.

Briefly, an amplifier takes an audio signal and
changes its volume. If you feed the module a high
control signal, the audio will be loud, while a low
control signal will quieten the audio. You can therefore
use this module to make an oscillator 'turn on' when
you hit a key and 'turn off' when you release it.
However, notes that just turn on and off suddenly
are not very interesting, which is where the envelope
generator comes in.

An envelope generator (EG) mimics the sound
of an acoustic instrument. When triggered by an
input control signal, often from a keyboard key being
pressed, the EG outputs a control signal which, when
connected to an amplifier or filter, can evoke the
sound of a guitar, a violin, or a piano (depending on
the settings).

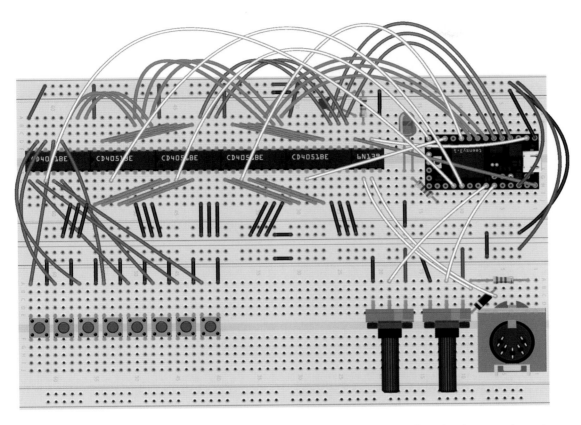

Figure 1 ◈
A diagram of the full synth (audio board and patch point wiring omitted for clarity) – note the diode, resistors, and capacitor required for the MIDI input

SPOT THE DIFFERENCE

Download the code from **hsmag.cc/issue17** and have a look at it – there are quite a few differences from part one. Firstly, the audio connection code (generated by the online Teensy audio design tool) has been moved to a separate file. This is because there are a lot more virtual connections this time, so keeping them in their own file makes the main sketch look a lot tidier. The code that handles polyphonic note data from the keyboard has also

been moved to separate files. Another new element is the MIDI library, which is included and initialised at the top of the code.

The next change is that the **inputMixers** array is now a much more complicated, multidimensional array. Instead of being a simple list of references to four modules, it now contains two separate arrays, which we need because we are creating a polyphonic (multi-note) synth with two copies of every module.

The other most significant difference is that the main **for** loop is now more complex. Previously it was a nested **for** loop with two levels, which was fine because we only had one chip sending data and one chip reading it, but our new circuit →

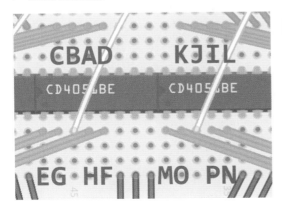

Figure 2 ◈
There are 16 'patch points' which connect to each other, creating the signal chain – run jumper wires from here to the second breadboard

HOW DOES POLYPHONY WORK?

A lot of classic synths, and the vast majority of modern modular synths, only play one note at a time. When designing a synth that plays multiple notes at once, you have to consider what the maximum number of notes playable will be, and which notes should be silenced if you go beyond this maximum.

In this synth, we have created two copies of every virtual module in the code, giving two-note polyphony. Try holding down three or more notes and see what happens. If you want to change the current behaviour, for instance to prioritise the highest note, you can edit the **KeyboardHandler** class files.

This synth's polyphony has been kept at two notes to make the code easier to understand, but you should be able to increase it to four notes or even more by tweaking the code, without changing anything in the circuit.

TUTORIAL ━━━━━━━━━━━━━━━━━━━━━━━━━━━━━━━━━━━

```
Patch 1: "sci-fi" test
A (LFO)      ————————▶ J (square CV)
C (square)   ————————▶ P (main output)

Patch 2: keyboard test
G (key CV)   ————————▶ I (saw CV)
H (key gate) ————————▶ O (envelope gate)
E (envelope) ————————▶ N (amplifier CV)
B (saw)      ————————▶ M (amplifier)
F (amplifier) ———————▶ P (main output)

Patch 3: throbbing filter
G (key CV)   ————————▶ J (square CV)
A (LFO)      ————————▶ O (envelope gate)
E (envelope) ————————▶ L (filter CV)
C (square)   ————————▶ K (filter)
D (filter)   ————————▶ P (main output)
```

necessitates a four-level loop. The principle is the same, but we are having to alternate which chips are active at a given time, hence the extra levels.

Inside the **for** loop, we also check for incoming MIDI data, pass it to the **KeyboardHandler** class so that polyphony is handled correctly, then convert the notes to virtual CV and gate signals so that they can be used for patching.

PLUG IN, BABY
Upload the code to the Teensy. If all has gone well, you should now have a synth that is very similar to part one, but with 16 patch points. Try some simple patches, such as the square wave going straight to the output – this should produce a simple tone. Now, referring to patch diagram, recreate patch

 It makes sense to build the circuit step by step, so we can check for errors

1 using jumper wires, and adjust the right-hand potentiometer – if it sounds like sci-fi effect, it's probably working. If not, check your connections.

Next, add and connect the final 4051 chip, plus the eight buttons that constitute our miniature keyboard. You should now be able to use patch point G (keyboard CV) to control the frequency of your oscillators, and patch point H (keyboard gate) to control the amplifier or envelope generator – try recreating patch 2 to see the keyboard in action. The sketch will allow the breadboard keyboard to function until a MIDI signal is detected, at which point the breadboard keyboard will be disabled.

Finally, add the MIDI input components. Because a MIDI input allows us to connect to another device, we use an optoisolator, which turns the incoming data into a series of pulses of light, then back into a digital signal again. If you would like more detail or ideas for troubleshooting, go to **hsmag.cc/vTjPpc** – the MIDI circuit for this synthesizer was based on this design.

If everything seems to be working, congratulations! You have built a semi-modular polyphonic digital synthesizer, and you're ready to make the world a more musically interesting place. ▢

Above ▱
Wondering what to do with your new synth? Here are some things to try

Right ◈
We've kept the patch points in order for this design (outputs on left, inputs on right), but you can easily rearrange them into a more convenient order

WHAT IS MIDI?
MIDI stands for 'musical instrument digital interface', and is a system whereby one instrument can control another via a special cable. The MIDI standard can deal with all sorts of musical information, such as tempo, pitch bend, and sustain pedal, but for this synth we're just going to implement the basic 'note on' and 'note off' commands.

WHAT TO DO NEXT
There are loads of things you could do next with this synth. You could add code to make it recognise more MIDI commands, allowing MIDI control of the filter and envelope. You could change what the patch points do – perhaps you would like a white noise generator instead of a second oscillator? If so, have a look at **hsmag.cc/WzjFUw** – there are lots of virtual synth building blocks for the Teensy detailed there.

Perhaps the most satisfying next step, though, would be to upgrade this design from a pretty mess of breadboard wiring to a more permanent form using stripboard. You could keep using jumper wires for patching, while soldering everything else in place, and make a sturdy enclosure from wood, metal, or 3D-printed plastic.

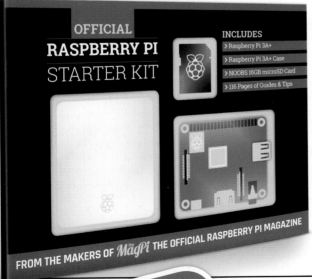

WiFi Tetris clock

An internet-driven clock drawn using Tetris blocks!

Brian Lough

🐦 @witnessmenow

Brian is a maker from
Ireland who primarily
creates projects
and libraries for the
ESP8266 and ESP32
microcontrollers. He
also designs and sells
boards on his Tindie
store. Check out his
stuff on his YouTube
channel and **blough.ie**

Tetris has been entertaining people
ever since it was released in 1984.
There have been many versions of
the game, including the multiplayer
battle royale-style Tetris 99 released
just this year. It is a timeless classic
that has spanned many generations of gamers.

Its iconic falling blocks are instantly recognisable
to almost anyone, regardless of their interest in
video games. But instead of using the blocks to
clear lines, we are going to use them to tell time!

This project draws out the digits of a clock using
the classic Tetris shapes on an LED matrix display.

Measuring in at roughly 19 × 9.5 cm, this is
physically quite a large display and is also very
bright, so the result is incredibly eye-catching.

Another twist with this project is, unlike
traditional Arduino clock projects, it does not use an
RTC module for keeping time – instead, the time for
the clock is set from the internet. One big

advantage of this is that you only need to set your
time zone and the clock will then automatically
display the correct time; it will even adjust for
daylight savings.

This is a surprisingly easy project to put together
that should only take a couple of hours in total. So,
armed with this guide, you should have no excuses
to not make one!

THE LED MATRIX DISPLAY

The intended purpose for these displays is to chain
them together to make up huge screens, as seen at
concerts etc., but they can be controlled individually
using a microcontroller. The displays come in a lot
of different configurations, but most should work
with this project.

When picking one of these displays, there are a
couple of key pieces of information. The first thing
is the pitch, which is the distance between the
centre of each LED. This is marked on the listing of
the displays by the number after the 'P'; for
instance, P3 indicates that the display has a pitch
of 3 mm. Displays with larger pitches will be
physically bigger.

The second thing to note is the resolution of the
display, which is how many LEDs are available to
use. A display with a resolution of 64×32 means it

A POTENTIAL FASHION ACCESSORY?

In HackSpace issue 16 (**hsmag.cc/issue16**), we showed how to hack a 'Pixel Purse' to
make use of the LED matrix it contained. The display in that toy uses the same HUB75
interface as the LED matrix used in this project, but it has a lower resolution (32×16).

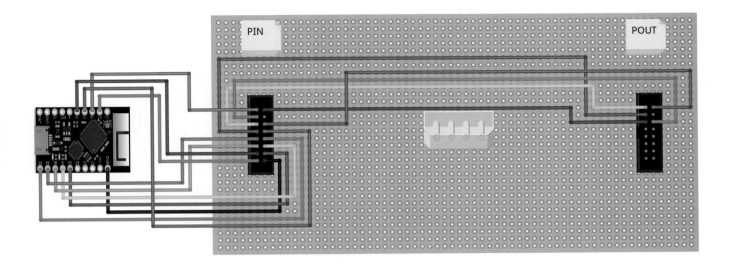

Above ◈
The wiring diagram for a TinyPICO. Details for other ESP32-based boards can be found at hsmag.cc/QXmJtz

Below ◈
The TinyPICO is an ESP32 development board that recently went through a successful crowdfunding campaign on Crowd Supply

Below ◈
Our display give us 64x32 LEDs to play with

will have 64 LEDs across, and 32 LEDs down. This project is coded to work on 64×32 displays, but it could be adapted for other ones if needed.

These displays can be driven with lots of different microcontrollers. People commonly use them with Raspberry Pi boards, but for this project, we are going to use an ESP32. An ESP32 is an inexpensive, Arduino-compatible, microcontroller with built-in WiFi.

> **"** The simplest way to power the ESP32 is to power it via a separate USB power supply **"**

When wiring the display up, pay special attention to the arrows that will be printed on the PCB of the display – the ESP32 needs to be wired to the connector that arrows are moving away from. These arrows can be seen in **Figure 1** overleaf.

To power the display, use a female DC jack to screw terminal adapter, and insert one of the prongs of the power wire that comes with the display into each screw terminal, connecting the black wire to the screw terminal marked with a '-' and the red wire to the one marked with a '+'. Once you're happy with the connection, use insulating tape or heat-shrink to provide some extra strength to the connection.

The simplest way to power the ESP32 is to power it via a separate USB power supply, but it can be connected to the same power supply as the display by connecting to the '5V' or 'USB' pin of your ESP32. The thing to be careful about with this is you don't want to get into a situation where the power from the USB of your PC is powering the entire display, →

QUICK TIP

The ESP32 is the successor to the widely popular ESP8266. It is more powerful and has more GPIO pins.

YOU'LL NEED

◈ **P3 64×32 RGB LED matrix** – Available on AliExpress, eBay, or Adafruit

◈ **TinyPICO – tinypico.com,** but any ESP32 board should work, e.g. HUZZAH32

◈ **5 V power supply** – 4 A or larger should do the trick

◈ **20 cm female to female DuPont cables**

◈ **Female barrel jack to screw terminal adaptor** – Depends on what head is on your power supply

◈ **3D-printed stands for LED matrix** – Or something to keep it upright!

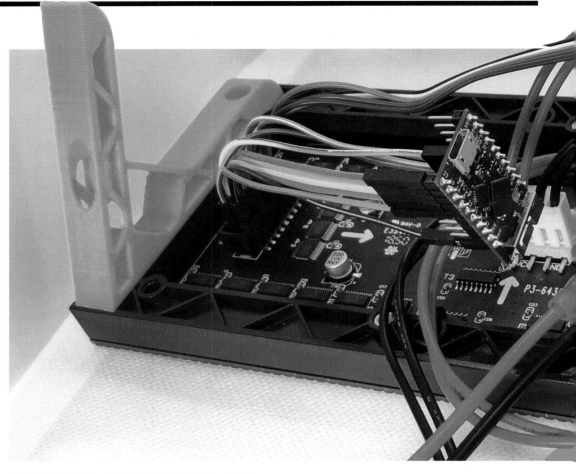

Right ⬧
What your wiring
should look like when
you are ready to go

Below ◼
Screw terminals
make it easy to add a
power connector

as the display will pull more current than your PC
USB port is able to provide. The best way to prevent
this from happening is to use a diode (Schottky
1N5817, for example). Put the negative side of the
diode facing the microcontroller, so 5 V from the
power supply can go to the ESP32, but 5 V from the
ESP32 cannot go to the display.

The display is pretty unsteady standing up on
its own, so it's highly advisable to create a stand
for it. If you have access to a 3D printer, these
stands designed for the P3 matrix work great –
hsmag.cc/bGLDTh. You will need to use some
10 mm M3 screws to attach it to the display.

If you wanted to port this project to the purse
display, you would only need to remove the text

QUICK TIP

If the ESP32 board
you are using does
not have the same
pins used in the
wiring diagrams,
you should be able
to swap any for
other GPIO pins, but
you'll need to reflect
this in the code.

PROGRAMMING THE ESP32

If you are not already set up for programming an ESP32, you
will need to do the following:

First, you will need to download the Arduino IDE from the
Arduino website and install it – **hsmag.cc/UHQfXs**.

Next, you will need to set up the Arduino IDE to be
used with an ESP32. Open the Arduino IDE, go to File
> Preferences, and paste the following URL into the
Additional Boards Manager URLs and click OK:
dl.espressif.com/dl/package_esp32_index.json.

Back on the main screen of the Arduino IDE, navigate
to Tools > Board > Boards Manager. When this screen
opens, search for 'ESP32' and install it. Note that this
may take a few minutes, depending on the speed of your
internet connection.

After setting up a new board, it is recommended to try
out a simple blink sketch before attempting anything more
complicated. This can save a huge amount of headaches
down the line!

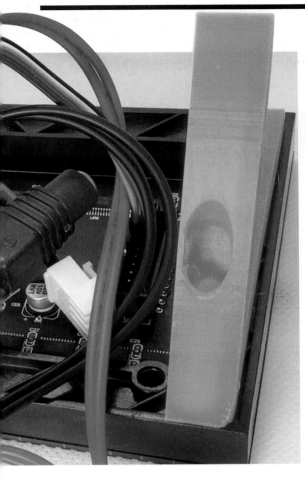

QUICK TIP

If the display doesn't look correct, or seems to be missing colours, double-check that your wiring is correct.

Figure 1 (top) ◈
Make sure to pay attention to the arrows on the board when you are wiring it up

Bottom ◈
A custom PCB that makes use of the ribbon cable that comes with the display to keep the wiring neater

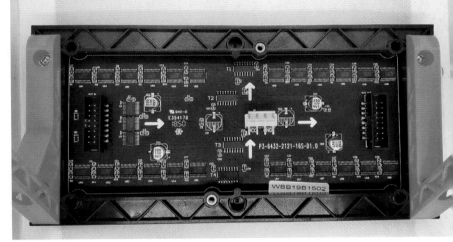

scaling and make some minor positional adjustments to the text, and it would work fine.

SETTING UP THE CODE

The code for this project is available on GitHub. Point your web browser to **hsmag.cc/rpULls** and click the Clone or Download button on the right-hand side of the page, and then Download Zip. Extract the zip file. Inside the extracted folder, open up the **ESP32** or **TinyPICO** folder, then the **EzTimeTetrisClockESP32** folder, and open the **EzTimeTetrisClockESP32.ino** file.

This sketch requires some additional Arduino libraries to be installed:

- Tetris Animation by Tobias Blum – handles the Tetris-style animating of the clock
- PxMatrix by 2Dom – for controlling the matrix display
- EzTime by ropg – used to get the time from the internet
- Adafruit GFX by Adafruit – the base library that PxMatrix is built upon.

Details of which versions of the libraries are needed, and where to get them, are contained up near the top of the Arduino sketch. After installing these libraries, you should click the →

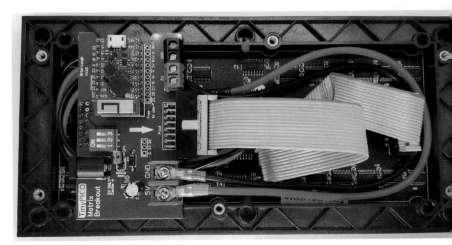

TUTORIAL

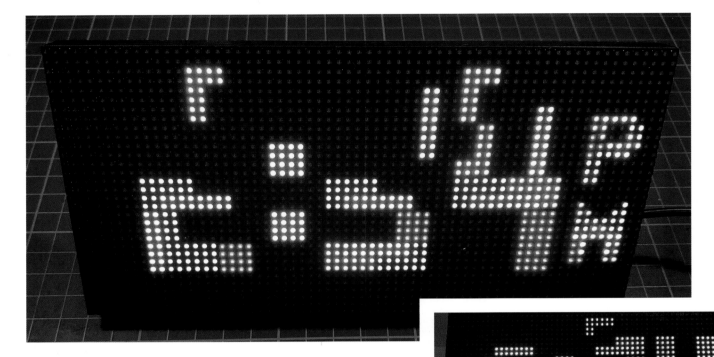

Above ↗
Numbers falling
into place

Right ◈
You could build your
own version of this
animated timepiece

'verify' button (shaped like a tick) on the EzTimeTetrisClockESP32 sketch to make sure that everything compiles fine.

You will need to make a couple of changes to the sketch so that the clock functions correctly for you. Inside the 'Stuff to configure section', set your SSID and password for your WiFi.

Just below that, set your time zone in the format 'Europe/Dublin'; there's a comment in the sketch with a link to a full list of possible time zones.

And finally, if you are using a different ESP32 board than the TinyPICO, you will need to change the wiring. Search for 'Generic' in the sketch and uncomment the two lines that you find, and comment out the adjacent lines that contain a 'TinyPICO' comment.

When you've finished configuring, upload the code to your ESP32, and you should see it animating in all its blocky glory!

THE POWER OF **OPEN SOURCE**

The Tetris Animation library is derived from a project created by Tobias Blum (toblum on GitHub), who created a clock using the Tetris animation, but it was hard-coded to work with a 32×16 display, and the code for getting the time and the animation code were intertwined. His sketch was open source and after discussing it with him, this author extracted just the animation part of the sketch into a standalone Arduino library so it could be used to draw any numbers, not just a clock. I also took the opportunity to change the library to use generic references to the Adafruit GFX library and add some additional features, such as the ability to scale the digits

Another developer, Mike Swan (n00dles101 on GitHub) then further improved the library by adding support for text characters. Each of the characters had to be manually coded to work, so Tobias and Mike did some amazing work on this!

TINKERING WITH THE SETTINGS

There are several adjustments you can make to the clock to so it works exactly as you would like it.

If you would prefer a clock with a 24-hour format, set `twelveHourFormat` to false.

The `forceRefresh` option controls how many of the digits get drawn every minute. If it is set to true, the entire clock will be cleared and it will draw all the digits again. If set to false, it will clear only the digits it needs to; for instance, if the time was currently '10:29' and it needed to update, only the '2' and the '9' would be replaced – the '10' would remain on screen.

And finally, you can adjust the speed at which the Tetris blocks fall by changing the value that triggers the `animationTimer`. By default in the sketch, it's set to 100000, which is 100,000 microseconds, or 0.1 of a second. Reducing this number will make the blocks fall faster. Changing the value to 50000 will result in the animation being twice as fast.

Once you've made those changes, upload the code again and you'll have the clock working just the way you like. All that's left to do is to while away the time watching the blocks fall. ▢

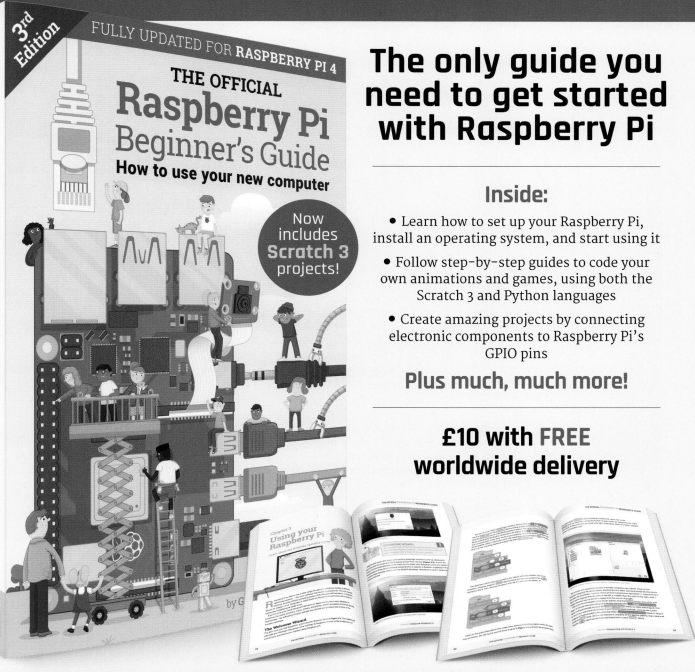

Let's learn LoRa!

Explore LoRa and LoRaWAN and transmit
temperature and humidity to an online dashboard

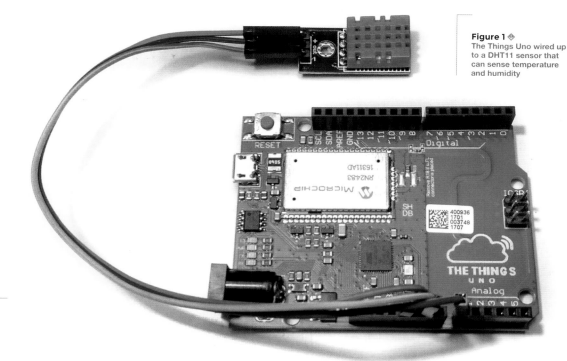

Figure 1
The Things Uno wired up
to a DHT11 sensor that
can sense temperature
and humidity

Jo Hinchliffe

🐦 @concreted0g

Jo is a contributor
to the Libre Space
Foundation, and is
passionate about all
things DIY space. He
loves designing and
scratch-building both
model and high-power
rockets, and releases
the designs and
components as open-
source. He also has
a shed full of lathes,
milling machines, and
CNC kit!

t seems that the terms LoRa and
**LoRaWAN are everywhere at the moment,
but what are they?** LoRa is a platform for
sensors to communicate wirelessly over long
range; LoRaWAN is essentially the same, but
when the receiver receives something from
a LoRa sensor device, commonly called a 'node', it
acts as a 'gateway', sending the information onto
the internet. In this tutorial, we're going to work
through some simple LoRaWAN activities and
connect a LoRa node to 'The Things Network', a
crowdsourced network of gateways. This enables us
to receive data from a node and transmit some data
across the internet to a nice dashboard displaying
our data.

We are going to work with The Things Uno, which
is essentially an Arduino-shaped board that has the
LoRa communications chip built into it. We can also
program The Things Uno using the Arduino IDE, so

the first thing is to download and install the latest
Arduino IDE software from **hsmag.cc/APNJVV**.

To test that The Things Uno board is working,
let's upload a simple program to check the board.
Connect your The Things Uno to your computer
using the micro USB cable. In the Arduino IDE, click
Tools > Board, and then check it's set to 'Arduino
Leonardo'. Next, click Tools > Port, and select the
port that includes the label 'Arduino Leonardo' to
ensure the Arduino IDE is communicating with the
correct port.

Next, click File > Examples > 01.Basics > Blink,
and then click the verify button (looks like a tick on
the top left of the screen), and then click the upload
button (the right-pointing arrow button next to the
verify button). All being well, after a few seconds
your The Things Uno should have a flashing LED
that is connected to pin 13 on the board (one of the
four green LEDs next to the micro USB port).

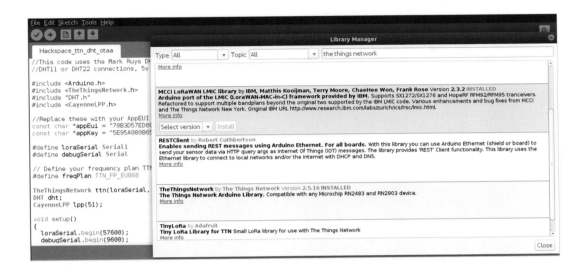

```
File Edit Sketch Tools Help

Hackspace_ttn_dht_otaa
//This code uses the Mark Ruys DH
//DHT11 or DHT22 connections, 5v

#include <Arduino.h>
#include <TheThingsNetwork.h>
#include "DHT.h"
#include <CayenneLPP.h>

//Replace these with your AppEUI
const char *appEui = "70B3D57ED0
const char *appKey = "5E95A080B65

#define loraSerial Serial1
#define debugSerial Serial

// Define your frequency plan TTN
#define freqPlan TTN_FP_EU868

TheThingsNetwork ttn(loraSerial,
DHT dht;
CayenneLPP lpp(51);

void setup()
{
  loraSerial.begin(57600);
  debugSerial.begin(9600);
```

Library Manager

Type [All ▼] Topic [All ▼] [the things network]

More info

MCCI LoRaWAN LMIC library by IBM, Matthis Kooijman, Terry Moore, ChaeHee Won, Frank Rose Version 2.3.2 INSTALLED
Arduino port of the LMIC (LoraWAN-MAC-in-C) framework provided by IBM. Supports SX1272/SX1276 and HopeRF RFM92/RFM95 tranceivers. Refactored to support multiple bandplans beyond the original two supported by the IBM LMIC code. Various enhancements and bug fixes from MCCI and The Things Network New York. Original IBM URL http://www.research.ibm.com/labs/zurich/ics/lrsc/lmic.html.
More info

[Select version ▼] [Install]

RESTClient by Robert Cuthbertson
Enables sending REST messages using Arduino Ethernet. For all boards. With this library you can use Arduino Ethernet (shield or board) to send your sensor data via HTTP query args as Internet Of Things (IOT) messages. The library provides 'REST' Client functionality. This library uses the Ethernet library to connect to local networks and/or the Internet with DHCP and DNS.
More info

TheThingsNetwork by The Things Network Version 2.5.16 INSTALLED
The Things Network Arduino Library. Compatible with any Microchip RN2483 and RN2903 device.
More info

TinyLoRa by Adafruit
Tiny LoRa Library for TTN Small LoRa library for use with The Things Network
More info

[Close]

Figure 2 ◈
Using the Arduino IDE library manager to install the libraries we need for our project

PUBLIC NETWORK

The Things Network is a community-hosted network that consists of gateways connected to the internet. LoRaWAN devices, in our case a The Things Uno, can be received by any gateway, and their data packets are then forwarded to an account registered by the device owner on The Things Network website. The website application can be set up to integrate or forward those pieces of information to other systems, allowing the user to create a visual web dashboard, a phone application, an SMS alert, an email, or other options triggered or populated by the data from the device or devices in the field. The Things Network website has a map of gateways – check and see if you have one locally that you may be able to connect to.

Next, we need to install some libraries we are going to use in this tutorial. We'll install two of them using the Arduino IDE libraries manager, and download and manually install one from the internet. Open the Arduino IDE and then click Tools > Manage libraries (**Figure 2**). The first library we are going to install is called 'The Things Network', so type that into the 'filter your search' bar at the top of the library manager. You should find a library whose description begins 'The Things Network by Johan Stokking, Ludo Teirlinck…' – select this library and click Install. Repeat the above process, searching for 'cayenne LPP' to install a library called 'CayenneLPP by Electronic Cats'. Finally, to install the third library, we need to download it from **hsmag.cc/pEDXUY**. Click the large green 'Clone or download' button and then click the Download ZIP option. Once downloaded in the Arduino IDE, click Sketch > Include Library > Add .ZIP Library, and then navigate to where you downloaded the zip file, and select it.

> ❝ We are going to work with The Things Uno, **which is essentially an Arduino-shaped board that has the LoRa communications chip built into it** ❞

GOING LOCAL

The next job is to upload an example sketch from The Things Network library we just installed. Click File > Examples > TheThingsNetwork > Device info in the sketch that is open – we need to make one small change before we can use this sketch. The Things Uno frequency for Europe is 868MHz, so we need to replace some text. Edit the sketch so that the 'REPLACE_ME' is replaced with 'TTN_FP_EU868'. Readers in other regions will need to replace it with the example that matches the frequency available in your region – it can be found on a sticker on the reverse of your The Things Uno.

Double-check your board is still connected and set to Arduino Leonardo, and the port is correct. Verify and upload the device info sketch to your The Things Uno. Once uploaded, you need to open the serial monitor in the Arduino IDE, this can either be opened by clicking the Magnifying Glass icon at the top right-hand side of the screen or clicking Tools > Serial monitor. In the serial monitor after a few seconds, you should see some details appear that are unique to your The Things Uno – copy and paste these details into a text document somewhere on your computer for later use.

We've now got the hardware set up and configured, it's time to take a look at the networking side of things. This is what gives us some where to send our data to. →

YOU'LL NEED

◈ **The Things Uno**

◈ **DHT11 or DHT22 temperature and humidity sensor**

◈ **Some breadboard connector wires**

◈ **Micro USB cable**

◈ **Access to a LoRa gateway** (see tutorial for details)

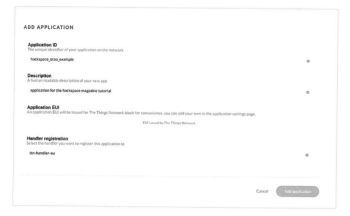

Figure 3 ◈
Adding an application
to our The Things
Network account

Figure 4 ▨
Registering a device
into an application on
The Things Network is
essentially introducing
The Things Network
to our The Things
Uno so that they are
connected and enabled
to communicate with
each other

TO THE THINGS NETWORK

We'll use The Things Network as the glue to hold our sensor together with dashabord (which we'll look at in a bit). Navigate to **hsmag.cc/BtGluJ** and register an account. Once registered and logged in, you should see a link for 'console' in a drop-down list when you click your username. Navigate to the console and you should see two large icons: one that says applications and one that says gateways. We are (hopefully) going to rely on you being in range of a gateway, so we are interested in setting up an application: click the Application icon.

An application, in terms of The Things Network, can be thought of as the area to which your devices or nodes (in this case, your The Things Uno) will send their data. It is here that the The Things Network will choose where to send and what to do with the data it receives. An application can receive data from multiple nodes or devices and can also be integrated into other online services that allow you to do things with the data (for example, send a text message when a temperature gets too high, populate a dashboard, send key information to an online spreadsheet).

For now, we are going to create one simple application to receive data from our The Things Uno, which will be the humidity and temperature from our DHT11 sensor. Click the 'Add application' button in the top right-hand corner and give it an application name – note that these have to be in lower case and also have to be unique, so if you try 'test' for example, you will probably find when you try to add the application, it has already been used. As instructed in the second section, add some human-readable text to remind you what this application is; for example, 'HackSpace tutorial temperature and humidity example'.

The last two input boxes should be as we want them, with 'Application EUI' set to 'EUI issued by The Things Network', and 'Handler registration' set to 'ttn-handler-eu'. Leave these as they are and click the turquoise 'Add application' (**Figure 3**) button in the lower right-hand side of the page.

The application should now be created and you will be pushed on to the Application Overview page. If you scroll down this page, you should find a section called 'Devices' which will show there are no registered devices. So let's add a device, which will be our The Things Uno, so that our hardware can connect to this application. On the upper right-hand

> **77** For now, we are going to create one simple application **to receive data from our The Things Uno** **77**

side of the devices box, click 'Register device'. In the resulting Device Registration page, give the device a device ID and then copy the 'Dev EUI' from the text document we made earlier when we got the device information off our The Things Uno via the device info sketch. Leave the App Key field on this page as it is (set to be generated by The Things Network) and click the turquoise 'Register' button in the lower right-hand corner (**Figure 4**).

You should now end up on the 'Device Overview' page for the device you just registered. There is a lot of information on this page, including the activation method (which should be OTAA) and the various keys that the device has or needs to communicate with the application. If we scroll down to the

QUICK TIP

Use The Things
Network website
map to see if you
are close to any
LoRa gateways.

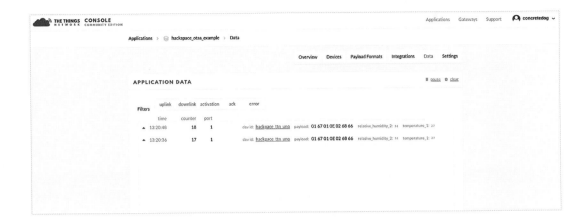

Figure 5 ◈
Success! Data
from our device
successfully being
received by our
application on The
Things Network

bottom of this page, we should see a box called 'Example Code'.

IT'S ALL IN THE CODE

Rather wonderfully, this is a snippet of code containing the two key pieces of information an Arduino sketch on our The Things Uno needs to connect it to our application on The Things Network. Copy these (either select and right-click and select 'copy', or press the copy button in the upper right-hand side of the box) and paste them into a text document or a blank Arduino sketch. Before we move on to the next part of the tutorial, we are going to make one last change to the application we have made on The Things Network. Return to the Application Overview page – navigate here by clicking 'Applications' in the upper right-hand side of the page near your profile name – then select the application we just created. Once back in the Application Overview, click the 'Payload Formats' tab on the upper right-hand side. On the resulting page, you should see a box called Payload Format, and it should show 'Custom' in it. Click on this box. In the drop-down menu, there should only be one other option, which is CayenneLPP; select this and then make sure to click the Save button in the lower right-hand corner of the page.

LET'S GET CONNECTED

Connecting our DHT11/22 sensor board to The Things Uno is pretty straightforward. Connect breadboard wires between the DHT11/22 and The Things Uno 5V and GND pin sockets. The data pin on the DHT11 sensor needs to be connected to pin A0 on The Things Uno (as seen in **Figure 1**).

Returning to the Arduino IDE, we will now upload the sketch for our sensor to The Things Uno; having

made some changes and added the keys, we need to allow it to communicate with the application on The Things Network. Download the sketch from **hsmag.cc/issue22** and open it in the Arduino IDE. There are only a couple of changes we need to

> **"** The data pin on the DHT11 sensor needs to be connected **to pin A0 on The Things Uno "**

make. The first is to check the frequency plan is correct for our The Things Uno; this is the same bit of code we replaced earlier in the device info sketch. In our code, it is set as the 'TTN_FP_EU868' European version and will only need changing if you are using the US frequency plan.

The second change is that you will see a section in the code which is similar to the code we copied from the 'Example Code' box on the Device Overview page on The Things Network earlier. (It's →

SPICY MESSAGES

Cayenne is an IoT platform by a company called myDevices. CayenneLPP (Cayenne Low Power Payload) is a format for data packages over LoRa that allows for some key types of sensors to be integrated into the Cayenne IoT platform simply via The Things Network. Put simply, if we can send sensor data in a CayenneLPP format, a lot of the work to unpack this data and present it in a straightforward and readable way is done for us in The Things Network and the Cayenne myDevices environment.

QUICK TIP

Remember, an application on The Things Network can support multiple devices – perfect for large, remote sensor array projects!

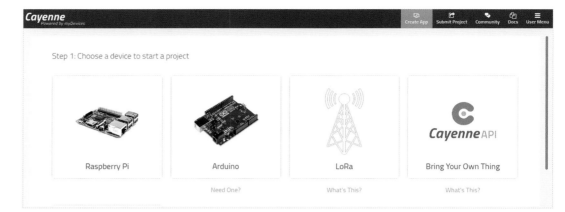

Figure 6 ◈
Beginning to set up
a dashboard on the
myDevices site

Figure 8 ◈
Selecting the
CayenneLPP options
for our dashboard

Figure 7 ◈
Select The Things Network from the left-hand menu

> Our payload is decoded and is nicely displayed,
> **labelled correctly 'temperature' and 'humidity',
> instead of just a raw collection of bytes**

Above ◈
The standard
dashboard showing
our data

the two lines under the comment '//Replace these with your AppEUI and AppKey') So, of course, copy and paste those entire two lines from your Device Overview Example Code box to replace the similar ones in the Arduino sketch.

DECODING THE PAYLOAD
Save your sketch and then click Verify. If the code compiles correctly, then double-check that your The Things Uno is still attached correctly as an Arduino Leonardo, and the correct port is selected, and then

upload the sketch to The Things Uno. Leave The Things Uno plugged into your laptop for power after the sketch has uploaded.

You now have a LoRaWAN node with a sensor hopefully transmitting its payload of the sensor data on humidity and temperature, if you are within range of a gateway (it's worth taking your laptop and The Things Uno outside to increase chances!) Returning to The Things Network website, click the applications tab and select the application you created, and then in the Application Overview page, select the 'Data' tab from the upper right-hand side. Wait for a short while, and you should start to see data packets appear with some information about the data, and most importantly, the payload in the end columns stating the temperature and humidity readings from your sensor (**Figure 5**). As we set the application to read the payload as being of the CayenneLPP type, our payload is decoded and is nicely displayed, labelled correctly 'temperature' and 'humidity', instead of just a raw collection of bytes. If you click on a particular data packet, you get a drop-down with more information, such as the signal strengths and which gateways the device sent the data through.

As things stand, we have our sensor data going to The Things Network, but you might notice that if you refresh the Applications Data page or close it and reopen it, it doesn't keep the data there. Simple applications on The Things Network don't retain data; they act as a holding area that can send and forward data to other places. We are now

> The myDevices dashboard elements can all be edited and customised **so you can swap the icons or the type of graph**

going to create a simple dashboard for our device to which our application will send the data, and the dashboard will keep our data more permanently so we can review it when we need to.

LET THERE BE DATA

Apart from it making it simple to get a payload in a readable form on The Things Network, we used the CayenneLPP library and payload format as it makes it very trivial to create a dashboard for our device online that will collect and display all the data from our The Things Uno device. To set this up, we first need to register a free account on the Cayenne myDevices website: **hsmag.cc/YlgAGf**.

Once logged in, select the large LoRa icon (**Figure 6**) and then select 'The Things Network' from the lower end of the menu bar on the left (**Figure 7**). Then scroll down and click the CayenneLPP option (**Figure 8**); in the settings window that should appear, you need to give the dashboard/device a name, and then add the Device EUI in the DevEUI box – leave the Activation mode set to 'already registered', and the tracking box locations as 'this device moves'. Save these settings and leave this tab open in your browser.

Finally, we need to go back to The Things Network site, and in our Applications Overview we need to select the 'Integrations' tab and click 'Add integration'. Scroll down and click the myDevices icon; in the Process ID box, give this a name such as 'hackspacedashboard', and in the 'Access Key' drop-down menu, when you click on the empty box,

it should reveal only one option 'Default key' next to two buttons that say 'Devices' and 'Messages'. Click on 'Default key' to select this into the 'Access Key' box, then click the blue 'Add integration' button in the lower right-hand corner.

If you now switch back to your myDevices page we left open in another tab, as soon as myDevices receives some data from your The Things Uno, it should automatically make a dashboard for you and display the data. It should create a dashboard with RSSI (received signal strength indicator), SNR (signal to noise ratio), and, of course, our sensor humidity and temperature data. This dashboard will update with the latest data and will store the data it receives, meaning you can come back and check it anytime – or, if you take your The Things Uno offline, it won't lose all the existing logged data. The myDevices dashboard elements can all be edited and customised, so you can swap the icons or the type of gauge or graph by clicking the settings menu for each widget.

TIME FOR ANOTHER PROJECT

Congratulations on setting up your first LoRaWAN device and application. There are dozens of different platforms for devices, and innumerable sensors that can be developed and added to them. In addition, as a rapidly growing community, there are lots of tutorials to explore online to help you develop your next projects. □

Below ◈
Our altered dashboard showing data in visual form

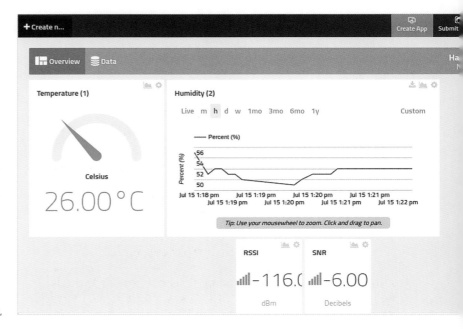

BUILD YOUR FIRST WALL

By Jenny List

We take for granted the ability of mammals and other creatures to walk. It's something that our young minds learn in infancy without understanding what a complex task we have mastered. We are blessed with some of the most intricate and capable actuators imaginable in the form of our arms and legs, but to master them takes a huge array of skills and sensory inputs that we process subconsciously. To try to replicate walking motion in a robot is hard, so it's little wonder that the majority of mobile robots employ wheels or tracks.

KING ROBOT

Make a robotic pet, butler or assistant

As humans, we are one of relatively few species that walk upright, on two legs. We are inherently unstable and prone to falling over, so our brains monitor our balance continuously and adjust our muscles accordingly to keep us upright. This is a particularly difficult task in terms of robotic programming, so even the fruits of multi-million-pound research programmes such as Honda's ASIMO or the Boston Dynamics' biped robots are only just starting to walk comfortably. By comparison, four-legged walking in the way practised by most walking animals is a much more stable process, and a four-legged walking robot is well within the capabilities of most people. →

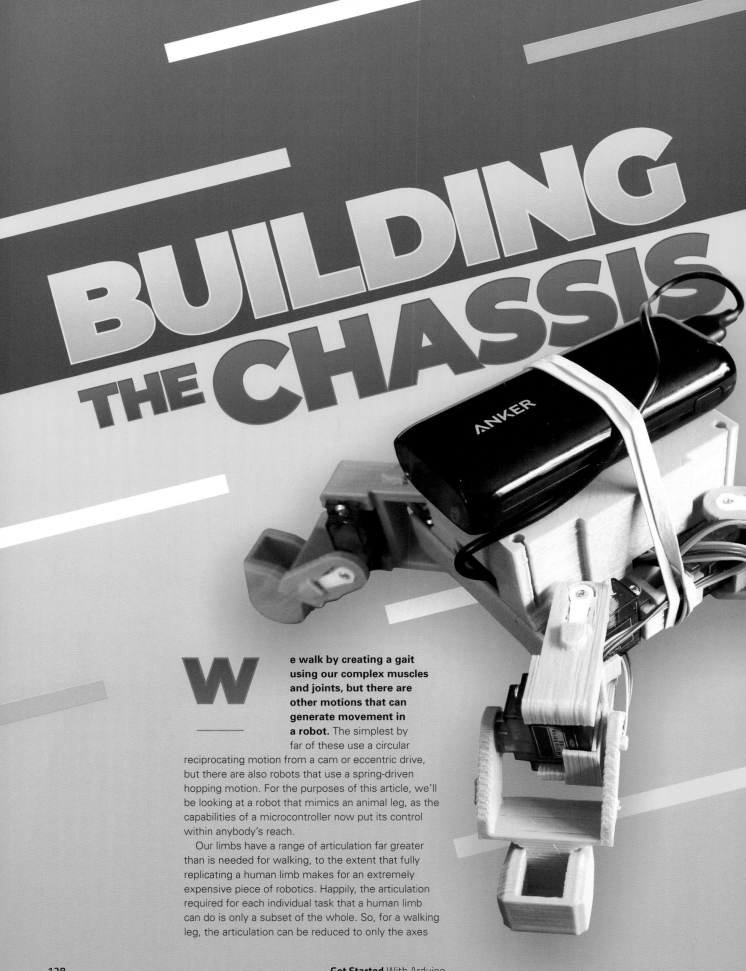

BUILDING THE CHASSIS

We walk by creating a gait using our complex muscles and joints, but there are other motions that can generate movement in a robot. The simplest by far of these use a circular reciprocating motion from a cam or eccentric drive, but there are also robots that use a spring-driven hopping motion. For the purposes of this article, we'll be looking at a robot that mimics an animal leg, as the capabilities of a microcontroller now put its control within anybody's reach.

Our limbs have a range of articulation far greater than is needed for walking, to the extent that fully replicating a human limb makes for an extremely expensive piece of robotics. Happily, the articulation required for each individual task that a human limb can do is only a subset of the whole. So, for a walking leg, the articulation can be reduced to only the axes

Left ◈
An assembled leg

needed for the job. Hip, knee, and ankle joints can be made to only move in one plane, resulting in a leg that only requires three servos. With a rounded foot design, the need for an ankle can be further removed, leading to a leg with only two servos. This is the design followed by the robot we are making here; it has four legs of two servos each – only eight servos for full walking mobility.

THE MINIKAME, AN INFINITELY VERSATILE ROBOT DESIGN

The Kame series of robots follow a 3D-printed open-source design that has been around for several years now, and which has seen significant refinement and alternative versions of the same basic four-legged robot. Elements from different versions can be combined for custom builds, and a wide array of other controllers substituted for the ESP8266 of the original. A search of the popular Thingiverse 3D model library will turn up a host of different Kame-derived designs. The MiniKame we built is a smaller version originally designed for the HuaDuino, a custom Arduino-based board which required a wait for Hong Kong postage, so we've opted to print a modified version of its body designed for the popular (and readily available in the UK) Arduino Nano expansion boards. If you can wait for a HuaDuino to be delivered, that option is a bit

more compact. Or if you really know what you are doing, choose another board entirely, such as an ESP8266 one with WiFi – but, for the purposes of this article, we're sticking with Arduino boards. This is the beauty of open-source: instead of a single take-it-or-leave-it design, there is instead a healthy ecosystem of remixes, meaning that every Kame robot build can be different to suit its owner's needs.

The different 3D-printed parts for our MiniKame came from Thingiverse, and the ›

THE STRANDBEEST, A WALKING ARTWORK

Since the early 1990s, the Dutch artist Theo Jansen has created a series of wind-powered walking sculptures. These Strandbeesten (Dutch for 'beach beasts') are typically made from PVC pipe, and are released on the beaches of the Netherlands as autonomous artworks. They are characterised by their multiple legs, using Jansen's own design of linkage, with a pair of rigid triangles linked by a diamond shape that can be manipulated by the crank to produce a practical walking motion in which the foot moves in an approximation to a walking human foot. Strandbeest legs have been enthusiastically taken up by the maker community and turned into all sorts of walking machines; they have even been used to replace the rear wheel on a bicycle frame.

THE PARTS
WE USED IN OUR BUILD

The parts used in this robot build are all completely standard and should be available from the usual maker sources. If you opt for a board such as the HuaDuino, it may have to be ordered from overseas, but that is beyond the scope here.

The body and leg components were 3D-printed in PLA. You may find that some commercial 3D-print services can sell you them ready-made, but they are easy enough to print yourself. Your local hackerspace will have a 3D printer – go and join up if you are not already a member.

The legs use eight standard SG90 servos that can be bought from multiple suppliers. Ours came from Amazon, but could just as easily have come from HobbyKing, or any other model parts shop. They should include all screws and servo arms.

The Arduino Nano and Arduino Nano Shield V3 boards are standard commodity items that should only cost a few pounds. Ours were Chinese clones rather than the genuine Arduino boards. Again, they are available from a huge variety of suppliers; ours were already on the bench. We suggest buying quality if you can.

The Bluetooth HC-05 module is yet again a standard component available from many suppliers. Ours came from Amazon.

Finally, the jumper cables are the rainbow ribbon cable variety with single DuPont sockets at each end. All the usual suppliers sell them; the chances are you already have some, but if you don't, you'll find them useful far beyond a MiniKame.

Above ◈
The servo arms fit into the insets in the 3D-printed parts

instructions came from its Instructables page. You'll find the resources at **hsmag.cc/CkdDMO**.

The main body of the Kame is a plastic box sized for its controller board, with a lid, and receptacles for the four SG90 servos that form its hip joints. There are two link bars underneath that clip onto the bottom of the body and locate with the lower part of the hip hinge; in our build, it was these and the main body assembly that both came from the Thingiverse repository for the Arduino Nano board. Meanwhile, the legs are the standard MiniKame items: a thigh assembly, and a combined lower leg and foot assembly that fit together with yet another SG90 servo. We printed four of these assemblies. They, and the body, were printed using PLA in two sessions on a HyperCube at MK Makerspace over the course of an evening.

The first step in assembling a MiniKame is to build all four legs. There are the two larger pieces for the thigh and lower leg, plus a small pin that fits under the knee servo and becomes half of the knee hinge. There is a circular hole in the assembly at the bottom of the thigh piece, into which the pin snaps, then the servo can be fitted above it with its shaft pointing in the opposite direction on the same axis as the pin. All MiniKame servo positions have holes ready for the servo fixing screws; your servo should come with the necessary fastenings in its accessory pack.

The first step in assembling a MiniKame is to build all four legs

There are two distinct mirror-image sets of leg prints; in each case, the spindle of the servo must face outwards away from the end of the robot when it is fitted. In all cases, the lower leg piece has an inset in the shape of a servo arm on the side of the knee which locates with the servo shaft, and a plain hole on the side locating with the pin.

WHAT WENT **WRONG?**

In this article, we have discussed the building of a toy robot by an engineer with years of experience in creating some extremely complex devices and systems. We've seen quite a few MiniKame builds over the years – it's a popular choice because it works. Despite the descriptions above sounding easy, however, this build turned out to be a difficult one fraught with problems and setbacks. It's important to own your mistakes and shortcomings, and it's also important, if you don't have huge experience, to understand that things go wrong for professional engineers too. Thus we'll run through some of the issues, so that with luck you can avoid them yourselves.

In theory, 3D printing is a press-and-go affair, like using a photocopier. In practice, a lot of care and patience is required, along with some failed prints. Our first set of MiniKame legs didn't have enough support material and were somewhat droopy, so we increased the support and tried again. The result was a perfect print, but the extra support proved very difficult to remove. Thus our feet have a messy remainder of chiselled-off support material on their underside. It's best to own up to these things.

Always read the instructions. We fitted the servo arms, then had to remove them again for the calibration step.

The servo arms can break if too much force is applied. We broke a couple, and had to cut one side off a double-sided arm to make a replacement.

Our Bluetooth module was extremely difficult to pair with our phone. It would appear in the list of devices, then disappear as if by magic when we tried to connect. A lot of time was expended getting it to eventually connect.

We have to admit it, our MiniKame has been temperamental. All the components appear to be fully working, yet sometimes they refuse to work together. A thought was that a power supply might be to blame, but they continue to have problems even when a bench power supply is used. If there is a lesson to be learned here, it is to always buy good-quality components if you want a robot that walks all of the time rather than some of the time, and be prepared to mistrust a cheap Chinese Arduino clone that has been sitting on your bench for a year or so.

Below ◈
**The thigh servos
mounted on the body**

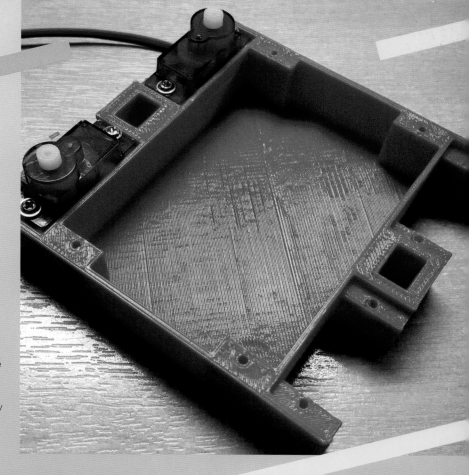

Once the pin and servo are fitted to the thigh piece, the lower leg can be fitted. Slide the pin into its knee joint hole, and then gently ease the other side of the knee over the servo shaft. Don't fit the servo arms yet – we need the servos to be able to move freely for the calibration step which we'll perform later.

The body is little more than a plastic box with mountings for four servos that form the hip joints, which should be easy enough to fit and screw into place. Match up the legs to the body corners, such that each corner has a leg whose knee servo shaft faces outwards. With the link bar held underneath across the robot, such that its pin is in the same axis as the servo shaft, fit the leg in the same way as the knee joint by locating the lower point of the hinge on the pin and easing the upper point onto the servo shaft. Again, don't yet fit the servo arms. Fit all four legs, and route all the servo wires to come together in the centre of the body. That's it: you now have recognisably built a MiniKame robot, albeit one with floppy legs, because the servo arms are not yet installed.

MAKING IT MOVE

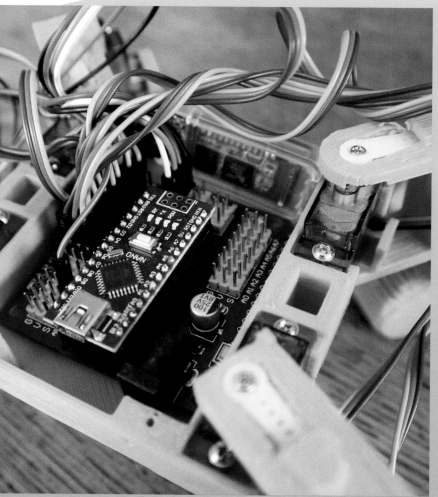

The next hardware task is to fit the control board and hook up the servos. We used an Arduino Nano clone and an expansion board with an added Bluetooth-to-serial board because that's the most basic MiniKame configuration, but there are versions of suitable software for multiple other controllers. Wiring is straightforward, with the Nano expansion board providing numbered headers for servos that should be connected as follows:

- D2 to front right hip servo
- D3 to front right knee servo
- D4 to back right hip servo
- D5 to back right knee servo
- D6 to back left hip servo
- D7 to back left knee servo
- D8 to front left hip servo
- D9 to front left knee servo

The Bluetooth module is then wired in with four socket-to-socket jumpers: two to 5V and GND pins, and the serial TX on the Nano board to the RX on the module, and the RX to the TX.

There's one further component that we've not yet mentioned: the power supply. There are a huge number of possible ways to power any Arduino project, almost all of which could give a MiniKame the necessary juice. We tried two methods: our robot was able to function from a mobile phone booster pack over a USB cable, or from a pack of AA batteries via the Arduino power jack.

Left ⬦
The Nano and its shield fit neatly into the body. The Bluetooth module is in the background

Other options you could consider might be a LiPo battery with a suitable regulator board, or even a long cable from an external power supply. It's worth bearing in mind, though, that the robot may not like too much weight; our MiniKame found the weight of eight AA batteries to be a bit much.

SOFTWARE

We are almost ready to install the software on our MiniKame, but there is one final step before we can proceed. It involves another piece of software, which sets up the Bluetooth module. This can be found on the Instructables page, but is also shown below. You'll need to use the Arduino IDE to load it onto your Arduino Nano and, ensuring that the Bluetooth module is connected, you should then reset the Arduino without USB connected and let it run.

```
void setup() { Serial.begin(9600); //change to fit
your ble initial baud_rate
Serial.println("AT+UUID0xDFB0\r"); // uuid
delay(50); Serial.println("AT+CHAR0xDFB1\r");
// characteristic delay(50); Serial.
println("AT+BAUD8\r"); // set baud rate to 115200
}void loop() {}
```

The stock software for a MiniKame comes in two halves: an Arduino sketch for the robot itself, and an app for your phone. The result is a simple remote-controlled robot which is fun enough to play with, but the real fun comes in the accessible nature of Arduino coding. You can choose to use it as a novelty robot toy, or you can get inside its mind and hack the software.

Installing the final Arduino sketch is as simple as downloading its repository from GitHub, unzipping

WALKING MECHANICS

To successfully make a robot walk, we have to understand something of the mechanics of walking, both the structure of a leg and the coordinated movements of its joints. One of the best sources for this comes from an unexpected source: not zoologists or roboticists, but animators. A cartoon character walking across the screen has to look like a cat, a dog, or an anthropomorphic standing-up mouse, and one of the key features it must possess to do this comes in walking in a convincing way. Thus animators make an extensive study of walking motion, so if you're interested in walking, a very good place to start is a web search on phrases such as 'animation walking tutorial'. You may not need to produce the natural motion that the animators require, but a grasp of the sequence of movement of a four-legged animal's legs is important in the understanding of how your robot can move without becoming unstable.

the archive, and compiling it to the Arduino itself using the Arduino IDE. Meanwhile, there is more than one suitable app for a Kame in the Play Store and the Apple App Store, which can be installed on your device of choice. Pair with the Bluetooth module and you should be ready to proceed.

You should now have a MiniKame robot with floppy legs

If all went well, you should now have a MiniKame robot with floppy legs, but with all software and wiring in place. The final step is one of calibration, the act of setting all the servos to a known position before fitting the servo arms. This is simple enough: fit a jumper wire between the Arduino Nano's D12 line and its 3.3-volt pin (made easy by the relevant pins being exposed on our Nano expansion board), and power up the robot. You will hear the servos move into their calibrated positions, then you can power down the robot, remove the jumper from D12, and install the servo arms.

Position the robot flat with its legs outstretched at 45 degrees to the body, and carefully snap in a single-sided servo arm into each inset. There should then be just enough room to slide a single-sided servo arm into the inset, and click it onto the servo shaft before screwing it into place. If you're lucky, you should now have a working MiniKame. Enjoy it!

Above ⬆
The Victorian photographer Eadweard Muybridge was one of the first people to study walking motion in detail

Below ⬇
The servo arms fit into the insets in the 3D-printed parts

MORE ROBOTS

You've built your first robot — what next?

MIKE'S WALKING DOG

Created by Mike Rigsby, this cheap and cheerful hound can be walking around your estate for under £500:

"Walking robot platforms can navigate buildings, climb stairs, enter cars, and traverse farmland. Potentially, they can become elder companions or herbicide-free weed removers. Excessive cost for such a platform — tens of thousands to millions of dollars — discourages students, makers, and startups from advancing the technology. My open, shared walking platform can be constructed using parts and materials that cost less than $600.

"The dog has evolved from a gangly beast that could barely stand to something that can now barely walk. The legs have been shortened, and joints strengthened. The servo motors selected represent the highest torque per dollar that I could find.

"I am a writer and a maker — the best place to keep up with the dog's progress (as well as files and build instructions) is **hsmag.cc/sBBErE**. The best video of the dog moving can be found at **youtu.be/kclfsCcEjcs**.

Right ⬥
You don't have to add a head and tail to your dog, but you can

OPEN DOG

The pinnacle of walking robots has to be the work coming out of Boston Dynamics, as we've already mentioned. But what if you don't have millions of dollars to spend on research and development? James Bruton is in the process of building an open-source, four-legged walking robot called openDog, and documenting the process on his YouTube channel so that anyone can follow in his footsteps. So far, it's cost him just over £2000 – you can see for yourself what the robot can do at **youtube.com/user/jamesbruton**

Below ◈
Is this an open-source dog or a terrifying vision of the future?

Credit
© James Bruton

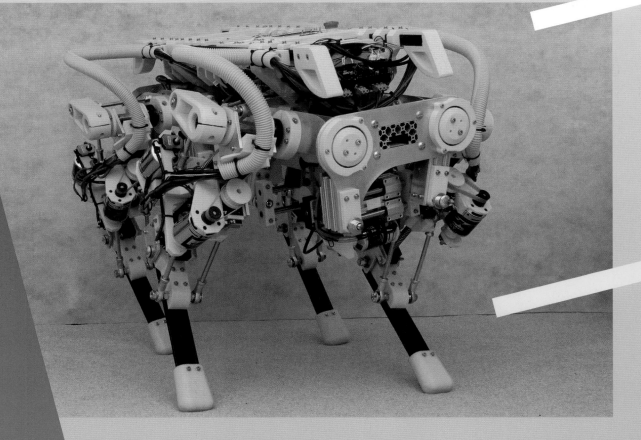

NYBBLE

If you're not a dog person and would rather have a robot cat, Nybble is for you. Its body is made of laser-cut wood, so it's easy and cheap to put together. It uses an Arduino-compatible microcontroller with the option of plugging in a Raspberry Pi to make it more intelligent, and can take inputs from built-in ultrasound, lidar, GPS, and more sensors.

Left ◈
Just like a real cat, Nybble understands voice commands; it just chooses to ignore them

MARTY THE ROBOT

If you're more comfortable following a script than going off-piste with your own design, give this a try. Marty is a two-legged walking robot which solves the problem of balance with an exaggerated hip sway and big, stable feet. Where it really comes into its own is the accessibility of its programming. It's controllable via Python, JavaScript, and even Scratch, so it's ideal for kids wanting to take their first step [pun intended] into ambulatory androids. ☐

Above ◈
An easy way to wobble along

BUILD A SYNTH

*BUILD YOUR OWN AMAZING
SOUND-GENERATING,
VOLTAGE-SEQUENCING,
GATE-TRIGGERING,
KEYBOARD-PLAYING
SYNTHESIZER AND
SEQUENCER*

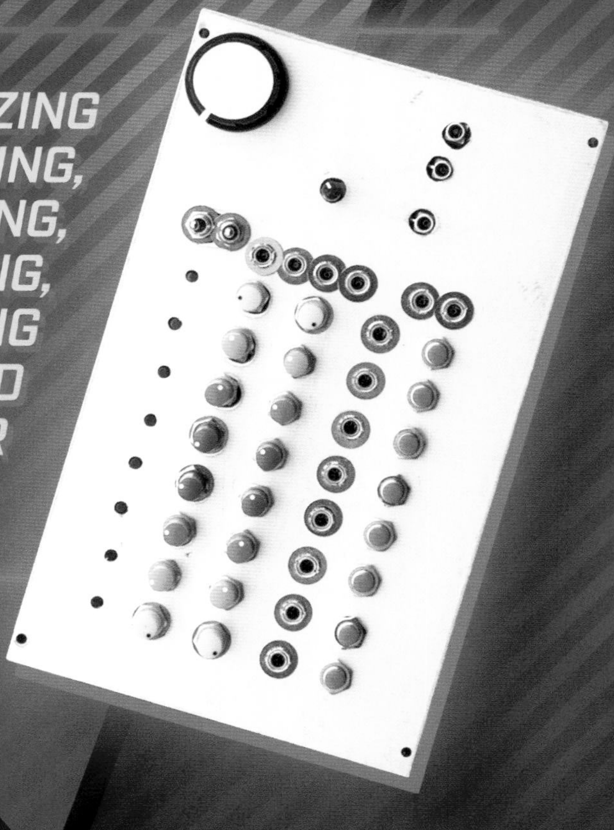

There is nothing in nature that sounds like a classic synthesizer. From Delia Derbyshire's incredible work at the BBC's Radiophonic Workshop, adding synthesizer sci-fi to the original *Doctor Who* theme, through to the modern minimalism of synthesist and composer Kaitlyn Aurelia Smith; it's a synthesizer's harmonic avarice that, quite audibly, sets the tone.

Much like computers, sound-making machines started off as monolithic analogue machinery that turned and crackled and sparked themselves into life. Though not huge, one of these early instruments was the theremin, a wooden box with alien antennas that modulated a tone when a performer moved their hand, like a Jedi conducting a disturbance in the force. And it was Robert Moog, building replicas of the theremin, who helped define what the modern synthesizer was and, most importantly, what it could sound like.

After bland digital synthesizers took over in the late 1980s and 1990s, analogue synthesis with an experimental edge is back, and stronger than ever before. The big manufacturers, like Moog, Korg, and Roland,

are building and selling experimental kit, and there's a growing global community of makers and hackers building and selling their own components, kits, and code, contributing to a new age of DIY sound design and experimentation. And it's this world we're going to visit over the following pages – helping you to build your own sequencer and sound generator, and

hopefully, causing you to get hooked into this brave new world of sound design, drone, and tonality. Or even just a few Brian Eno-like earworms. But before we get ahead of ourselves, we need to briefly cover exactly what these wonderful machines are, and how they're formed.

Below ◈
Nearly every synthesizer sound is made up of one or more of these waveforms – clockwise from top left: square, sawtooth, triangle, and pulse (which is an asymmetrical square wave)

SIGNAL PATH

Synth sounds start with an oscillator, because it's the oscillator that generates the raw initial audio. This sound then passes through whatever other stages a synthesizer offers before arriving at the final output.

A waveform, like a mathematical function, has a specific shape, and the most commonly used shape for a synthesizer is a sawtooth.

> ## Analogue synthesis with an experimental edge is back, and stronger than ever before

A sawtooth, predictably, looks like the jagged teeth on a saw. It's perfect for audio because the hard edges in the waveform result in lots of harmonics. A sawtooth is basically the sound equivalent to a chunk of malleable clay, ready to be moulded and reduced into an infinite number of other sounds. Other common synthesizer waveforms – including square, triangle, and sine – aren't quite so flexible, but they can add to the timbre. But it's the next stage that adds the character: the filter. The filter cuts out some of the frequencies in the harmonically rich oscillator output, and it's the filter that often gives a synthesizer its definitive sound.

There are only a couple of other elements you can use to make a synthesizer, and they affect how the sound changes over time. These are known as modulators, and there are two common types. The first is an envelope generator, and this is used to specify a level for each stage that a sound is being played, from the initial attack to the point when the sound is released. The second is an LFO, or low-frequency oscillator. This is a slower version of the oscillator used to generate the initial sound. Its frequency will typically be too low to generate audio (not always!) but is used to modulate the amplitude, filter frequency, or pitch.

Having all these separate parts in one setup is known as a modular synth, and that's what we're going to build. Our two modules – a sequencer and a voltage-controlled oscillator – will get our synth started, and you can expand it from there. →

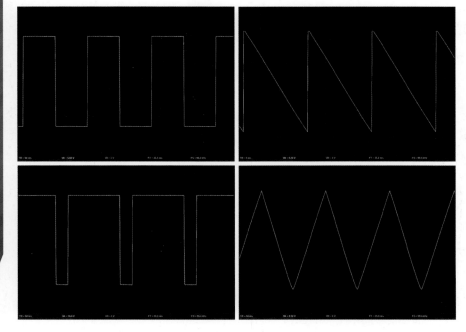

BUILD A SEQUENCER

BUILD YOUR OWN VINCE CLARKE TIME MACHINE

ur synthesizer has two parts: a sequencer and a voltage-controlled oscillator (VCO). The sequencer is used to create a tune. It has eight steps that will play one after another, before looping back to the start. At each step, there's a button to set it to play or not play, and two knobs (controlling potentiometers) that dial in the notes to play if that step's enabled. This allows us to program in simple tunes, and edit them as they're playing.

There's quite a lot of outputs from this sequencer and you can integrate it with other sound modules in different ways. However, the key ones are CV1 and CV2. These are the control voltages that can be used to generate sounds (as we'll see next in our voltage-controlled oscillator). CV1 takes the sequence from one row of potentiometers, while CV2 takes the output from the other. In this way, you can connect this sequencer to two different oscillators to create more complicated sounds. There's no need for it to be exactly this setup (eight steps and two outputs) – this is just the setup we've chosen. If you want more or fewer of either, then that's fine – it's your synth. The only limits are your imagination and your microcontroller's GPIO pins (and you can switch to a microcontroller with more GPIOs if needed).

All the output connectors take audio jacks (as will the inputs on your sound generators). You can connect the two together with jack-to-jack cables. These cables (known as patch cables) are used to set modular synths up to output different sounds. They are, in a sense, the way you program modular synths.

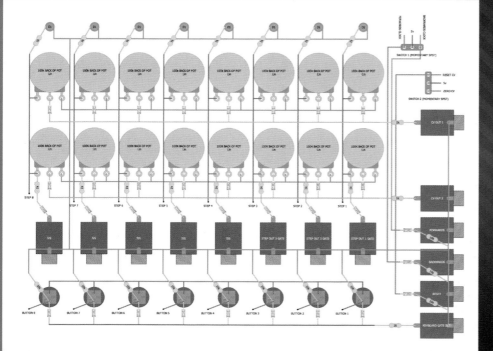

Figure 1 ←
This is what we're going to build – a sequencer for outputting voltages and an oscillator (VCO) for turning those voltages into notes

Credit
look mum no computer

1 WHAT YOU'LL NEED

Before we start, we want to mention a couple of things about this specific project. Firstly, it is actually quite straightforward and easy to build, despite what it may look like from the jumble of wires in the end product. We're not going to create complicated circuits with difficult-to-understand components. This sequencer is actually the opposite of a black box, using just a handful of resistors, capacitors, potentiometers, input jacks, and buttons, mostly wired directly to pins on the Arduino, with only simple code to manage them all. But it can also easily become a web of interconnections as you try to wire everything together and make room for everything you want to fit it. We advise you take lots of breaks, and don't do the whole project in one go. Take it a bit at a time, then step away. When you're feeling refreshed, come back and check over the work you did on the previous step. If you've not made any mistakes, carry on! If you have, consider leaving the next step until tomorrow. Take your time and enjoy the process.

The second important thing to note is that you can, and should, change things to suit your needs and imagination. In particular, our project is designed to coexist with other Eurorack modules, and that makes it small. We're soldering most of our components onto a 15×9 cm double-sided PCB. If this is your first soldering project, we'd strongly recommend using a larger form factor. Similarly, you may want to avoid the regimented order of the PCB. The PCB format is perfect for prototyping a final circuit, but it needs wires to criss-cross each other to make connections.

Below ◈
See the Ingredients list for all the components you'll need to build the sequencer

2 PCB LAYOUT

This is exciting! You now get to create your own utterly unique instrument that operates in the way you want it to. Start by temporarily arranging the components on a tabletop to find a layout that suits your needs and style. As when handling all electronic components, it's a good idea to ground yourself first. For our layout, we've used minimalism and the utilitarianism of musique concrète for our inspiration, so we've gone for a purely functional approach: equally spacing eight LEDs, two rows of eight potentiometers, eight jack outputs, and room on the side for the control outputs, inputs, and switches. You could alternatively try arranging the pots and LEDs in a circle, or an arc, in a 4×4 grid, or any way you choose.

Unlike stripboard, the double-sided PCBs we're going to solder our components to don't bridge any connections, so we'll need to wire or solder everything manually. You need to take this into consideration when you're placing LEDs, pots, buttons, and jacks that are going to be connected together, or to the same input or output on the Arduino. By placing many of our adjacent components horizontally, for example, we can easily create a ground bus to connect them all, and then connect together the same steps in columns and the same devices in rows. But we'll get to that step later.

When you've worked out where everything is going on your PCB, make any adjustments you need, and don't be scared about drilling them. We needed to drill holes through the PCB for the buttons and for the switches, as their legs are too wide for the standard holes. Now slot your potentiometers, jacks, and buttons into their positions. As the pins clip through the holes in the PCB, they should hold their positions, even when the PCB is turned over so that you can solder the legs into position. You can then start by soldering one leg of each component. This allows for some movement in their positions when you make sure everything is aligned, and that the height where the panel will rest on each component is the same. →

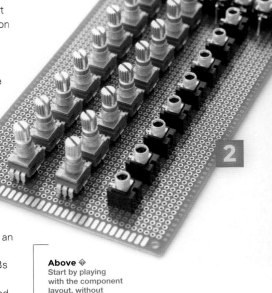

Above ◈
Start by playing with the component layout, without soldering anything

INGREDIENTS

◈ **Arduino Nano**

◈ **An IC socket or pin headers** for the Nano

◈ **14 × jack sockets** (3.5 mm jacks for Eurorack)

◈ **16 × 100 kΩ potentiometers**

◈ **8 × push-buttons**

◈ **2 × momentary toggle switches**

◈ **8 × LEDs**

◈ **35 × 1N4148 diodes**

◈ **1 × 78L05 voltage regulator**

◈ **Prototyping PCB or stripboard**

◈ **18 × 1 kΩ resistors**

◈ **Female socket strips**

◈ **Eurorack power cable**

◈ **Panel or container**

◈ **Mount screws**

◈ **Lots of wire**

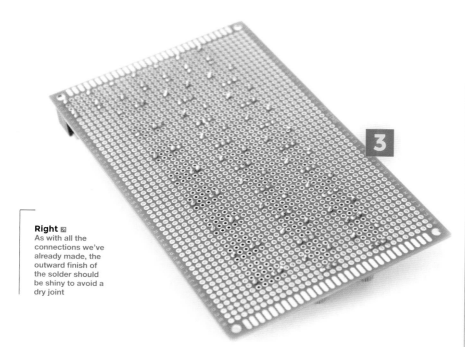

3 SOLDER NEARLY EVERYTHING

At this point, you should really drill the holes in the front panel. If you're sensible, go and do that first, because all of your components are still wobbly enough to wiggle into the holes you make. You can then leave as many components as you are able to in place, especially the LEDs, to make sure their positioning and heights are perfectly aligned with the panel. This is a lot harder to do later when everything is fixed in place. We went ahead and started soldering, however, because we changed a few things while we started to work with the components on the reverse side of the PCB.

We did the soldering in two steps, starting with the pots and jack inputs because these will stay in the PCB when it is turned over. One advantage of doing many components in line like this is that they're quicker to solder, much like a production line. But it's also easier to see when something has gone wrong. One of our input jacks, for example, had a leg folded beneath its plastic, which was easy to spot alongside all the others.

Make sure that all the LEDs have the same orientation. The long leg is positive, while the short leg is negative – if there's no difference in the leg lengths, there should be a flat edge on the plastic of the LED alongside the negative pin. These are also the trickiest pieces to solder without the front panel,

because you not only have to make them exactly the same height – solved by turning the PCB over and placing something of equal height beneath them – you also need to make sure they're the correct height to remain visible when you do fit the panel to the boards. Our solution was to measure carefully, but you're better off poking them through the actual drilled panel and soldering from there. Similarly, our buttons needed to be soldered individually. This is because we'd drilled holes to fit their legs through the PCB, but a blob of solder on either side of the legs on the reverse of the PCB solved the problem.

4 GROUND BUS

You're now at the point where you can start making the circuit. You may want to look at the circuit diagram in figure 1 and tackle this your own way, depending on the layout you've used, but this way worked for us. It's still worth referring to the circuit diagram before each stage to make sure you know what's being connected to where. In particular, you need to pay special attention to the diodes.

We'll start with the ground bus. This snakes its way across many of the components on the PCB. We created five stripped lengths of wire to go the width of the LED row, both potentiometer rows, and the step gate jacks, and across one of the pins for each of the final row of buttons. Connect the negative (short) legs of the LEDs to their wire, the third pin of every potentiometer to theirs, and the outside pin of each gate jack (usually found halfway up the outside of the case) to their wire. Finally, lay down the ground bus for the buttons, and connect each of the rows together with a sixth stripped wire going vertically up either one of the edges. Don't forget, you can anchor any wire down on the PCB if you need to. It also helps if you can leave enough space for other wires you know are going to connect to the other pins on the potentiometer, as well as the jacks and buttons we haven't touched yet. Finally, make sure every ground bus is connected to the others using your multimeter.

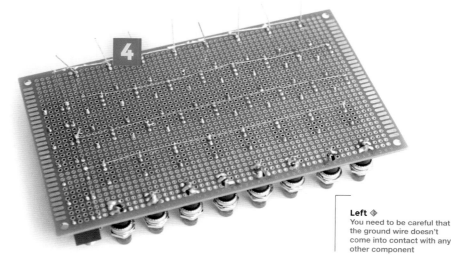

5 DIODES AND 1K RESISTORS

You're now going to add lots of 1N4148 diodes and resistors, so tread carefully and take your time. Diodes need to be oriented correctly. Start with one of the potentiometer rows, placing eight diodes across the PCB so that the end without the black band is next to the third pin of each potentiometer. If you can, place the other leg somewhere conveniently spaced, so that you can join them up. We did this by pushing the diode through from the top side of the PCB so that both legs were protruding on the side we'd done all our soldering on. We then soldered the leg away from the black band to each leg of the potentiometer, and the diode leg closest to the black band was folded flat and soldered to the next closest diode flat leg. In this way, we were able to solder all the legs closest to the black band to create a bus across the PCB.

Do the same with the other row of potentiometers, creating a bus for their 'black band' pins that stretches across the width of the PCB. The final row of diodes are not connected to each other, and are

oriented the other way around because they're going to connect to the output jacks, where the flow of current is the opposite to the potentiometers (pots). Solder one diode onto each output pin of the jack (not the earth).

It's now time for the resistors – unlike the diodes, you can solder these either way around. Insert them into the PCB next to the positive leg of the LED (the leg that isn't attached to our ground bus), and also next to the jack outputs. This is so that you can solder one leg of the resistor to the other leg of the diodes you just added, while the other leg of the resistor connects to the leg of the closest potentiometer in each column. Finally, add three further 1 kΩ resistors to the two CV output jacks and the keyboard gate output alongside each row of pots, and connect the final three diodes to a pin on the input jacks for the forwards, backwards, and reset jacks.

It's still worth referring to the circuit diagram before each stage

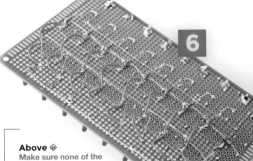

Above
Make sure none of the connections touches any of the others, and only expose the very tips of the wires when stripping their ends

6 CONNECTING COLUMNS

You now need to connect each of the active parts of each column step together so that they can ultimately be controlled by the step output from the Arduino. To do this, cut 16 small lengths of wire and eight long lengths of wire. Each column will use three wires. The first short wire connects the third pins of each potentiometer together, connected directly to the same pin as the resistor on the lower potentiometer. The second short wire connects the third pin of the top potentiometer to the 1 kΩ resistor attached to the LED in that column, effectively tying each column together. The long third wire connects to any point on this 'column bus' and will need to stretch to the Arduino board. To make the cables, strip each end of each cable, and 'tin' the end in solder. This can be done by touching the end to the soldering iron and a section of solder at the same time, so that some solder attaches itself to the end of the cable. This makes it much easier to solder the joint. →

Above
Make sure the diodes and 1 kΩ resistors don't go any higher than the lower edge of the top panel components

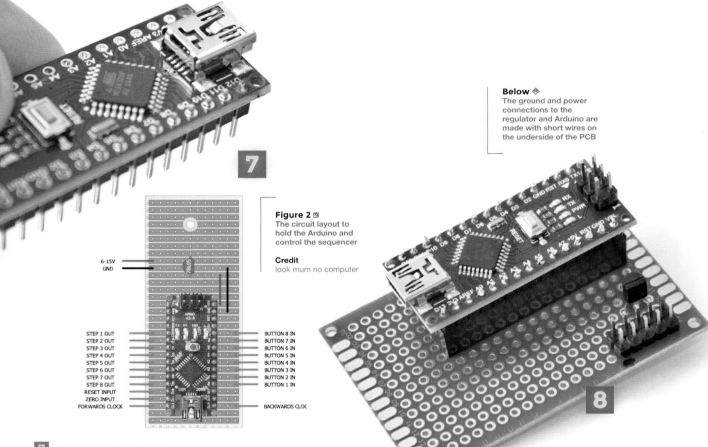

Below ◈
The ground and power connections to the regulator and Arduino are made with short wires on the underside of the PCB

Figure 2 🗗
The circuit layout to hold the Arduino and control the sequencer

Credit
look mum no computer

6-15V
GND

STEP 1 OUT
STEP 2 OUT
STEP 3 OUT
STEP 4 OUT
STEP 5 OUT
STEP 6 OUT
STEP 7 OUT
STEP 8 OUT
RESET INPUT
ZERO INPUT
FORWARDS CLOCK

BUTTON 8 IN
BUTTON 7 IN
BUTTON 6 IN
BUTTON 5 IN
BUTTON 4 IN
BUTTON 3 IN
BUTTON 2 IN
BUTTON 1 IN

BACKWARDS CLOCK

7 ARDUINO HEADER

To be able to connect things to the Arduino Nano, you need to start work on the board that's going to hold the Nano and the power supply. We've put the Nano on a separate PCB and, crucially, planned for the Nano to be socketed. Before we could tackle the board, we had to solder strips of pins onto our Nano (although your Nano may have its pins already connected). To do this, heat up one corner pin first, slightly, and then dab on the solder. It should melt and immediately move into the hole and surround the pin, keeping the row of pins in place.

You need to be a little careful when soldering the pins onto an Arduino, as the heat is directly transferred to the electronics. If in doubt, always take iterative steps, gently heating and soldering rather than trying to move too quickly. When soldering long lines of pins, it can be easier to solder a pin at one end and then a pin at the other, so that you can make sure it's straight. This is because you can still manipulate the row into the correct position. When you're happy that all is straight, solder all the pins in between.

You now need to perform a similar action on the second smaller PCB to create a socket for the Arduino. We used two strips of female socket strips that we cut to the correct lengths and soldered onto the PCB. It's easier to do this with the Arduino connected to the two strips, but once again, be careful you don't heat the pins for too long, to protect the Arduino.

8 ADDING POWER

With the Arduino socketed and ready for fitting onto the smaller PCB, you now need to add power for the entire project. How you do this will obviously depend on how you intend to power the sequencer. The easiest way is actually to do nothing at all, and to use the USB connection on the Arduino to supply the power. This is enough to run the entire sequencer and the Arduino. However, a more permanent solution is to use external power, and we can easily use the power delivered via a Eurorack power bus, which is what other modules will be using.

The typical smaller Eurorack power connector consists of ten pins in two columns of five. Each row is identical, and carries +12 V, GND, GND, GND, and -12 V respectively. We need to create a pin header for this connector on the PCB and then make a connection from the +12 V and one of the grounds to a voltage regulator, which sits between the power coming in and the power and ground we connect to the Arduino. The sequencer power will simply take the 5 V and the GND directly from the Arduino.

Start by creating the ten-pin header for the Eurorack power. This should be easy after having just done the same for the Arduino. Place the 78L05 regulator on the PCB too, and connect the power to the bottom pin of the 'D' shape of the regulator and the ground to the middle pin of the regulator. From there, on the underside of the PCB, take the power from the regulator and connect it to where the Arduino's 'VIN' pin is going to connect to the header, and do the same to connect ground from the regulator to the GND adjacent to the VIN on the Arduino. That's all there is to it. →

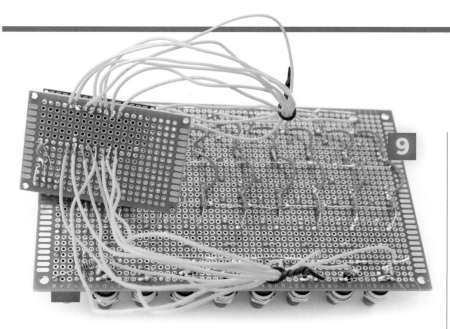

Above ◈
If you have the time and space, it would be better to use four headers and two ribbon cables to connect the main PCB to the Arduino

9 BUTTONS, SWITCHES, JACKS, POTS, AND LEDS

We're now going to connect each of the steps, all the buttons, and the various remaining jacks and switches together with the Arduino, so there's going to be a lot of wire. The button bus we created earlier, which is isolated from everything else on the PCB, is going to carry the 5V from the Arduino, as are the middle pins of both momentary switches. As with all our Arduino connections, we're taking one wire from the main PCB to the underside of the PCB with the Arduino. It would be neater if we routed all these wires to a separate header and then used a ribbon cable to connect the two, but we'll leave that as a further exercise. Now that we can see how much space there is on the PCB, we also insert the two switches into the top-right of the PCB. They could equally be left free, attaching only to the faceplate. It's important that these are momentary switches as this means they won't stay in position. Press them once to go backwards and the other way to go forwards.

The ground bus now needs to be connected to the underside of the GND pin on the Arduino. This is a good point to check continuity again by making sure your multimeter emits a sound when one connector is on the Arduino GND and the other is on any one of the ground buses you created on the PCB.

Now prepare twelve cables and solder eight from each button before the diode to pins A0 through to A7 on the Arduino PCB, left to right (see above image). Likewise, solder the eight cables we previously attached to the LEDs, potentiometer, and

jack columns to D9 through to D2 on the Arduino, from left to right. Now connect the reset jack to one side of one switch, and from the switch to D10 on the Arduino. The other side of the switch needs to be connected to D11. For the final switch, connect one side to the forward input jack and the other side to the backward input jack, also connecting the forward side to D12 and the backward side to D13 on the opposite side of the Arduino.

10 DRILL CASE

We did lots of things wrong in this step. Firstly, and most importantly, we should have done it earlier, before soldering everything in permanently. We didn't because we were still making up the layout as we went along. Secondly, we drilled holes into an aluminium panel using a hand-held power drill. This works, but won't give the most professional-looking results. If you've got access to a drill press, use this instead.

As we have carefully placed all the components on a PCB, you can easily duplicate your layout on a piece of mathematical paper. We did this and traced the places where we needed holes onto a piece of cardboard, which we then pierced to make holes and mark the aluminium panel for drilling.

11 FLASH ARDUINO AND GO!

You need to download the Arduino IDE for your operating system (**hsmag.cc/OYiLpN**). Plug your Nano into your USB port, then open up the code for this project (**git.io/fpz1h**), select the Arduino Nano as your device, select the USB port it's connected to, and click 'Upload'. You're now ready to insert the Arduino into your sequencer! Plug in the Arduino and then add the power. With a bit of luck, you shouldn't see anything. Try pressing a button. Its LED will light. If you connect the gate output to an oscillator or sound source, it should trigger a sound. Connect CV1 or CV2 outputs to pitch on the oscillator and it will play whatever pitch is dialled into the potentiometer. If you have a clock source, plug this in and the sequencer will start stepping through each column at a time.

If things aren't working, don't be disheartened. Projects rarely work perfectly first time. If an LED is skipped over, make sure all the LEDs are connected properly. If things flash and flicker, look for bridged connections. And sleep on it. With a fresh mind, any mistakes will be obvious and you can start enjoying your new modular sequencer and synthesizer. →

Below ◈
If you place your sequencer into a rack, consider running a USB extension to the outside so you can still flash your Arduino

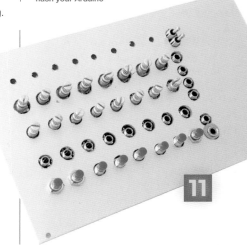

BUILD A VOLTAGE -CONTROLLED OSCILLATOR

YOU'VE BUILT THE SEQUENCER, NOW YOU JUST NEED TO BUILD SOMETHING THAT MAKES A SOUND

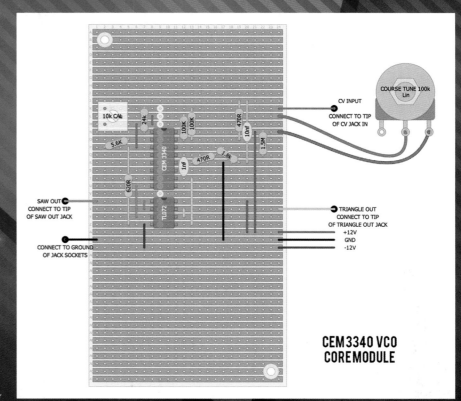

Figure 3 →
Here's the circuit layout of the project we're building. Huge thanks to Look Mum No Computer

Credit
look mum no computer

1 WHAT YOU'LL NEED

This project isn't as complex as the sequencer, and is easier to put together. However, with the form factor we're using, it's more fiddly to solder all the connections together.

The most important part of this build, and the most exciting, is the chip that generates the sound. This is the venerable Curtis CEM3340, a chip that helped pave the way for the mass production of analogue synthesizers. It was used in many classics, including the Memorymoog, Oberheim OB-8, Roland SH-101, and Sequential Circuits Prophet 5 (rev 3).

The reason why the chip was so revolutionary then is the same reason why we're using it now. It's a completely self-contained VCO that generates multiple waveforms, and needs very few additional components to work within a circuit. Before the CEM3340, a VCO would need to be constructed from lots of different and difficult-to-source parts, especially when you needed them to sound the same and stay in tune. By using a real CEM3340, we get exactly the same source sound as those old synths, and if the genuine chip is too expensive (typically around £12), there are replicas that perform the same function for around half the price.

Below ◈
Here are most of the things we'll need to build the oscillator. It's fiddly, but there aren't too many parts

By using a real CEM3340, we get exactly the same source sound as those old synths

2 SOCKETS

As the VCO is the most valuable part of this build, and the part most sensitive to electrostatic damage, we're going to seat it within a socket. This makes it easy to replace the chips, and also means we can solder the socket, and the socket's pins, without the chip being seated, protecting the chip from the heat. We'll do the same for the TL072 too, which is used to condition the output. We've positioned the sockets in the centre of the PCB as we'll be adding components to each side. Make sure the notch in each socket is facing the top – this is so we can orient the chips into the circuit when we plug them in.

To solder the sockets, dab solder onto the pins on opposite corners to hold the sockets in place, and then proceed to solder all the points in between. As we'll be using both sides of the PCB, we'll often need to bridge adjacent connections from the socket pins, which is worth considering as you start adding components and wires. Take a look at some of the later steps to see how we routed wires around the chips and legs of the pins, and keep this in mind when you create the power header.

This step will be different if you want to power your module from a battery or other power source – unlike the sequencer, which can alternatively be powered via a USB connection on the Arduino. We're using a standard Eurorack power supply. This needs eight pins on the PCB, with +12V delivered to the top pair, -12V to the bottom pair, and ground (GND) in the middle section. We can use these directly with the VCO. The header is created in the same way as the sequencer header, cutting off two rows of eight pins, placing them within a Eurorack power cable, and then soldering them through the PCB, ensuring the connector is on the same side as the PCB. →

Below ◈
Don't insert the chips into the sockets until the very end of the build process

INGREDIENTS

- ◈ **3 × jack sockets** (3.5 mm jacks for Eurorack)
- ◈ **10 kΩ trimpot, or potentiometer, for front panel access**
- ◈ **100 kΩ potentiometer**
- ◈ **TL072 amplifier**
- ◈ **Eurorack power cable**
- ◈ **VCO: CEM3340,** or the copy AS3340
- ◈ **IC socket: 1 × 8-leg, 1 × 16-leg**
- ◈ **46×24 dotted stripboard** or PCB
- ◈ **Resistors: 2 × 100 kΩ, 2 × 470 Ω, 1 × 620 Ω, 1 × 1.8 kΩ, 1 × 5.6 kΩ, 1 × 24 kΩ, 1 × 1.5 MΩ**
- ◈ **Capacitors: 1 × 1 nf, 1 × 10 nf**
- ◈ **Knob for potentiometer**
- ◈ **Lots of wire**

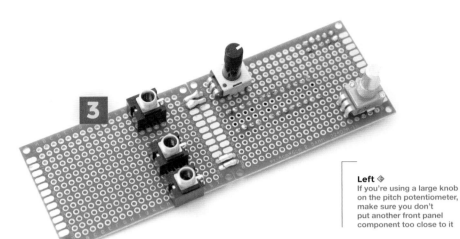

Left ◈
If you're using a large knob on the pitch potentiometer, make sure you don't put another front panel component too close to it

3 POTS AND JACKS

Let's start with the big components first, as we want to make sure these fit onto the PCB before attaching the many wires.
These are two potentiometers, one of which is used to set the pitch of the oscillator, while the other tunes it, and the three jacks. One jack will take an incoming voltage so the pitch can be controlled, while the other two output sawtooth and triangle waveforms from the CEM3340. These go on the reverse side of the PCB from the chips and power header. This is so they're presented to the front panel while the chips and power header remain accessible from the rear. It's worth keeping the jacks on the same row as we'll need to connect their ground pins together, usually by running a wire across all the top pins.

Make sure your pins aren't too close to be soldered and that nothing will be obscured by elements on the front panel. Our 10kΩ potentiometer also needed to have its anchoring legs trimmed to fit through the PCB. With everything in position, you just need to dab the soldering iron against a little solder and the pins to solder them in place.

Above ◈
Check each solder afterwards with a multimeter

4 GROUND CONTROL

We're going to refer closely to the circuit diagram in figure 3 to make sure we don't miss any connection or component. You may find it useful to tick off each as you make them. Also, don't forget that stripboard has the horizontal rows implicitly connected, which isn't the same on the PCB. This means you need to make sure everything on one row is interconnected, either with a wire or by soldering across adjacent holes. But before we get to that stage, we first need to feed the jacks a connection to ground.

All the GND connections are going to come from any of the middle pins on the power header. The header is on the rear side, facing away from the pots, which is also the side we want to use to solder the connections. This creates a slightly tricky situation where we need to solder a hole adjacent to a pin, bridge the connection to the pin, and make sure the solder runs through the hole to the other side of the PCB, from where we can solder a wire to the destination. It sounds harder than it is. We first need to do this for the ground connection, bringing a GND connection from the power header through to the reverse side of the PCB so that we can solder a wire to the earth pins of the input and output jacks. We did this in two stages, first by connecting the ground pins together with a spare piece of bare wire, and then by connecting this to the ground connection. Though not in the original diagram, we also connected ground to the third pins of each potentiometer.

5 CHIPS AND PINS

We now need to work through all the connections on the board. You will need around 20 sections of wire in total, but they'll all be slightly different lengths. Don't forget to 'tin' each stripped end of wire first with a little bit of solder.

For the overall strategy, we found it easier to start with the left side of the chips on the rear side of the PCB, working upwards from the CV input jack. Take time to see where the connections need to be made and take it step-by-step, working up from the input jack.

The -12V connection from the power supply is connected to the lower left pin of the TL072 socket. This is pin 4. Pin numbers on chips go from the top left, which is always pin 1, down the left side and then continue from the bottom right to the top right, which is pin 8 on the TL072 and pin 16 on the CEM3340. You also need to bridge pins 1 and 2 on the TL072 socket, which you can do directly from the pins on the front-facing side of the board. You'll also need to bridge and flow the solder through for the jack connection and for the first resistor, the 620Ω, which connects this pin to 3 on the CEM3340. Continue like this for the three resistors on the left side, plus the trimmer pot and the sawtooth output, which will need to connect to the pin opposite the ground on the jack you're using to output the sawtooth.

Below ◈
It would be tedious to cover every connection in this tutorial. It's easier to methodically step through each wire and resistor in the circuit diagram

6 POWER AND CAPACITORS

The left side of the PCB is completed when pin 3 of the CEM3340 is connected to one leg of the trimmer, and pin 1 (via the 24 kΩ resistor) is connected to the other leg. As mentioned earlier, our trimmer had three legs, and we connected this third leg to ground. It's now time to tackle the right-hand side of the circuit, and this is just more of the same, albeit with a higher component and wire density. Pins 6 and 7 on the TL072 are bridged, and pin 7 connects to the tip of the triangle output jack. Pin 5 then connects to pin 10 of the CEM3340. The tightest soldering is off pin 15 of the CEM3340, near the top right of the chip. This pin needs to connect to two 100 kΩ resistors, the 470 Ω resistor, a connection from the +12 V power connector, and the output to pin 3 of the coarse tune potentiometer. Getting these soldered in an orderly way was almost impossible with our small PCB, but each pin of the resistor can be soldered together or used to bridge a horizontal stretch of the PCB for the other connections.

Just take your time and make each connection in turn. There are far fewer to make than the sequencer, and there's usually plenty of room when you start soldering legs together.

Above ◈
If you need to remove the chip, use a plastic tool to carefully pry one end up, followed by the other end

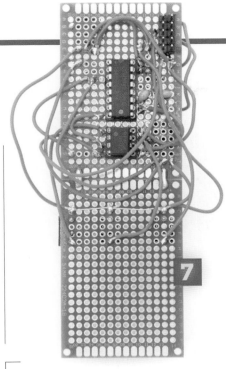

Above ◈
We found it easier to push the capacitors through from the side with the sockets and chips

7 CHIPS AND POWER

Once everything is soldered together, you can insert the two chips into their sockets. New chips will have their legs slightly too far apart to fit into the socket. This is normal and you need to use a blade, or something with a straight edge, to fold both sides in slightly. Regarding pressing the chips in, ensure the notch in the chip is aligned with the notch in the socket. If either chip doesn't have a notch, look for a circle next to one of the corner pins; this is used to mark pin number 1, and should be oriented into the top left position of the socket.

You're now ready to see whether your oscillator works. This is the most exciting step – if it doesn't work, disconnect the power and look at your circuitry. To test the oscillator, connect the power, making sure the red stripe on the Eurorack power cable is facing down where the -12 V needs to be.

Connect the sawtooth output to a mixer or a PC audio input, or something you can listen to. Now turn it on. There's a chance you won't hear anything. You need to first use the tuning potentiometer to bring the pitch within range. Try to sweep across this until you hear anything, even if it's a loud occasional thump. As soon as you get a sound, use the pitch knob to dial in a tone. Congratulations: you've just built your own classic oscillator!

8 TESTING AND FRONT PANEL

The oscillator will generate a constant tone, with the pitch being set by either the 'pitch' potentiometer or an incoming control voltage to the pitch input jack. The CV input is used to play notes, and the pitch potentiometer can then be used to control the root notes from which the CV input will diverge. Standard voltage tuning for almost every Eurorack module and keyboard is 1 V per octave, meaning the twelve semitones in an octave are divided across a single increase or decrease in one volt. And the great thing about the CEM3340, and why we didn't need any more complicated circuitry, is that it also tracks pitch at 1 V per octave. Connecting one of the CV outputs from the sequencer to the CV input on the oscillator means you can now create your own sequences.

All that's now left is to create the front panel. This is going to depend entirely on how you're going to use your VCO. We sneakily kept space next to the sequencer front panel so that both modules can be mounted into the same unit, so all we needed to do was drill five new holes for the potentiometers and the jacks. As with both of these projects, our aim has been to create a great-sounding and useful sound engine. When you strap in the VCO alongside the sequencer and connect them together, you'll have a powerful and capable proto-synthesizer from which you can expand in almost every direction, and yet it already sounds absolutely fantastic. →

Below ◈
Here's the completed module fitted alongside the sequencer. The only job remaining is to spray-paint the panel so you don't see the scratches!

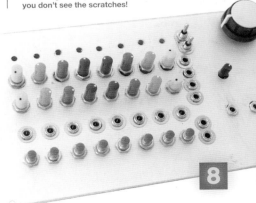

TAKING SYNTHS FURTHER

NOW YOU'RE HOOKED, SPEND THE NEXT TEN YEARS BUILDING YOUR PERFECT STUDIO

With a sequencer and VCO, you now have something that can be used to make awesome music, even just by feeding the pitch from the sequencer into the oscillator. This is what Kraftwerk did, and Wendy Carlos had only a few more oscillators when performing *Switched-On Bach*. But this is just the beginning, and you've hopefully got the itch to take both of these projects further, and to look at extending your new 'studio' into something with more possibilities.

POWER-UP YOUR RIG

If you're going to stay with the Eurorack, and you should, you're going to need a Eurorack power supply. You can obviously buy these along with the racks to hold your modules, but you may also want to build your own – and for just £10, you can. The Frequency Central Power DIY kit (**hsmag.cc/oNEViK**), as recommended by Look Mum No Computer, is perfect for creating +/-12V, ~100mA at 5V from a 12V AC power supply. You'll then be able to connect your modules

Right ⏎
Recapture the sound of your old games console or computer by turning it into a synthesizer

directly to the same source, and add new modules with ease.

We've barely tapped the potential of the Curtis CEM3340 chip. In particular, it can also generate pulse and square waveforms without too much extra circuitry. From a technical perspective, both of these waveforms are actually generated from the same source, as the 'width' of the square shape can be modulated using another voltage control input. With a 95% width, for example, the waveform is a sharp pulse, whereas at 50%, it's half-way up and half-way down, which is the shape of the square wave. Changing this percentage is called pulse-width modulation (PWM) and is another classic synthesizer sound source

changes like these, share them with the community. You never know where that might take you.

ADDING HARDWARE

While the sequencer and oscillator are capable of generating some excellent sounds, they still don't quite fulfil the role of an entire synthesizer. For that, you're going to need a few more modules, as we explained at the beginning, and these are a great place to start if you want to expand your module collection. Your first addition should be a filter, as this will add much needed character and harmonic control to your synthesizer sound. There are as many different filter designs as there are

> ## It's built around an Arduino, and that of course means you can change its functionality

that's amazing for bass as a square, and amazing with sawtooth when it's closer to a pulse, and amazing when you adjust the PWM amount with an incoming voltage.

If you don't feel like doing any extra soldering, the great thing about the sequencer project is that it's built around an Arduino, and that of course means you can change its functionality through the code without having to change any of the hardware. In this way you can make it truly unique and specific to your own needs. You could add a random step mode, for example, or add swing timing so that the clock isn't so regimented. You can also change the functions of the switches – especially as the backwards and forwards switches may be unnecessary if you're using both clock inputs. The switches could even be used to change between various playing modes for the sequencer, and you could show which mode or preset you're using by briefly hijacking the LEDs to show a patch number. And, if you're only using one clock input, change the code to use the other input for something else, such as changing direction, or doubling the speed. This really is the best thing about building your own modules. If you do make

synthesizers, and this being modular, you can (and should) aim to have more than one.

Your second and third additions should be a VCA, a voltage-controlled amplifier, and an EG, an envelope generator. This is because there's currently no way to attenuate the output from the oscillator, so the sound is always on. By plugging the audio output from the oscillator into a VCA, you can control the VCA levels over time with the EG, and you can trigger when the EG starts using the gate outputs from the sequencer or button keyboard. If you want the gate to match the pitch change, use a 'multiple' to split the clock into two, with one end going to the sequencer and the other to the EG. This is exactly how modern synthesizers respond to input from a keyboard. Many synths will have two or even three EGs, because they can also be used to change the amount of filter over time, or adjust the pitch of the oscillator over time, although you could equally use one and patch the control outputs to multiple destinations. A multiple is a module that takes a single source and provides multiple outputs; certain modules can take 'banana' cables that allow you to connect more than one cable to a single jack output. →

VCV: VIRTUAL MODULAR SYNTHESIZER

If you're still a little intimidated about the various elements that need to come together to make a synthesizer, of even the nascent beginnings of a Eurorack system, the answer is to experiment with software first. And there's an amazing piece of open-source software that not only teaches you about how all these various synthesizer modules fit together, and what they sound like, it teaches you about the exact modules you can build, buy, and install on your own system. VCV (vcvrack.com) is a virtual rack for virtual recreations of real hardware. The software is free and open source, and accurately models everything about a module, from its panel design and interface, through to loading the actual firmware that digital modules run, and the emulations of all the components in the circuitry.

You can even recreate our humble project without soldering a single component. Just install and run VCV on your chosen operating system (Linux, Windows, and macOS are supported). The main view is an empty rack for you to fill with modules, and you don't have to worry about power. Just right-click and select 'Fundamental' to open the menu of basic modules and select 'SEQ-3' to add a sequencer almost identical to the one we built. Similarly, select 'VCO-2' to add a simple oscillator. We also need to get the audio out from the virtual rack into your headphones or speaker, and you do this by adding 'Audio' from the 'Core' module. Now connect the CV output from one of the rows on the sequencer to the FM input on the VCO and turn up the 'FM CV' knob, and connect the output from the VCO to an input on the audio module. If you select an audio device with a right click, you'll immediately hear the pitch of the VCO being modulated by the potentiometer on the sequencer, just like our real hardware. You can now experiment with additions and new configurations without having to build the real hardware.

Below ◈
If you don't want to play with a soldering iron, you can create a perfect virtual Eurorack using the open-source VCV software

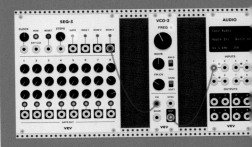

OTHER PROJECTS TO TRY

IF YOU'RE NOT YET READY TO PUT DOWN THE SOLDERING IRON, THESE ARE THE PROJECTS WORTH TAKING A LOOK AT FOR INSPIRATION

There's a considerable community that's grown, and continues to grow, around build-your-own synthesizers, catering for all kinds of different styles of music and all kinds of engineering capability. These projects range from simple circuits that will take an hour or two to complete, to fully fledged re-creations of old classic synthesizers that could take a year of work, and salary, to put together. Many people who started off building their own creations will now sell their own PCBs and faceplates, and buying one of these kits is a great way to grow your own collection without having to design everything from scratch or drill your own holes through aluminium plates.

RADIO MUSIC

One of the simplest projects you can start with, and one of the most creative, is called 'Radio Music'. Radio Music was designed by Tom Whitwell and inspired by early musique concrète experimentation by the likes of John Cage, Karlheinz Stockhausen, and Don Buchla, as they each played with loops of randomly recorded lo-fi radio. It takes an SD card crammed full of raw audio files you

make yourself or source. Radio Music then lets you control how those files are played back, from which point, and from which 'channel'. It's a wonderful sound source that can operate as a VCO with a completely non-traditional sound. But the hardware is also completely open, and that means the schematics, along with the designs, the bill of materials, and the code that runs on the Teensy microcontroller are completely open source (CC-BY-SA). It's also suitable for all levels, because not only is it an easy project for beginners to put together, you can even buy it fully completed if you'd prefer. You can build it yourself from the information on its GitHub page, you can buy the PCBs and the front panel, and you can buy kits that include everything you need, bar the soldering iron and the solder.

Another great thing about Radio Music is that it can also be something else completely different – a chord organ and rather gritty VCO. With exactly the same hardware, only with a different Teensy firmware, it switches from being a digital playback device to something that can play different chords. The 'station' knob now switches between chords, for example, while the 'start' knob adjusts the root note and octave for the chord. Finally, the 'reset' button now selects

Right →
Small kits, like Radio Music, are a brilliant way to start with modular synth building, as they're cheap and can be expanded, upgraded, and subverted easily

between sine, square, sawtooth, and pulse width. It's brilliant for generating complex chord progressions from a single module and a simple kit. For more details, check out Tom's GitHub page: **hsmag.cc/UPiAJO.**

There are hundreds of other Eurorack modules that you can build yourself from designs shared online, or from kits put together for usually modest sums of money. In the UK, there's even an annual meet-up of these home-grown modular synth moguls in Brighton. At the 2018 event, you could rub shoulders with these makers and their hardware, listen to music made with the equipment, and even attend workshops to help you build your own modules – from beginners to experts.

ADVANCED PROJECTS

Another great source of projects that require varying amounts of commitment is MIDIbox. Rather than fitting into the Eurorack format, many of MIDIbox kits and circuit designs create self-contained units that can be used to control other devices, or turn old and esoteric sound hardware into a

Above ◈
Our sequencer in its natural home, alongside other synth modules

reverse-engineer the original PCBs of some old equipment and design new circuits to include more easily available components, putting the whole thing together over multiple revisions and kits until a final stable version becomes available. At this point, the PCBs are usually manufactured in small runs, and a BoM for the build is created for other people to follow.

For the ultimate in synth sound nostalgia, many people consider the Yamaha CS-80 to be the definitive synth of the 1970s, and even this has succumbed to DIY enthusiasts.

The CS-80 was famously used by Vangelis in his late 1970s and early 1980s golden era, on soundtracks such as *Antarctica*, *Blade Runner*, and *Chariots of Fire*. The sound of the CS-80 is what many people consider the sound of synthesizers, with sweeping pads and strings dripping in eight seconds of reverb, and yet its signal path is rather unusual, consisting of two parallel voices and eight notes of polyphony. That makes 16 voices in total, alongside a strange parallel filter control and polyphonic aftertouch. And like the ARP 2600, you can now embark on a DIY project to build a synth with the same character if you're prepared to spend hundreds of hours and pounds on the components, PCBs, and cases. This DIY recreation is called Deckard's Dream (**deckardsdream.com**) and may well be the sonic equivalent of a unicorn running through a forest clearing. ◻

MIDIbox kits create self-contained units that can be used to control other devices

synthesizer. There's a PCB for generating sound out of a Commodore 64's SID chip, for example, and another for creating a bank of faders that can control various synthesizers over MIDI. Many of these projects also have points that can be used to add control voltages, and many builders bend the designs to suit their own requirements and form factors.

But if you've mastered the soldering and you're looking for a real challenge, there are plenty of hundred-hour-plus projects that synthesizer affectionados pour their time and money into. Many of these projects involve recreating classic and unobtainable synthesizers from the 1970s, and they are a huge challenge for a number of reasons. They usually centre on a few individuals who

One such project that followed this path is TTSH – an acronym for 'two thousand six hundred', which just happens to be the number for a very classic and now very expensive 1971 synth, the ARP 2600. TTSH is a complex project that has itself been refactored into another clone, the STP 2600, which promises to be much easier to build without compromising the sound. Take a look at **diysynth.de** if this sounds like your kind of endeavour.

Below ◈
A Yamaha CS-80 synthesizer can now cost tens of thousands of dollars, and you need a full-time engineer to keep it tuned. If you have the patience and the time to solder thousands of components, you can get close to the CS-80 sound with a DIY Deckard's Dream synthesizer

We have to give huge credit to Sam Battle's 'Look Mum No Computer' for the circuit designs we've used as the basis for both the oscillator and the sequencer. It's his website, **lookmumnocomputer.com**, and in particular his Patreon page, **patreon.com/lookmumnocomputer**, we'd recommend looking at for your next steps. His site includes the extra circuitry and components needed to tap into the missing elements on the oscillator, and he also has schematics for extending the sequencer to use an Arduino Mega and add another eight steps, if you can handle the extra wiring.

Inspiration

Be inspired by these amazing Arduino projects

158

160

162

Freeduino

By **Jiří Praus** jiripraus.cz

Since its creation in 2003, the Arduino Uno has breathed life into the world of open-source electronics. There are more powerful boards, but the openness of the hardware means that it's gained a community, which is worth more than a little bit more processing power or faster ins and outs.

Being open, the Arduino is also highly clonable – you'll see all sorts of cheap knock-off versions on the market. This clone, by developer, maker, and artist Jiří Praus, is anything but a simple clone. He's recreated the Arduino's PCB in free-form wiring, connecting all the real components to create a skeleton version of the board that's functionally identical to the real thing. Why, you may ask? Well, we say, why not? ◻

Right ◰
The build took a few days, and yes – it works!

Chartreuse

By **Anna Lynton & Alex Fiel** hsmag.cc/NmChjn

Chartreuse is an interactive face that follows you when you walk by. When she sees you, her eyes turn yellow, and she gets a happy expression in her eyes. As you walk away, her eyes change to blue, and she sadly turns away.

Chartreuse is powered by an Arduino Uno, two servos, and a stepper motor and a couple of addressable LEDs. She's constructed from a few pieces of 1/8″ hardboard.

The creators, Anna Lynton and Alex Fiel, are both Technology, Arts, and Media Students at CU Boulder. □

Far left ◈
There's an ultrasonic distance sensor hidden in the base, watching you

Word clock

By **Mosivers**  hsmag.cc/SwgwCw

"**A** friend of mine and I were making a regular word clock for his girlfriend as a Christmas gift.** During this, we noticed that it is possible to project the letters from the back onto a white sheet of paper. Moreover, we were able to create interesting effects by bending the paper so that individual letters change size and become blurred. After that, we tried to come up with a design for a word clock which makes use of this effect by being able to move each of the 114 letters and dots using a servo.

"We knew that this would be a challenging project, but it turned out to be even more tedious than we thought, because you basically have to repeat every step 114 times. However, in the end, I think we created something original and unique." □

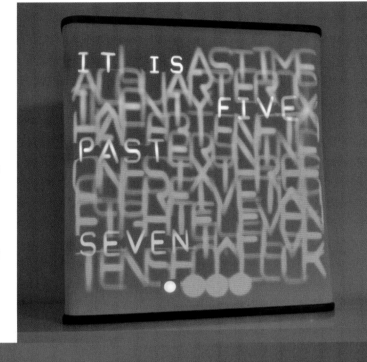

Right ⊿
While we've seen many word clocks in the past, this is by far the best-looking

Get Started With Arduino

Assistive spoon

By CuriosityGym   hsmag.cc/jHHMIS

"**P**arkinson's disease is a progressive nervous system disorder that affects movement.** Symptoms start gradually, sometimes starting with a barely noticeable tremor in just one hand. Tremors are common, but the disorder also commonly causes stiffness or slowing of movement.

"We were greatly inspired by Liftware Steady (see **liftware.com/steady**), which is a product sold for this very purpose. We realised early on that this was expected to be a challenging project and would take the team into the arenas of motion control, physics, and 3D maths that we had a working knowledge of, and this project helped us put our theory into practice.

"The design was expected to be held in hand, and be able to help cancel out any tremors the person's hand felt, thus providing the ability to level and steady out a spoon held at the end of the prototype." □

Left ◰
The project was made by CuriosityGym team members Siddhesh Murudkar, Rupin Chheda, and Jehangir Khajotia

Arduinoflake

By **Jiří Praus** ✈ hsmag.cc/wwRjLy

" **I** **am a senior engineer for Samepage.io, and hardware enthusiast.** I started with a simple Arduino kit two years ago, and I fell in love with the platform. Now, I am having fun making free-form sculptures and electronics. My Arduinoflake has 30 LEDs interconnected by 0.8mm brass wire by the so-called 'dead bug' method [where wires are soldered directly onto the upside-down integrated circuit] into the shape of a snowflake. It runs on Arduino Nano, and you can interact with it by the capacitive touch sensor. I wanted to build it as a toy for my daughter, but it turned out to be more – it's circuit art." □

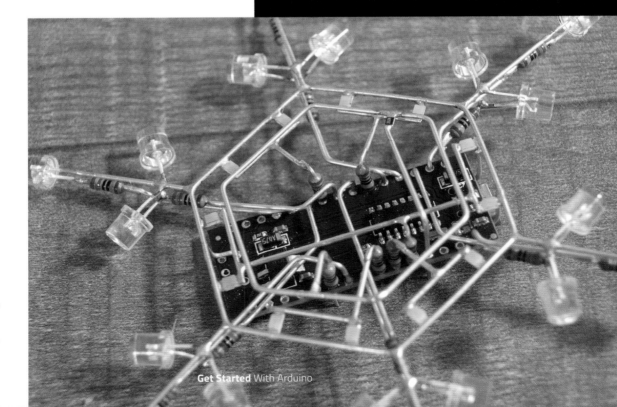

Right ⏷
This sculpture was entered into the Hackaday Circuit Sculpture Contest (hsmag.cc/whrlzk)

Field Test

Expert reviews of some of the
most interesting Arduino kit around

174

172

170

Grand Central M4 Express

One board, so many inputs

ADAFRUIT ◈ **$37.50** | adafruit.com

By **Ben Everard**   @ben_everard

There's no shortage of microcontrollers built in the Arduino form factor. **However, almost all of these are built in the style of the Uno.** The Mega form factor (with its vastly expanded range of IO pins) has seen only one significant insurgent in the last nine years – the Arduino Due, which, despite some advantages, never became popular. However, this has now changed with a new board supporting a large number of IO pins: Adafruit Grand Central M4 Express.

This board houses an impressive 54 digital IO pins and 16 analogue inputs (two of which can be used as analogue out via a 12-bit DAC).

Below ◈
If you Charlieplex all the GPIO pins, you can drive 3782 LEDs. Let's get blinking!

There are a few clues about the processing power of this board in its name. M4 refers to the version of the ARM core on the board, while Express – in Adafruit terminology – means that there's more than 2MB flash space (there's actually 8MB). You can fit a lot in 8MB, but if that's not enough, there's also a microSD card slot, so you can pile (almost) as much data as you like into storage.

The M4 core runs as 120MHz, and has both hardware DSP (digital signal processing) and floating point support. It's a little hard to compare the speed of different microcontrollers because there are a lot of differences in the underlying silicon, as well as the speed it runs at. Floating point can be really slow on some microcontrollers, so the speed-up may be much faster than the numbers alone may suggest.

To test how much faster, we compared this board to a Circuit Playground Express, which has an M0 core running at 48MHz (this is a fairly quick microcontroller by many standards) without a floating point unit. Using the Arduino IDE, we programmed this to perform a million integer multiplications and a million floating point multiplications. On the CPX, this took 189 milliseconds for integer, and 8308 milliseconds for floating point.

On the Grand Central, the integer operations took 67 milliseconds – which is about in line with the expected speed-up, as the core is 2.5 times faster and slightly more powerful. The floating point operations took 75 milliseconds – only slightly slower than the integer operations. As well as floating point, the M4 cores have hardware support for integer divide, with a similar speed-up of about 40 times. This speed means that the Grand Central

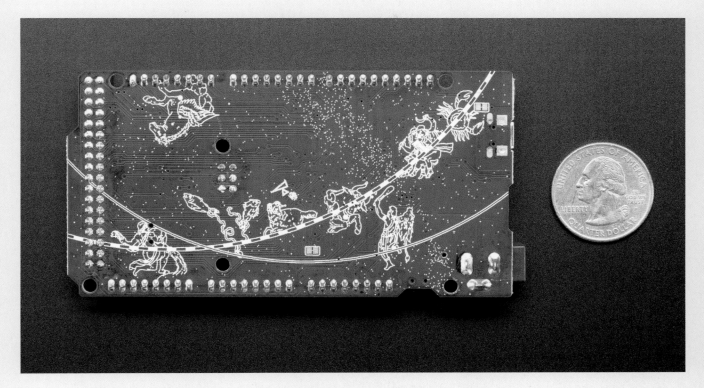

can be pushed into areas that many microcontrollers just can't cope with – such as audio manipulation, and calculating complex LED patterns.

The DSP can provide a huge speed boost, however, using it isn't easy. Unless you're interested in diving down into the minutiae of compiler optimisation, it's

> **The M4 core runs as 120MHz,** and has both hardware DSP and floating point support

probably only going to be relevant if you're using libraries that support it. The most popular example of this is the Audio Library originally designed for the Teensy (the Teensy 3.x also use an M4 processor). As M4 processors become more widely used, more libraries supporting the DSP are likely to be created.

The form factor – as we mentioned at the start – is based on the classic Arduino Mega, which is an extension to the Arduino Uno, and this means that there are a range of shields already available. Like most modern microcontrollers, the Grand Central is a 3V board, so you need to make sure that any shields are compatible with this voltage.

The Grand Central has a huge amount packed into it, but all microcontrollers are about compromise – you simply can't make a board that has it all,

especially when 'all' often includes small size and low price. The most obvious compromise on the Grand Central is the lack of any wireless connectivity – there's neither Bluetooth nor WiFi. This doesn't mean you can't use it wirelessly, but you will need extra hardware, which means extra cost and complexity.

A SOFT TOUCH
On the software side of things, both Arduino and CircuitPython are supported, but Adafruit has this to say: "We have a working Arduino board support package, with lots of stuff working, but our primary target for this board is CircuitPython".

While this does sounds a little pessimistic on the Arduino front, it does need to be taken into account compared to Adafruit's usual excellent support. For most uses, the Arduino environment should work as expected, just don't expect loads of libraries and examples targeting the more esoteric features of the board, such as the PCC camera interface.

CircuitPython using Mu requires version 1.0.2 or later to detect the serial connection, and works as expected. There are already official guides for creating a soundboard and a MIDI interface.

The Grand Central M4 Express packs a huge amount onto a microcontroller board. There's enough IO to control almost anything, and the processing power to crunch through the massive amount of data it's capable of bringing in. As the name suggests, it's not the smallest board, but if you've got the room, this is a great brain for IO-hungry projects. ▢

Above
The silkscreen image is taken from the ceiling of Grand Central Station in New York

VERDICT

Inputs, outputs, and processing power galore. This is a great board for complex controls and interfaces.

9/10

NeoTrellis M4 Express

Buttons, lights, and lots of sound

ADAFRUIT ◈ From $59.95 | adafruit.com

By **Ben Everard** @ben_everard

Below ◈
The NeoTrellis
is small enough
to be operated
while holding it
in two hands, like
a gamepad

The NeoTrellis M4 express is an 8×4 array of buttons powered by a SAM D51 chip (with an ARM Cortex-M4 running at 120MHz with hardware DSP and floating point). There's an audio-out 3.5 mm jack connected to two 12-bit DACs, and two exposed GPIO pins which can run I²C or analogue in. There's also a three-axis accelerometer.

NeoPixels behind each button give you the ability to light up each switch to indicate a different use, and create an endlessly variable display. As this display can be configured on the fly, the button-and-NeoPixel format is great for creating novel user input devices. There's also 8MB of flash storage, which gives enough space for quite a few audio samples, and an electret microphone amplifier (accessible through the fourth pin on the audio jack).

If this particular setup isn't what you're after, you can get other bits in similar forms. 4×4 Trellis keypads are available both with regular LEDs ($9.95 for the PCB + $4.95 for the silicon buttons) and with NeoPixels ($12.95 for the PCB + $4.95 for the silicon buttons). These can be daisy-chained both vertically and horizontally to form groups of up to eight. These don't include a microcontroller, so you can add one of your choice.

Putting the device together is just a case of lining everything up and securing it together with five bolts. The laser-cut case feels sturdy and the silicon buttons are soft enough to feel comfortable, yet still click firmly under your fingers.

There are, at the time or writing, two ways of programming the board – with the Arduino IDE and with CircuitPython.

If you want to unlock the full audio power of this board, you'll have more luck with the Arduino IDE. There's a port of the popular Teensy Audio library for the NeoTrellis M4 which allows you to create sounds and apply all sorts of audio effects. For those more interested in controlling other music-generating hardware, the Trellis can output either USB or five-pin DIN MIDI (with a simple circuit described here: **hsmag.cc/RhptgC**).

Just as a simple example of the power, this reviewer created a synth (based on the examples)

Left
Three connections –
USB, Grove, and jack
– provide a wealth of
expandability, even
though there are only
two GPIOs

that can output sine, triangle, square, or sawtooth waves with the attack and release of the modulation controlled by the x and y values from the accelerometer. Holding the device in different orientations gives different sounds (and you can get the source code from: **hsmag.cc/DLHQYI**). This button-plus-tilt interface is hugely flexible for all sorts of weird (and occasionally wonderful) sound generators, and having the Audio library available gives you a huge range of effects and options at your fingertips.

PYTHONIC

CircuitPython doesn't quite have the same performance as Arduino, if you're really pushing the audio effects, but it is still running on a powerful M4 chip, so it's no slouch. It's still powerful enough to work with audio: for example, there's a CircuitPython beat sequencer at: **hsmag.cc/zrtnfN**.

The NeoTrellis is a really useful – and slightly unusual – input device packaged up with a powerful processor. At first glance, it doesn't seem as flexible as some maker devices – especially given the lack of GPIOs. However, this is deceptive. The USB is native and can be used to create a MIDI or other USB device, there's audio in and out, and the I²C connector is enough to control almost any hardware, and that's what this device is about. It's a way of creating novel user interfaces. In this review we've focused on audio and we think that this will be a popular use for this board. However, there's nothing that ties it to this particular use.

From the audiophile perspective, perhaps the most disappointing thing about the NeoTrellis will be the sound fidelity. 12-bit DACs are fine for general playback, but they don't have the same resolution of high-end audio hardware, and you're never going to get great input from an electret microphone. This belies the usefulness of this device, though. Sure, the DACs aren't perfect, but it's a handheld controller and if you need high-fidelity audio, you

 This button-plus-tilt interface is hugely flexible for all sorts of weird (and occasionally wonderful) sound generators

can use this and a MIDI controller to get sound out of a wide range of hardware – and if you need high-quality samples, you can record them off-device and load them on.

Some hardware just makes you smile. It's hard to put a list together of exactly what it takes to do this, but it's some combination of a good human-circuit interface, interesting outputs, and documentation that makes it easy to get started and experiment with the features. The NeoTrellis M4 express is one of these – it's just great fun to use.

The particular form-factor of the NeoTrellis M4 won't suit all projects, but for those projects it does suit it's unrivalled. At $59.99, it's fantastic value as well. ☐

VERDICT

A quirky and great fun device with an unusual set of inputs.

9 /10

REVIEW

Arduino Every and 33 IoT

The tiniest Arduino board gets an overhaul

By **Ben Everard**   🐦 @ben_everard

The Nano line of Arduino boards has been a staple of makers for over a decade. They're small and cheap (compared to other official boards), yet still come with the USB connector and all the power of the larger boards. Technology has moved on since the first version of the Nano came out, and Arduino has released a line of new boards in the Nano form factor – we're taking a look at the Nano Every and the Nano 33 IoT.

The Nano Every is based on the ATmega4809 microcontroller running at 20MHz. This is broadly compatible with other AVR chips from Arduino,

Below ◈
The new Nanos are tiny, but the 33 IoT is very slightly larger

including the one in the original Nano. This board is running at 5V, so should be a completely drop-in replacement for the original Nano, but with more flash (48kB) and more RAM (6kB). At eight euros, this is the cheapest board that Arduino makes by a fairly significant margin.

The Nano 33 IoT also comes in the same form factor as the Nano, but it's built on the 32-bit ARM SAMD21G18A microcontroller. It runs at up to 48MHz and has 256kB of flash and 32kB of RAM. Overall, this is a significantly more powerful processor than the AVR chip in the Nano Every. As well as this, there's an ESP32-based u-blox module for WiFi and Bluetooth, and a six-axis inertial measurement unit. All this comes in at 16 euros, which is twice the cost of the Nano Every, but it's still one of the cheapest boards that Arduino produces.

Both of these devices are tiny, solidly made, and as easy to use as you'd expect from devices made by Arduino. Unlike many small boards, there are four mounting holes, so you can easily secure the board in your projects.

They're completely flat on the bottom, and have castellated pads so they can be soldered onto other PCBs to make a sort of permanent shield setup – a sign that Arduino is targeting the small-run electronics industry by making it easier to build products out of Arduino projects.

POWER SUPPLY

The world of small microcontrollers is pretty crowded at the moment, but these new Nanos do have their niche within it. They're among the smallest boards around, yet still pack in quite a healthy amount of IO (12 digital, 8 analogue in, and 1 analogue out). They achieve this feat by cutting out one key feature found in most slightly larger

Above ↗
The ATmega4809 is
more powerful than the
AVRs in older Arduinos

boards – battery management. You'll need a source of power, whether via the USB port or up to 21 V via Vin. The rather beefy on-board regulator can provide up to 950 mA for peripherals.

In a world of 3 V microcontrollers, the Arduino Nano Every is probably one of the best choices for 5 V microcontroller right now from a price to performance ratio, as long as you don't need battery charging or networking. There is less 5 V hardware around these days, but if you find yourself needing to control some, this will save you the hassle of level shifting. With 950 mA of current available from the regulator, and 5 V IO, this is a great choice for small to medium-sized NeoPixel projects.

The Nano 33 IoT is in the fuller marketplace of 3.3 V WiFi-enabled development boards, but it does have a few stand-out features. It's the smallest, cheapest board that's compatible with the Arduino IoT Cloud. While this online development environment is still in development, it's shaping up to be a really easy way to get started with IoT devices. The Nano 33 IoT has the sprightly performance that we've come to expect of boards based on the SAMD21 microprocessor, and the off-chip WiFi gives solid networking performance. □

BENCHMARKS

Overall, the 33 IoT is about four times the speed of the plain Nano Every. The only exception to this is in floating-point multiply and divide. Each test is running a million instances of each instruction, except the analogue input which is only 10,000. The result is the number of milliseconds that the process took to run.

Benchmark	Nano 33 IoT performance	Nano Every performance
Analogue input	4,234	1,124
Integer sum	147	884
Integer multiply	211	829
Float sum	2,609	8,560
Float multiply	14,757	12,684
Float divide	32,485	46,542
GPIO test	3,303	72,722

VERDICT

Arduino
Nano Every

If you need a small, 5 V microcontroller board, this has to be top of your list.

9 /10

VERDICT

Arduino Nano
33 IoT

A no-nonsense WiFi microcontroller that fits in the tiniest of spaces.

8 /10

Teensy 4.0

A 600MHz microcontroller

 TEENSY ◆ $19.95 | pjrc.com

 By **Ben Everard**   🐦 @ben_everard

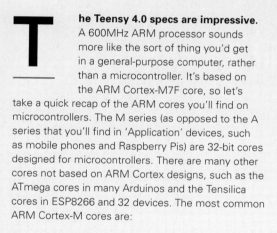

The Teensy 4.0 specs are impressive. A 600MHz ARM processor sounds more like the sort of thing you'd get in a general-purpose computer, rather than a microcontroller. It's based on the ARM Cortex-M7F core, so let's take a quick recap of the ARM cores you'll find on microcontrollers. The M series (as opposed to the A series that you'll find in 'Application' devices, such as mobile phones and Raspberry Pis) are 32-bit cores designed for microcontrollers. There are many other cores not based on ARM Cortex designs, such as the ATmega cores in many Arduinos and the Tensilica cores in ESP8266 and 32 devices. The most common ARM Cortex-M cores are:

M0 Small instruction set, optimised for small size on silicon, low price, and low power (at least, relatively speaking as these are still significantly faster than AVR chips, such as those found in the Arduino Uno). Based on the ARMv6-M instruction set.

> **In microcontrollers, it doesn't really make sense to have a notion** of one of these being overall 'better' than the others

M0+ A machine-code-compatible upgrade on the M0 that adds a bit more oomph.

 Above ⊿
The Teensy 4.0 really lives up to its name – it's tiny

M3 Based on the ARMv7-M instruction set with instructions not present in M0 cores such as divide and multiple-accumulate. Code should run faster than on an M0 core.

M4 The same basic core as an M3, but with digital signal processing (DSP) instructions. These are used extensively in audio processing libraries.

M4F An M4 core with additional acceleration for single-precision floating-point calculations.

M7F This includes single-precision and (optionally) double-precision floating-point accelerations, as well as DSP instructions. It's a significantly more powerful core than that in the M3 and M4, with a larger pipeline and branch speculation (this is a bit of a confusing feature, but it can result in faster code run time). There's also the option of tightly coupled memory, which allows you to use a small amount of very fast memory.

CORE CONUNDRUMS

There are a few others, but they're not commonly used in the hobbyist world. In microcontrollers, it doesn't really make sense to have a notion of one of these being overall 'better' than the others, as it depends so heavily on use-case. M0 cores are the least powerful in this list, but on the scale of microcontrollers, they're still fairly powerful and should accomplish many tasks without draining your power supply or bank balance. However, if you need to do any DSP or floating-point operations, then you'll really benefit from an M4F or faster core.

The M7F core in the Teensy 4.0 is more powerful than an M4F core (such as that in the Teensy 3.6), and it can also run at higher clock speeds – 600MHz in this case (though it may be possible to overclock it in the future). The one feature that really has a dramatic speed increase is the support for accelerated double-precision floating-point operations, but this is quite a specialised use-case.

BENCHMARKS

We ran a series of benchmarks on some of the fastest microcontrollers we've got, to compare them to the Teensy 4.0. In each case, the benchmark result is the time taken to complete a task intensive in that particular area. Lower is better.

Benchmark	Teensy 4.0	Teensy 3.6 (240MHz)	Adafruit PyPortal (SAMD51 – 200MHz)	ESP32
Integer arithmetic	6.00	38.00	40.00	54.00
Float arithmetic	28.00	79.00	85.00	151.00
Double arithmetic	30.00	620.00	739.00	614.00
GPIO output	65.00	271.00	451.00	265.00

Below ◈
The Teensy breakout isn't available for sale, but you can create your own with instructions at hsmag.cc/ZyDVhx

Take a look at the box above for a comparison of performance with other high-speed microcontrollers. There's no doubt that the Teensy 4.0 is, for almost any case, the fastest microcontroller geared for hobbyists by a factor of about three to five (depending on exactly what you're doing with it). There are a few applications that can really benefit from this speed-up.

The Teensy range has been a favourite device for people working with real-time audio, both because they've historically been fast boards, and because there's a great set of support libraries written by Paul Stoffregen (who also sells the Teensy boards). This includes a drag-and-drop creator and a set of libraries that help you write Arduino code to both create and modify audio signals. The Teensy 4.0 is much faster than the previous version (Teensy 3.6), and has four times the memory. This means that you can do a whole lot more. In audio terms, this means you can do more computationally intensive effects, and more of them.

AUDIO ADAPTORS

The Teensy 4.0 does work with the Teensy Audio Adaptor Board, but the pins are in slightly different positions, so you have to connect it with jumper wires rather than soldering the two boards directly together, as you could do with the earlier board.

Another area where powerful microcontrollers are looking promising is running neural networks, such as using the TensorFlow framework. At the time of writing, there's a lot of work going on with this. On paper, the Teensy 4.0 looks like it would make a good platform for this, and there is some support for M7 processors, but as yet, there's not a straightforward process for getting all this running. If you're interested in running TensorFlow on microcontrollers, it's certainly worth keeping an eye out for Teensy 4.0 support.

The Teensy 4.0 is a significant step up on performance over any other hobbyist microcontroller board, and available at a great price. If you find yourself lacking the processing power to do what you need, then there's really no competition at the moment – this is the board you need. ▢

VERDICT

The most powerful hobbyist microcontroller available at the moment.

DIRECT FROM SHENZHEN

Black and Blue Pills

Two cheap boards built on the same microcontroller

By **Ben Everard** @ben_everard

T he **'Blue Pill' – a generic design of microcontroller, based on the STM32F103 – has been around for a while.** The Black Pill is a newer, similar design based on the same MCU. These names are given to the boards by the community, so you won't find them for sale under these titles. Instead, they're usually called things like 'STM32F103C8T6 ARM STM32 Minimum System Development Board Module', and you'll have to pick them based on the image (as there are other board designs sold under similar names).

There used to be a red version as well, but this doesn't seem to be available any more. The two we got were 'STM32F103C8T6 ARM STM32 Minimum System Development Board Module For Arduino Kj' for £1.79, including delivery, from GadgetsCloud on eBay for the Blue Pill, and 'STM32 Minimum System Development Board STM32F103C8T6 ARM Module for Arduino M' for £1.99, including delivery, from Ukings on eBay for the Black Pill. Similar boards are available for similar prices on most direct-from-China websites.

The CPU is based on an ARM Cortex-M3 running at 72MHz with 64kB of flash and 20kB of RAM. There

Right ◈
The Black Pill is more robust, and more likely to have working USB

Credit
Thomas Gravekamp
GNU documentation licence

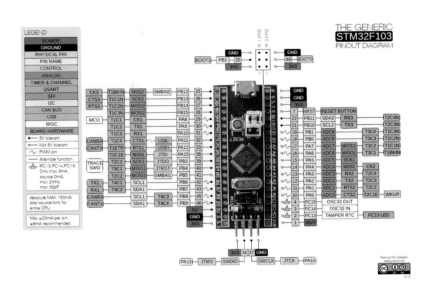

THE GENERIC
STM32F103
PINOUT DIAGRAM

Right ◈
Both boards have an impressive selection
of GPIOs and peripherals

are 37 IOs (35 on the Black Pill), including ten which
can handle analogue input. All this comes for typically
under £2.

While the MCU on both is the same, there are a
few differences on the board. Most notably, the Blue
Pill often has the wrong resistor on the USB port,
which can cause problems for USB connections on
some computers. It is possible to replace it, but it
might be easier to get the Black Pill and avoid the
problem. It's hard to know exactly what hardware
you're getting as the board isn't version-controlled –
there's not an official name, let alone official versions,
so you just pay your money and see what turns up.
Such is the nature of bargain-basement boards from
no-name suppliers. For under £2, it can be worth the
risk though.

DESIGN WOES

Another common problem is the soldering on the
USB port. Although we didn't have any problems,
some users have reported that it was weak and prone
to coming off the board – it's usually fixable with a
drop of solder. Again, this problem is solved on the
Black Pill. For these two reasons alone, the Black
Pill is worth the extra 20p, unless you specifically
need the Blue Pill (such as if your other hardware is
designed for it, or if you need the extra two GPIO pins
on this board).

Although the board does have a USB port, it
doesn't come with a USB bootloader by default, so
you'll need to burn a bootloader to it. This can either
be done using a JTAG adaptor or by using a USB to
serial adapter. The USB to serial adaptor is cheap,
and the setup is just a case of connecting the wires
together, so this shouldn't be enough to put off
people used to working with microcontrollers, but
for beginners, it might be best to start with a more
straightforward board.

Once the bootloader is burned, you can program
as you would any other Arduino-compatible board.
Install the correct board definition, then connect the
USB port and upload the programs as needed. Not all
libraries will work out-of-the-box, but many have been
ported to the STM32 (and you can see the list of those
here: **hsmag.cc/LvLKDu**).

As well as acting as a programming port, the
USB port can be used to allow the board to act as
a USB device. For example, the Venabili Keyboard
(**venabili.sillybytes.net**) uses a Blue Pill to convert

> **These boards aren't as plug-and-play as boards
> made by hobbyist companies, and they don't have
> WiFi like the similarly priced ESP8266 boards**

physical key presses into a USB communication
your computer can understand (look out for more
detailed coverage of this in a future issue). Similar
processors were even used as the USB controller on
the announced, but as yet unreleased, Arduino Cinque
which featured an open-source RISC-V microcontroller
at its heart (**hsmag.cc/xhybzr**).

While there's a bit of tweaking necessary to get
this board up and running, and no support from the
manufacturers, there's a community of hobbyists
who have got a lot running, and help each other out.
You can find most of the information you need to get
started at **hsmag.cc/LzqAqj**.

These boards aren't as plug-and-play as boards made
by hobbyist companies, and they don't have WiFi like
the similarly priced ESP8266 boards. However, they do
have a fast processor and plenty of IOs.

There's something inherently nice about working
with a board that doesn't quite work correctly
alongside a group of other enthusiasts. You'll probably
hit a few bumps along the way as you try to get a Blue
or Black Pill to work, but those have probably been hit
and documented by other users and, as you perform
the workarounds, you'll find you learn a bit more about
the workings of microcontroller boards. Of course, this
is only interesting (rather than frustrating) if you've got
the time and skill to go through the workarounds. For
£2, we think they're well worth the money, purely for
something to have a bit of a tinker with. You might find
they fit your use-case perfectly, but bear in mind that
there's a chance you might not be able to get them to
work as expected. ▢

DIRECT FROM **SHENZHEN**

A whirlwind tour of the Arduino Uno WiFi Rev2

A Headers

An Arduino is nothing without extra hardware. It exists to control lights, buttons, motors, and all manner of other gadgetry. These are connected via the headers – either in the form of 'shields' which connect a whole circuit board on top of the Arduino, or by using individual jumper wires to connect particular pins.

B Processor

An 8-bit 16MHz processor may not sound like much, but it's plenty of power for controlling most hardware. Some of us remember playing arcade games on much less powerful systems. It's got ten times the speed needed to control a pair of Italian plumbers, so most projects shouldn't struggle for power.

C USB

This two-way communication channel lets you upload code to your board, and also enables you to send data back and forth between a computer and the Arduino. This serial communication is vital for debugging and sending diagnostics as well as offloading data for processing.

D Power

Electrons are the lifeblood of your electronics project, and you inject them via this port. It can take between 7 and 12 volts, which means you can power your project off a 9V battery or a 12V charger. Note that this is only needed if the USB isn't connected.

E WiFi

The internet is everywhere, and connecting your project to a WiFi network gives it a huge potential for interactivity. You could send data to a cloud server for later processing, control it with your phone, or let other people see what's going on. The Internet of Things is here, so let's connect our own devices to it.

F Security

The internet is great (see above), but opening up your projects to it does carry risks. Security is paramount – fortunately, this board comes with an ECC608 crypto chip to ensure that you're using speedy, best-in-class encryption on data sent across an unsecured network.